Charleston Conference Proceedings 2008

Edited by Beth R. Bernhardt, Tim Daniels, and Kim Steinle

Katina Strauch, Series Editor

Libraries Unlimited

An Imprint of ABC-CLIO, LLC

A B C   C L I O

Santa Barbara, California • Denver, Colorado • Oxford, England

Copyright 2009 by Libraries Unlimited

Library of Congress Cataloging-in-Publication Data

Charleston Conference (28th : 2008 : Charleston, S.C.)
  Charleston Conference proceedings 2008 / edited by Beth R. Bernhardt, Tim Daniels, and Kim Steinle.
     p. cm.
  Includes bibliographical references and index.
  ISBN 978-1-59158-933-4 (pbk : alk. paper) 1. Library science—Congresses. 2. Library science—United States—Congresses. 3. Collection management (Libraries)—Congresses. 4. Acquisitions (Libraries)—Congresses. 5. Electronic information resources—Management—Congresses. 6. Libraries and electronic publishing—Congresses. 7. Library cooperation—Congresses. I. Bernhardt, Beth R. II. Daniels, Tim, 1963- III. Steinle, Kim. IV. Title.
  Z672.5.C53 2009
  020—dc22   2009027012

13 12 11 10 9   1 2 3 4 5

This book is also available on the World Wide Web as an eBook.
Visit www.abc-clio.com for details.

ABC-CLIO, LLC
130 Cremona Drive, P.O. Box 1911
Santa Barbara, California 93116-1911

This book is printed on acid-free paper ∞
Manufactured in the United States of America

Table of Contents

Content Development

Format

Management

Out-of-the-Box Thinking

Techie Issues

Miscellaneous

Charles Dickens' *A Tale of Two Cities* was the inspiration for the theme of the 28th Annual Charleston Conference—"The Best of Times…The Worst of Times," which was held November 5–8, 2008, in Charleston, SC. The theme seemed oddly prescient as we entered a year of economic uncertainty, elected a new President, and voiced questions about the Google Book Settlement and what it might mean for libraries. Still, Charleston was as collegial, informal, and beautiful as ever, and attendance hovered at close to 1,200—the maximum allowed by the Francis Marion Hotel. The Conference boasted nine preconferences that covered eBooks, newspapers, open source, innovation, weeding, negotiating, serials management, new service models, and many other relevant topics.

For the first time in 2008, we instituted what we called "threads" to help attendees categorize the hundreds of concurrent sessions that were offered. Over 120 concurrent sessions dealt with licensing, copyright and technical issues; budgeting, allocation, fund-raising, and statistics; management, organization, leadership, workflow and collaboration; education of librarians and library workers; content development and collection assessment; consortia; formats of content (books and ebooks, journals and ejournals, microform, video, etc.); end user issues, use statistics, usability; and out-of-the-box thinking, entrepreneurship opportunities. This book is divided into eight parts that correspond with most of those threads, Budget, Collaboration, Content Development, Format, Management, Out-of-the-Box Thinking, Techie Issues, and Miscellaneous.

Fourteen plenary sessions opened and closed each day of the Conference. Two humorous 15-minute skits held each morning forced us to laugh before tackling the more serious subjects at hand. **Derek Law** (University of Strathclyde) opened the festivities with his paper "Standing in the Company of the Dead: Preserving the Past and Forgetting the Future," in which he examined the issue of collection building with born digital materials and emphasized that librarians are neglecting their traditional roles and obligations in building collections. **Law** cleverly characterized Dickens' characters as a publisher, a poor librarian, a subscription agent, a consultant, and the university finance officer.

Pat Schroeder (President and CEO of the Association of American Publishers) outlined the recently announced (one week before the Conference began) terms of the Google Book Settlement with the AAP and the Authors' Guild which is still due to be finalized this fall. **Geoff Builder** (Director of Strategic Initiatives, CrossRef) persuaded us that we needed to make the Internet more trustworthy. **Greg Tananbaum's** panel included **James Neal** (Vice President for Information Services and University Librarian at Columbia) and **John Sack** (Director, High-Wire Press, Stanford University) and explored what is around the bend in scholarly communications.

On Thursday afternoon, **Roger Schonfeld** (Manager of Research, Ithaka) addressed "Community Goals in our Decentralized Environment."

Friday's plenary speakers began with **John Unsworth** (Dean, School of Information & Library Science, University of Illinois) who spoke about text-mining and how such tools are intended to tell you what something is about without reading it. **Andrew Pace** (Executive Director, Networked Library Services, OCLC) brought us further into the world of library automation and services and asked "what is web scale in library terms and what will it take to play on the network?" **Deanna Marcum** next discussed the subject of "Bibliographic Control and the Library of Congress" for an informal look at many of the issues of interest to both the Library of Congress and the library profession. **Heidi Hoerman** (Instructor, Specializing in Technical Services) filled in for **Tim Spalding** (Founder and Lead Developer, The LibraryThing) when she spoke about cataloging, subject headings, and authority control in general and where these practices might lead in the future.

The final Friday morning plenary panel—"The Role of the Library in a Fully Googlized World"—was chaired by **Rick Anderson** (Associate Director for Scholarly Resources & Collections, University of Utah). Speakers included **Nancy Eaton** (Dean of University Libraries, The Pennsylvania State University), **Rick Luce** (Vice President and Director of Libraries, Emory University) and **Joyce Ogburn** (University Librarian and Director, J Willard Marriott Library, University of Utah). These three distinguished directors looked toward 2020 and what the library world might look like. The Friday plenary session featured "OA Exposed" and the ins and outs of dealing with negotiating OA licenses. Speakers included **Arend Kuester** (moderator, Director, PCG Europe); **Ralf Schimmer** (Head of the Department of Scientific Information, Max Planck Digital Library); **Rick Luce** (Emory University); **Wim van der Stelt** (Springer) and **David Hoole** (Nature Publishing Group).

After the Saturday morning Beastly Breakfasts, **Tony Ferguson** (University Librarian, University of Hong Kong) began the first plenary session and enlightened us on "The Top 10 Ideas He Heard (and can copy) at the 28th Charleston Conference." The final plenary speaker was **Brian E.C. Schottlaender** (Audrey Geisel University Librarian, University of California, San Diego). Brian spoke about archiving, local print storage facilities, local digital asset management systems, and shared preservation initiatives. Concurrent sessions dealing with innovations rounded out the morning. **Hyde Park Corner**— where each participant can "sound off" about an issue, topic, or discussion heard during the Conference—closed the Conference.

You will find many of the papers in this volume. I extend a special thanks to **Beth R. Bernhardt, Tm Daniels**, and **Kim Steinle** for working so hard to put these papers together. And also my thanks to the staff at **Libraries Unlimited** and **ABC-Clio**, especially **Emma Bailey** for their support.

The 29th Charleston Conference will take its theme from Plato's *Republic*—"Necessity is the Mother of Invention" and will be held November 4–7, in Charleston, SC, as always. Be sure and join us for the very best conference around! See you here/there! www.katina.info/conference

Cordially,

Katina Strauch, Founder, Charleston Conference

Bruce Strauch, Owner, Charleston Conference

The Charleston Information Group, LLC

MSC 98, The Citadel
Charleston, SC 29409
www.katina.info/conference
kstrauch@comcast.net

The Charleston Conference continues to be a major event for information exchange among librarians, vendors, and publishers. Now in its twenty-eighth year, the Conference continues to be one of the most popular conferences in the Southeast. This year's Conference attendance was the largest ever. Conference attendees continue to remark on the informative and thought-provoking sessions. The Conference provides a collegial atmosphere where librarians, publishers, and vendors talk freely and directly about issues facing their libraries and information providers. All this interaction occurs in the wonderful city of Charleston, South Carolina. This is the fifth year that Beth R. Bernhardt has put together the proceedings from the Conference and the fourth year for Tim Daniels and Kimberly Steinle. We are pleased to share some of the learning experiences that we, and other attendees, had at the conference.

The theme of the 2008 Charleston Conference was "The Best of Times…The Worst of Times." While not all presenters prepared written versions of their remarks, enough did so that we are able to include an overview of such subjects as content development, budgeting, management, and technology issues. Topics also include issues collaboration, end users, and out-of-the-box thinking. The unique nature of the Charleston Conference gives librarians, publishers, and library vendors the opportunity to holistically examine these and other points of interest.

Katina Strauch, founder of the conference, is an inspiration to us. Her enthusiasm for the Conference and the proceedings is motivating. We hope you, the reader, find the papers as informative as we do and that they encourage the continuation of the ongoing dialogue among librarians, vendors, and publishers that can only enhance the learning and research experience for the ultimate user.

Signed,

Co-Editors of the 28th Charleston Conference proceedings

Beth R Bernhardt

Beth R. Bernhardt, Electronic Resources Librarian, University of North Carolina at Greensboro

Tim Daniels

Tim Daniels, PINES Program Manager, Georgia Public Library Service

K Steinle

Kimberly Steinle, Library Relations Manager, Duke University Press

Introduction

As good custodians of our collections budgets, we all need to be concerned about making responsible decisions. Budgets and fiscal matters continue to be an ongoing topic at the Conference. The key topics that were covered included new pricing models and how to deal with end of the year monies.

Budget

FULL SERVICE OR À LA CARTE: EXPLORING NEW PRICING MODELS FOR SUBSCRIPTION AGENTS

Jose Luis Andrade, President, Swets North America, Runnemede, New Jersey

Kim Maxwell, Associate Head Acquisitions and Licensing Services, Massachusetts Institute of Technology, Cambridge, Massachusetts

Abstract

Historically, subscription agents have largely used a full-service pricing model, with libraries paying a service charge based on this full-service offering. An alternative menu-based model was first proposed over 15 years ago, with agents offering a selection of services from which libraries could choose. By allowing libraries to select only the services they wanted, they would pay a lower price in return for fewer services. However, agents and libraries never adopted this model. Does today's e-environment present new opportunities to reconsider menu-based pricing models? Our agent and library panel will examine these questions and explore new pricing possibilities with attendees in an open-forum session to encourage feedback.

Introduction

With today's changing digital landscape, it may be time to take a fresh look at pricing models that have been in place for decades. Historically, subscription agents have largely used a full-service pricing model, with libraries paying a service charge based on this full-service offering. Considering the plethora of new products and service choices, a menu-based pricing model could allow libraries to select only the services they want, which could permit lower fees in return for fewer services. Although the menu-based approach was initially proposed more than 15 years ago, agents and libraries never adopted the model.

During the Lively Lunch, our presenters will describe the current situation, as well as offer ideas and options to help attendees explore new pricing alternatives. Topics focus on the types of services offered and how libraries may need to reevaluate their requirements to achieve the desired pricing outcomes. For example, with new electronic interfaces that help manage processes online, libraries may choose to (or be required to) take on certain tasks in exchange for lower prices. When libraries use EDI (Electronic Data Interchange) and other automated, paperless options that streamline invoicing, renewal, claiming, and reporting processes, agents may (or may be expected to) offer discounts.

Current Situation for Subscription Agents and Libraries

As the universe of online information rapidly expands and user demand for access to the wide range of available resources increases, librarians are challenged with resource provision under the constraints of shrinking budgets. Agents are competing to respond to market needs, attempting to provide online subscription management systems and electronic access interfaces faster, better, and cheaper than their counterparts. With lofty goals in mind, these solutions are designed to streamline processes, reduce operational costs, and improve the quality of management information.

In addition, publishers competing for a portion of libraries' smaller budgets offer a host of e-resources, access platforms, and variety of unique and often complex pricing models to go with them. Libraries struggle to compare pricing for similar e-resources and deal with daily challenges of training staff and patrons in the use of various platforms while maintaining reasonably constant e-access.

No one anticipated the scale of issues associated with e-resources in the early days of the Internet. Many expected the intermediary would no longer be required. In recent years, it has become apparent that e-resource complexity requires working with an organization offering comprehensive capabilities for electronic subscription and access management. From Swets' viewpoint, alleviating the administrative burdens of libraries and their staff is a primary responsibility of the intermediary in our digital world.

Simplifying the Complex Online World—A New Paradigm

When we look to simplify the complexities of e-resource management and access, it is helpful to analyze other industry examples. Let's review banking, for instance. Financial institutions learned early-on the importance of providing an online tool that satisfies customers' needs.

With banks, most transactions can be performed online in the comfort of the home or office. Basic transactions are also conducted at convenient off-site locations, including kiosks in high consumer traffic areas, such as malls, convenience stores, and restaurants.

As a result, the following outcomes occur:

- Customers save time and money (depending upon the service model).

- Customers can attend to their real priorities.

- Most important, customers are generally happy and satisfied.

Reevaluation of Needs—Uncovering Costs

Today's electronic environment provides libraries with an opportunity to reevaluate needs. In some organizations where budget constraints are extreme, the process of examining needs is imperative. Presenters offer some general guidelines, such as the following:

- What does your library/user community really need? List the top 10 areas and rank according to organizational goals.

- Have your needs changed with the advent of e-resources? How? What are the differences and what impact does this have on collection decisions and provision.

- Do you have a handle on your costs?

    Can something be outsourced?

        For cost savings?

        To allow you to spend time on more essential concerns?

Do you have a clear picture of personnel costs?

Have you analyzed hard costs vs. soft costs for essential processes and support?

Are costs under control?

From Kim Maxwell's perspective, libraries could benefit from considering creative solutions such as service unbundling to help with budget pressures. An à la carte approach could work well depending upon the individual needs of the library. Having the flexibility to pick and choose from a set of services is not something most libraries are accustomed to doing, but with continuing pressures on serials budgets, the need to add new discovery and access tools, and the changing dynamics of staffing requirements, unbundling may be an option for libraries to explore more seriously with their agents.

As many libraries also move a larger percentage of budgets to electronic packages, service needs change. For example, when MIT made decisions to increase the number of e-journals and considered an "e-only" transition, processes for claiming and invoicing may require adjustment in terms of tasks that staff or the agent should handle. Determining whether it is practical to continue to claim e-only titles is also important to review and something that MIT concluded was no longer necessary. Print titles essential to a specific department or research need may be ordered on a title-by-title basis outside a package to ensure they could easily flag for claiming purposes. A logical next step is to outline with the agent service levels that may be tailored according to some of these decisions.

Another consideration for the future is the basis of payment. Should it be according to fee per subscription or a percentage applied to the full list? The panelists conclude that the approach must fit the need of the institution, requiring flexibility from the agent.

To assist libraries with discussing aspects of cost analysis, Swets provides a spreadsheet listing the key elements of license management tasks, just one facet of the overall picture. The analysis is comprehensive to evaluate both the costs and business impacts. This spreadsheet can be applied to other functions. Following is a sample.

The upper section of the spreadsheet focuses on the "hard costs." The first column of the spreadsheet lists the main tasks. Examples include software costs; personnel costs such as collecting, duplicating, and archiving licenses from publishers; connecting licenses to the corresponding resources, updating licenses, standardizing licenses, and so forth. The second and several subsequent columns to the right list the hours per month spent on the tasks. Calculations permit the analysis of costs per month and year.

The second section of the spreadsheet identifies other impacts, which are often overlooked during analysis. These costs pertain to objectives or tasks that go unmet as a result of time or budget spent on tasks that could be handled differently and more efficiently. For instance, perhaps a task or two should be outsourced or supported via automated solutions.

As a result of conducting such an impact analysis, libraries and information centers can better determine the cost of the activity, in terms of both hard costs and business goals.

À la Carte Alternatives

Alternatives to the full-service pricing approach may include one or more of the following:

- Can you do without claiming print versions if you have an electronic version?

- Can you use automated tools for the majority of your work?

  Subscription management tools are more comprehensive and robust today.

- Can you go paperless for many tasks?

  Subscription agent can aid libraries with campus "green" initiatives using EDI solutions and online services.

  Integration with primary ILS (Integrated Library System) is becoming more common.

- Is content discovery important to you and your users?

  Would you consider adding other value-added services for better overall cost?

- Other scenarios—suggestions from the attendees.

Conclusion

Our electronic environment provides an opportunity for all parties in the information chain to reevaluate their needs. While agents are investing in value-added services for the electronic environment, libraries are in need of creative solutions. But creative solutions begin with understanding the internal and external costs, and the expected value of services. Organizations should carefully examine both hard costs and potential business impacts of continuing "business as usual" to determine desired pricing outcomes. From Swets' perspective, it is a perfect time for libraries to propose service and pricing alternatives because we are listening. Let your agent help serve in ways that most closely meet your needs.

Q & A Session

Presenters: Jose Luis Andrade, Swets and Kim Maxwell, Massachusetts Institute of Technology

1. Question: What are the most painful concerns libraries have?

   Responses:

   a. Budget cuts

   b. Managing usage of collections

   c. Understanding usage/value

   d. Service fees—understanding what they are really getting for the money

2. Discussion: Managing change resulting from e-resources, some suggestions from the attendees:

   a. Identify the areas libraries really need help managing.

   b. Have the ability to customize an array of services.

3. Question: Would you have a service agreement?

   Response:

       a. Yes, a service agreement is needed that outlines expectations.

4. Question: Should the pricing be a flat fee or per claim?

   Response:

       a. Must relate to the budget.

5. Question: What do vendors prefer?

   Response:

       a. When libraries cut journals, this action affects the volume of subscriptions being processed. Therefore, the price increases. Libraries should consider the array of services offered and even those that they have not considered in the past as potential tasks for their agent to perform, especially as staff is reduced.

6. Questions/Discussion: What about the RFP (Request for proposal) process? The financial page lists the fees. Would you consider a package of services rather than line-item services with fees?

   Response:

       a. Customers want to know "hidden" costs. Some attendees work closely with their agent to develop a pricing approach to better fit their situation. Others do not view the agent relationship as a close business partnership but simply as one of many suppliers.

7. Question/Discussion (from attendees): Why not sit with your agent to determine or renegotiate pricing? Would this bring a better understanding and closer relationship? Isn't there a conflict of interest for agents to receive commissions from the publisher and charge service fees to the customers?

   Response:

       a. Similar other supply chains, agents, or "resellers" get a commission for reselling a product or service and that's what publishers pay for. The service fee we charge to customers includes a broad variety of services that are not tied to reselling the content or acting as an agent. The goal of this meeting is to discuss openly the concepts of pricing, so we can talk about a fully integrated service or libraries can pick and choose the services they want or need. It can be as simple as wanting us to act just as an agent and receive no other value added services, then we would get our commission for facilitating the process, and there would be no additional service fees.

8. Question: What is the biggest service the agent charges for?

   Responses:

       a. Claims (some librarians think they need to do e-claims themselves).

       b. Multiple scenarios of invoicing.

c. Extremes: some libraries cancel subscriptions without considering things such as archiving and didn't negotiate for this.

d. Negotiation needs to be done with the publisher for billing, claiming, and platform integration.

9. Question: Would an "à la carte" model require justification with other management?

   Response:

   a. In some cases. MIT example: The acquisitions department maintains a close relationship with collections to determine what to claim. Stats from Swets are provided, and there is an indicator in the system to know.

OPENING THE DOORS TO COLLABORATIVE COLLECTION DEVELOPMENT: MEETING THE JANUS CHALLENGES IN FLORIDA

Michael A. Arthur, Head of Collection Development and Acquisitions, University of Central Florida Libraries, Orlando, Florida

KEYWORDS: Collection development, resource sharing, collaboration, core collections, licensing principles, publisher relations, scholarly communication, archiving, born digital, digitization, retrospective conversion, preservation, remote storage

Introduction

In October 2005, Cornell University hosted the Janus Conference on Research Library Collections, and the audience consisted mostly of the chief collection development officers from upper-tier research libraries. The name "Janus" was chosen because Janus was the Roman god of gates and doorways, and this symbolized the desire to forge a new pathway toward resource sharing and collaboration between research libraries. The theme for the conference and the structure for discussion began when Ross Atkinson of Cornell University presented the "Six Key Challenges for the Future of Collection Development." During his presentation, Atkinson passionately expressed his desire that research libraries would begin to forge new ways to cooperate in order to share scarce resources and to take advantage of economies of scale in purchasing and negotiation. His six key challenges included the following:

- RECON (Converting the Scholarly Record)

- PROCON (Prospective Conversion/Ensuring future publications are in digital form)

- Creating Core Collections

- Licensing Principles/Publisher Relations

- Archiving Print

- Alternative Channels of Scholarly Communication

The conference generated much excitement about the challenges facing research libraries, and a steering committee was formed to address these problems. By the 2006 American Library Association (ALA) Annual Conference in New Orleans, the Janus Challenges were a major discussion topic for the Chief Collection Development Officers of Large Research Libraries (CCDO). Following the discussions, six working groups were formed with the specific charge of addressing the challenges. By 2007 ALA Midwinter in Seattle, there had been no progress, and it seemed that this initiative had faltered at the national level. This may be attributed to the amount of time necessary for planning and implementation at the national level and a feeling among those charged with exploring the challenges that it was just too difficult to implement when facing budgetary and other pressures.

In February 2007, the Council of State University Libraries' (CSUL) Collection Planning Committee (CPC) heard from some members who were aware of the current status of Janus at the national level. It was believed that the Janus Challenges could be reformed to address the difficult issues that the state universities in Florida were facing due to shrinking budgets for materials and personnel. The Janus working group met in May 2007, and the discussion focused on ways to make the six challenges work within the State of Florida. The CPC accepted the Janus Challenges Report for Florida, and it was forwarded to the library directors. The directors approved the concept, and six Janus task forces were created with the purpose of addressing implantation strategies. The CPC Janus steering committee developed charges for each task force, and the planning process began.

Janus at the National Level

The Janus Conference was held at Cornell University, October 9–11, 2005. Members of the Chief Collection Development Officers of Large Research Libraries (CCDO) primarily attended the conference. The late Ross Atkinson, then Associate University Librarian for Collections at Cornell University, presented the structure for the discussion. His presentation on the "Six Key Challenges for the Future of Collection Development" highlighted what he believed were six areas in which research libraries could collaborate at the national level to address major challenges affecting collection development.

Atkinson presented the six challenges that included the following:

- RECON (Converting the Scholarly Record)

- PROCON (Prospective Conversion/Ensuring future publications are in digital form)

- Creating Core Collections

- Licensing Principles/Publisher Relations

- Archiving Print

- Alternative Channels of Scholarly Communication

Atkinson considered these issues to be fundamental to collection development in research libraries, and he challenged those in attendance to keep attention focused on ways in which libraries can work together to share limited resources, address space problems, ensure the long-term preservation of materials, and take advantage of buying power. Several key ideas were developed during the Janus Conference. It was pointed out that changes brought about by the previously mentioned factors, along with changes in publishing and user needs, are all impacting the future of collection development.

Atkinson emphasized that research libraries would have to move toward establishing core collections both in print and online, and defining collectively what would be shared. This in turn would free up funds for purchasing materials that make each library unique and would free up time to select these materials. This new push toward collaboration would also have an impact on the way in which libraries negotiate for price and content. Libraries would be encouraged to create the market, stipulate the conditions, and be willing to pass on products when acceptable conditions are not met.

Following the presentation by Ross Atkinson, breakout sessions were held and attendees were encouraged to develop ideas for how to address the six challenges. Goals were identified and there seemed to be considerable interest. A steering committee was formed and members agreed to regular meetings. Things were going well and by the 2006 American Library Association (ALA) Annual Conference in New Orleans the Janus Challenges were a major discussion topic for the CCDO. Six working groups were formed with a charge to develop action items for each challenge. By 2007 ALA Midwinter in Seattle, there had been no progress, and it seemed that this initiative had faltered at the national level. The question was, could it work in Florida?

History of Collaboration in Florida

The CSUL consists of eleven universities in Florida and the director of each library attends regularly scheduled meetings. The eleven universities that comprise this group include:

Florida A&M University (FAMU)

Florida Atlantic University (FAU)

Florida Gulf Coast University (FGCU)

Florida International University (FIU)

Florida State University (FSU)

New College of Florida (NCF)

University of Central Florida (UCF)

University of Florida (UF)

University of North Florida (UNF)

University of South Florida (USF)

University of West Florida (UWF)

The CSUL sets the policy and direction for collaboration among the universities. The size of the cooperative is impressive with an FTE of 191,619 in 2007–2008. The universities are supported by the Florida Center for Library Automation (FCLA). For over 25 years, FCLA has supported collaboration by providing automation support and services to the university libraries. FCLA receives state monies that are used to enhance university collections through the purchase of shared resources. FCLA spends about $5 million per year on electronic databases and automation support with roughly 185 shared databases. FCLA supported databases received 23,632,556 hits in 2007–2008, and through this collaboration the group was the beneficiary of approximately a 50% cost reduction on shared statewide licenses. Although there has been a history of cooperation, it is accepted by all members that it must increase and expand into new areas. The goal is to provide a framework for increased cooperation among the members.

Addressing Janus in Florida

In February 2007, the Council of State University Libraries' CPC heard from some members who were aware of the current status of Janus at the national level. The committee discussed the merits of Janus, reviewed the process at the national level, and explored why Janus had stalled as a national initiative. The committee felt strongly that Janus represented a basic structure to build on the collaborative collection development already in place among the eleven universities in Florida. Although the original Janus Challenges were seen as too provocative, it was also the feeling among the committee that they formed the basis of a strategic plan that could be adopted and provide benefits in the long run. In fact, the consequences of not acting were a bigger fear to the group than the struggle to begin a process for wider cooperation. Other states had implemented statewide consortia, and the group consensus was that Florida's universities had to move down that road.

The Janus working group met in May 2007, and the discussion focused on ways to make the six challenges work within the State of Florida. The CPC accepted the newly updated Janus Challenges Report for Florida, and it was forwarded to the library directors. The directors approved the concept, and six Janus task forces were created with the purpose of addressing implantation strategies. The CPC Janus steering committee developed charges for each task force, and the planning process began.

As the working group moved forward, several issues were identified that will impact the future of cooperation. Space issues are critical in academic libraries, and Florida is no different. In addition, the size of the state and the distance between the libraries presents real logistical problems when considering cooperative measures. Flat or declining budgets year over year combined with inflation, and reductions in staffing are eliminating the ability of libraries to meet the needs of patrons. This comes at a time when demand for unmediated borrowing and seamless delivery of content from patrons is stretching resources to the breaking point. Finally, concerns over preservation of print and ownership rights for online content along with the impact of constant changes in technology are adding even more concerns to this growing list. The process has moved along with each of the six task forces submitting reports to the Janus Steering Committee.

The RECON task force focused on ways to convert to digital format the holdings of the eleven universities. They envision a move away from individual institutions and toward a statewide framework. This will be realized through enhanced communication between areas such as special collections, cataloging, collection development, and digital services. In order to take advantage of talent and reduce duplication, the task force recommended resource sharing in the area of university-owned resources with a focus on maximum exposure to hidden collections, and increased visibility for unique collections. Other recommendations include central scanning, a statewide RECON team, and development of a priority list for RECON projects. The later would serve as a planning document for allocating shared funds toward realization of increased cooperation.

The PROCON task force began by proposing shared e-book collections, possibly starting with reference materials. They established various models for collective spending and suggested that each institution should set benchmarks for the total amount of funds that could be redirected toward cooperative purchasing. They recommended a standing e-book working group, which would be similar in scope to the existing Electronic Resources working group. The task force stressed the importance of perpetual rights when negotiating with publishers and developed ideas for preferred purchasing models.

The Core Collections task force focused on ways to define a core monographic collection with the understanding that individual institutions could then focus more energy on unique content. Suggestions for reaching this goal included a preferred statewide vendor and the use of approval plan profiles to guide purchasing. This task force explored the idea of having each institution be responsible for specific disciplines. Each member would identify their collection strengths and assign collection levels by discipline to develop a statewide plan for building and maintaining core monographic collections.

The Licensing Principles task force explored ways to streamline purchasing through establishment of a shared license agreement and development of approved purchasing models. The task force discussed the importance of stipulating the conditions the group would accept and also of encouraging more cooperation to build on previous success. A best practices document was developed for the licensing of e-resources.

The Archiving challenge was actually addressed outside of the Janus Steering Committee. There had been discussions about a possible statewide storage facility and the likelihood of it increased, so the CSUL created a task force to explore the issues involved. It was determined that a facility would be planned, and it would be located at the University of Florida in Gainesville. It was recommended that the task force continue for an unspecified amount of time to monitor the progress. Some of the major issues discussed included, digitization, interlibrary loan, delivery and circulation policies, funding, and preservation. Also of importance was deciding on best copy for inclusion in the storage facility and whether or not to create a separate Aleph instance and OCLC symbol. The final recommendation was for a separate Aleph instance and OCLC symbol.

The Alternative Channels task force recommended that members actively support scholarly communication initiatives and statewide education regarding IR (Institutional Repository) and open access. It was recommended that an environmental scan be completed to explore IR and open access. Finally, improved communication and sharing of knowledge was emphasized, along with building an online collection of resources on scholarly communication and open access issues.

Learning from the Janus Process

The Janus Steering Committee began this process in May 2007. It was always the intention of the group to move things along quickly. The fact that awareness of the issues has been raised is promising, and having specific recommendations in place equals success in some ways. Broad representation from the member libraries was important, and several good ideas were generated. Seeking and obtaining approval from the directors gave the project much needed support right from the beginning. Overall, it is the feeling of the steering committee that things went well, and the goal was met. However, there are things we learned along the way that may help other groups considering such an initiative.

The directors appointed the Janus Steering Committee, and all task force members were selected from those who volunteered. Looking back on it, the task force believes that all members should have been appointed based on what each could contribute to the individual task force. On occasion, it was difficult to get buy in, and so it is important to remember that tough decisions should be made by a small group of people, and policy is easier to implement when it comes from the top down.

Developing a structure to guide and monitor such an initiative will be difficult. Will the Janus Steering Committee be charged with this? Will the directors appoint a new committee? Either way the leadership structure will have to be cohesive and focused on being more directive than it was with the task forces.

The Janus Steering Committee will be meeting in Gainesville in November 2009 to review the final reports from each task force and write the final report. The report will then be reviewed by the CPC, edited as needed, and then forwarded to the CSUL. It will be interesting to see what happens from there regarding implantation of this long-term vision for increased cooperation within the state universities in Florida. Implementation of this new vision will be difficult. However, it is essential if the group is going to build library collections in the digital age and do it under harsh conditions that include severe cuts to funding and personnel.

Special Thanks

I wish to thank my colleagues who joined me on the Janus Steering Committee for their help in developing the content for this presentation:

Roy A. Ziegler, Associate Director for Collection Development

Florida State University Libraries

Claire T. Dygert, E-Resource Licensing Specialist

Florida Center for Library Automation (FCLA)

Rebecca Donlan, Assistant Director, Collection Management

Florida Gulf Coast University Library Services

Links and References of Interest

http://www.lib.fsu.edu/events/resourcesharing

http://csul.net/cmc/janus/janus.shtml

http://ecommons.library.cornell.edu/handle/1813/5426

Atkinson, Ross. "Six Key Challenges for the Future of Collection Development." *Library Resources & Technical Services* 50, no. 4 (October 2006): 244–251.

Ziegler, R. "Janus in the Sunshine." *Florida Libraries* 51, no. 2 (Fall 2008): 10–12.

END OF YEAR MONIES: THE CASE FOR CONGRUENCE

John P. Abbott, Coordinator, Collection Management, Appalachian State University, Boone, North Carolina

Georgie Donovan, Lead Acquisitions Librarian, Appalachian State University, Boone, North Carolina

Libraries in public universities and colleges, and sometimes within private institutions as well, are frequently called upon at the end of the fiscal-year cycle to spend-out not only the library's allocated budget but also the unspent residue of the entire university budget. With dozens of individual accounts, the university must juggle all of the physical plant orders that did not arrive as expected, costs for benefits such as health insurance that were lower than projections, and leftover monies from departmental lines and campus units that failed to spend all of their allocations. As nonsensical as it often seems, spending out the budget to the last penny before fiscal year close is a regular routine and an annual challenge.

Libraries often play a role in end-of-year spending because libraries typically either have invoices in hand or may quickly acquire products that are one-time purchases such as books, microfilm, datasets, or digital collections that we can order, pay the invoice, and have delivered within a very short turnaround time as required in the closing days of fiscal year. Sometimes the turnaround is measured in hours before the close of business for the last day of the fiscal year. If the library has a well-established relationship with the university budget office, often the library will be among those units who first receive a contact call asking whether they can help spend money within a short time period. Furthermore, if the library is well prepared with wish-list items, it can sometimes make a case for end-of-the-year funds to purchase items beyond their invoices in hand.

In this paper, we discuss our particularly notable case of end-of-the-year money during the end of fiscal year 2007–2008. During the final two weeks of the fiscal year, we received an amount of end-of-year money equal to 62% of our regular annual allocated budget, and we spent that amount within 10 days. The vast majority of those funds were spent on new digital purchases, which were one-time expenses with limited ongoing costs. During this time, and in years past, we have been able to make a significant impact on the level of research materials available to Appalachian State University faculty and students.

We believe that with significant preparation, clear communication with vendors, and a strong relationship with the university budget office, other libraries could take advantage of the end of the fiscal year for purchasing digital collections or paying invoices. We also believe that through good communication with customers and preparation on the vendors' part, the vendors themselves can learn more about the details of the university spending calendar and take advantage of this opportunity to increase their sales. We offer here a narrative of our experiences, followed by advice for both vendors and acquisitions and collection management librarians. Interesting problems and issues are covered as well.

What Is the End-of-the-Year Phenomenon?

A fiscal year or budget year is the period used to calculate annual expenditures against budget allocations. In universities, the fiscal year sometimes coincides with the calendar year, January through December. However, it more often runs on a July through June cycle with some variation across universities. The latter cycle places the busiest time of year in the summer rather than during the December holidays when most campuses in the United States and beyond are on holiday.

As the fiscal year progresses, campus units, such as the library, monitor budgetary allocations against expenditures, while the campus budget office as a whole keeps a watch over projected revenue from the state, endowments, and tuition and fees and compares that revenue to expenditures. Often it's hard to predict the future well enough to make these numbers match up. For example, during 2008, as endowment portfolios lost a third of their value (see *The Chronicle of Philanthropy,* http://philanthropy.com/news/updates/6881/many-foundations-have-lost-almost-one-third-of-their-assets-chronicle-study-finds), many private universities have frozen expenditures and started to develop plans for wide-scale budget cuts (see http://www.dailyprincetonian.com/2008/11/12/22071/). The same scenario occurs in public universities, but with revenues typically tied more to state income taxes as well as tuition, with some impact from endowment income.

University budgets by and large do not roll over from year to year. This inability to carry over money from one fiscal year to the next necessitates careful and precise spending in the last weeks of the fiscal year to spend as much of the budget as possible. This is a political process in the sense that spending to the last dollar proves to funding agencies that all of the money was needed; it is also a procedural process, ensuring that there is a speedy turnaround for delivery of goods, materials, and resources. No matter how diligent the attempt to spend money within a fiscal year, there are often items that don't arrive as planned or projects that haven't reached a completion point as the fiscal year draws to a close. Examples would be large HVAC units for a gymnasium that are not delivered on time and cannot be paid for before the fiscal close or benefits overhead that is allocated but not used because personnel leave.

However absurd it may sometimes seem to spend the university's budget to the last penny, this process is part of the regular working procedure of many universities and colleges and not unfamiliar to librarians. Within our own acquisitions departments, we try to pay invoices and purchase materials to the precise amount of our allocations. Operations and staffing budgets are usually managed in the same way by university units.

Background Information about Appalachian State University

Appalachian State University, in the mountains of northwestern North Carolina, is classed as a Carnegie Masters-L university (larger masters universities), is part of the University of North Carolina System, and is home to well over 12,000 undergraduates and 2,000 graduate FTE (Full Time Equivalent). The Library at Appalachian State has an annual collections budget in the range of $3 million, and our book collection is nearing 1 million items. The mission statement of the Library is "to assist those who pursue knowledge," and the most recent strategic plan focuses on four areas: learning, scholarship, engagement, and effectiveness. With a high level of participation in teaching and information literacy activities, the Library is well regarded on campus and receives very high marks in quantitative surveys such as LibQual+ and in qualitative measures such as anecdotes and feedback on our Web site and via e-mail.

For the past eleven years, Appalachian has focused increasingly on electronic databases and electronic serials, allocating a larger portion of the budget every year toward materials that are available 24/7 online. Seventy-five percent of our typical annual budget is allocated for continuing expenditures. This may indicate perhaps that a larger percent of our budget is spent on monographic purchases than is the case at larger universities, but our smaller budget and FTE keeps our costs for electronic products on a lower scale in some instances, while book unit costs are the same for us as for any institution. In addition, Appalachian focuses a great deal of purchasing power on special collections, notably on the Appalachian Collection, one of the best of its type in the country, a strong Music Library, and a strong teacher-preparatory Instructional Materials Center. These and our other special collections may tip the budget more strongly toward monographic purchases, but even though we are aware of these factors, expenses for continuing resources continue to grow, and the online resources are among the most desired and requested by students and faculty.

In the Appalachian Library, end-of-the-year funding from the university has been common over the years. Normally this money has ranged from several thousand dollars to pay on-hand invoices to a hundred thousand dollars used to buy new resources, and as a percentage of the university's almost $150 million budget, the numbers are small. Working collaboratively, the acquisitions team and the collection management team have almost always dedicated these end-of-year monies to one-time purchases. A decade ago and earlier, we purchased microform sets and paper backfiles of serials to which we subscribe, and encyclopedia-type sets that selectors found cost-prohibitive but valuable.

Appalachian State University's FY2008 Experience

For FY2008, there was no signal that life would be different. In retrospect, we did hear rumor that university-wide, staff and faculty retirements were up almost 300 percent over previous years, but we didn't appreciate the impact of that. During February and March, we, the head of the collection management team and the head of acquisitions, asked selectors to prepare wish lists of materials and to then make the preliminary contacts with vendors to determine the approximate pricing, access information, and licensing required for any digital products on their wish lists. Because our budget had grown through increased-enrollment formulae and tuition revenues during the year, selectors had already gone through a process of selecting new serials and databases—an atypical year for us, when normally, adding new continuing resources can be difficult. With the busy work of the past semester of adding new serials and databases slowly coming to a close, the heads of collection management and acquisitions decided on a guideline to help make the end-of-the-year process more time-manageable. We placed three restrictions on all wish-list items selected: (1) wish-list resources had to be electronic or online only, rather than paper, microfilm, or in another physical format; (2) items had to be one-time purchases with little if any ongoing fees; and (3) all recommended purchases had to cost over $10,000.

These restrictions were uncomfortable for many librarians who had their eye on an expensive encyclopedia set or a set of newspaper backfiles on microfilm. The restrictions also favored the humanities and social sciences to some extent, because many new digital collections available from ProQuest, Thomson Gale, and ReadEx are in the humanities and social sciences. Collections of digitized documents are crucial to work in the humanities and many social sciences, as opposed to disciplines such as many in science or technology that are more centered on very current information. However, we believe that any subject collection manager can, with adequate research and preparation, find electronic backfiles and one-time purchases of data sets or other materials that are expensive and valuable to their patrons. These materials do exist and comprise a part of the world of resources not typically available to universities with our size collections budget. The best examples of cross-disciplinary resources that would have met our guidelines include:

- online journal backfiles such as those available from Wiley-Blackwell, Oxford, Springer, Sage, and Elsevier

- Table of Contents services from vendors such as Syndetic Solutions

- e-book collections such as those from Sage, Springer, and Gale, as well as the larger e-book vendors including ebl, eBrary, and netLibrary

- online newspapers backfiles such as those collections available from ProQuest and ReadEx

For the selectors, there were many steps in the process, and those who prepared the most thoroughly made it easiest for the acquisitions and collection management heads to negotiate the final deal. We did divide the roles so that selectors were in charge of doing much of the legwork in identifying and researching products and prices, but the head of acquisitions or of collection development was in charge of negotiating and agreeing to the final deal, negotiating licensing terms and access details, and essentially triggering the order and invoice. A breakdown of responsibilities is shown here:

Concurrently with the selectors compiling their wish lists, the heads of acquisitions and collections management began to contact major vendors to give them a heads-up about our potential for end-of-year money. In many cases, we asked vendor representatives to review our holdings for their products and to make suggestions for collection additions from their products, using the same criteria we gave to library selectors. Although perhaps unorthodox, these requests pushed some of the research onto the vendor's plate; yet with so much information about Appalachian's degree programs and the databases to which we subscribe available on the university Web site, vendors had a wealth of data available to them to help self-identify products that would meet the research needs of our faculty. Also, vendors often had heard directly from our faculty members about products that were attractive, because of the companies' participation in disciplinary conferences and the vendor's outreach directly to faculty.

Some vendors jumped at the opportunity to prepare their lists of top products that would complement Appalachian's needs and current holdings. The best information came from a few vendors who took the ball and ran with it. They provided a quick list of five to ten products that could be purchased with one-time funds and would complement our teaching and scholarship programs on campus. In the best cases, they gave us pricing estimates with discounts for the products, so that we could work with real numbers. We agreed that these were not price guarantees, and sometimes there would be room for negotiation, but the pricing quotes were invaluable in our attempts to advocate for the right resources at the right time. Now we were ready and waiting.

Role of the Selector	Role of the Head of Acquisitions/Head of Collection Management
• Identify the product.	• Prompt selectors for wish-list items and give clear guidelines about any restrictions. Make sure that everyone understands the process and has the training and understanding in place to accomplish their goals.
• Be ready to make the case for why it is needed and not duplicative of current subscriptions. Knowing faculty advocates for this resource is ideal.	
• Define exactly what the product is: many products are confusing, with different subscription levels and puzzling nomenclature. A precise description of the exact product desired is crucial to moving quickly on deals.	• Compile a list of wish-list items from selectors.
	• Vet requests to identify items that meet the restrictions. Focus on bringing a balance to the disciplinary foci of the requests so that there is either "something for everyone" or that urgent needs are met as priorities.
• Identify the vendor contact person and their direct phone/e-mail.	
• Obtain a .doc/.pdf of the license if possible. (Because we use Ebsco as a subscription agent, we can often find sample product licenses in EbscoNet.)	• Ask tough questions to the selectors. Attempt to run the process equitably and transparently.
• Get a price quote in an e-mail. We would also ask selectors to inquire about a getting pro-forma invoice from the vendor which would allow us to pay quickly if needed. This wasn't always possible, but when pro-forma invoices are a part of the suite of end-of-the-year tools, it makes the process of spending money faster and simpler.	• Talk openly and honestly with vendors about the possibilities for funds and purchasing. Talk with vendors before money may be available and follow-up whether or not money is made available. Be honest about the library's needs and resources.
• Provide a thorough summary for the head of acquisitions and be able to answer questions.	• Negotiate the price if possible. It never hurts to ask about discounts available consortially or otherwise. Sometimes there is a great amount of flexibility available in the pricing, especially if it means the difference between making a sale at the end of the fiscal year for a sales representative and not making the sale. Keep this in mind and negotiate accordingly. Negotiate fairly, reasonably, and with an attitude of professional friendliness.
• Do *not* trigger an order or agree to terms, pricing, or indicate a probability that we will be able to purchase the item. The most serious problems in our process occurred when selectors indicated that we would certainly purchase a product. When we decided not to purchase, or wanted to negotiate pricing further, that flexibility was no longer possible, and vendors can be highly frustrated—and rightly so. It is unethical to misrepresent our intentions to buy something, and selectors had to understand this implicitly.	
	• Request the license and provide a fast turnaround to the vendor.
	• Trigger the order, pay the invoice, and hook up the product.

The Real Fun Begins

In some instances, all of our preparation work would have been in vain. Perhaps the university would not have had any end-of-year funds, and our preparation would have been a nice exercise in fiscal preparedness and a learning opportunity to find the research materials available in the world and their approximate costs. However, in our case, the preparation paid off. In late May, Academic Affairs, the unit that administers all of the disciplinary schools and departments, asked the Library whether we had any end-of-the-year expenditures were money to become available.

Because of our preparation work, we had a spreadsheet containing $1.6 million worth of fantastic resources (we also had another $750,000 in our pocket of second-tier items based more on high prices than the worth of the content). Of that $1.6 million, $216,000 included invoices on hand that we were holding until the next year's budget was made available. An additional $270,000 could be spent on invoices that were expected by fiscal year end but were not currently in-hand. The rest of our wish list included digitized newspaper collections, backfiles of serials and indices such as *Biological Abstracts*, and e-book collections.

In response to the e-mail to the University Librarian from Academic Affairs, we answered with the most flexible position possible: we could spend any amount that they needed us to spend, up to $1.6 million. We put the $1.6 million into tiers: $300,000 would be helpful at paying invoices on hand and expected. Were we to receive $500,000, we could pay the invoices and purchase four new products. And if we had more money, we had identified several other digital resources that could be turned on within the guidelines (and therefore "received") by the end of the fiscal year and that would make a significant impact on research and teaching on the Appalachian Campus. Our response tried to impart a sense of flexibility: we weren't asking for $1.6 million, but we could spend any amount of money they needed and could make it happen with a very short turnaround time.

On June 16, we received a heads-up phone call from the Office of Business Affairs that we would be receiving $1.6 million to spend by June 30, essentially 11 business days. In retrospect, our preparedness and flexibility likely helped the business office to make an easy decision to trust us with a large portion of the end-of-the-year money from the university's budget—a much larger amount than normal caused by projected expenses for employee benefits that were never realized. We were surprised, to say the least, but excited and ready to jump into gear.

Starting on the afternoon of June 16, the head of collections and the head of acquisitions began telephoning vendors to start the process of targeting the exact products from our wish-list spreadsheet, agreeing to a final price—and negotiating discounts whenever possible—and triggering an invoice, ideally a one-line invoice to be paid. Accompanying these responsibilities were complementary tasks such as reviewing licenses and getting them revised and signed, asking the right questions about the cataloging issues when relevant, and talking to the vendor technical support representatives to turn on access before the end of the fiscal year. To follow accounting policies, we explained to vendors that we had to "receive" the product, which meant turning on access that was available to our campus IP addresses before June 30.

The Fine Art of Negotiating

With every new product that we add to the collection, but primarily and especially with databases and journal packages, we have made it a policy to negotiate the price. To do this, we always ask questions such as:

- Can the price be lowered? We have often seen the price for products drop by as much as 75 percent, and it is not unusual for the cost of an electronic product to be cut in half after negotiations. Vendors do want the business, and the cost for them is rather scalable, because it involves more customer service, billing, and technical support—but the electronic "product" already exists.

- Are we eligible for any discounts through consortial opportunities or other arrangements? Appalachian State is a part of the Western North Carolina Library Network of three university libraries; SOLINET, the Southeastern Library Network; the Carolina Consortia which is a loosely affiliated buying group of public and private colleges and universities throughout North and South Carolina; and the University of North Carolina System. Sometimes discounts are available through one or more of these avenues.

- Could other products of interest be included in our purchase? With so much money to spend with a short turnaround time, we found ourselves asking about corresponding products or more coverage years. Perhaps we had priced out backfiles for five out of ten available collections and were able to negotiate for bigger discounts upon purchasing more collections, which made the total cost still in our ballpark.

- What are the ongoing access fees, and can those be negotiated? Many vendors will allow you to pay the ongoing fees for a certain number of years, if local accounting policies allow for this. Also, there may be ways to lower the ongoing access fees, if there is a product with a large one-time cost.

We approached our vendors with an attitude of professional friendliness, and tried to make the best match between our needs and their needs. We did require a fast turnaround time: we needed those invoices and the access within days, which was difficult for some companies to manage. Because of the time pressure we were under, we learned quickly that when vendors weren't able to meet our turnaround-time needs or weren't quickly responsive to our questions and needs for information, we abandoned our efforts to work with them and moved on to vendors who were more agile.

Sometimes vendors were surprisingly unresponsive: the end of the fiscal year sometimes falls at conference time, and this year, the Special Libraries Association annual meeting and the American Library Association annual meeting both fell during the last few weeks of the fiscal year. Many vendors' sale staffs were away for conferences. After leaving voice mail and e-mail, we sometimes abandoned our plan to procure a large backfile or collection, because no one was in the office to take our calls at the end of the fiscal year.

Also, at times, vendors were unable to negotiate and sometimes unable to get us an invoice within the short timeframe we needed. As unfortunate as this situation can be for both the vendor representative and for us, the constraints on us were firm and imposed by the university. The constraints gave us a structure within which to work, and only the vendors who could respond to that structure could we finally use. Vendors can help remedy this situation by having better mutual understanding and communications between the sales, licensing, billing, and technical support branches of the company about the urgency of requests that come at year's end. They may also want to instill a practice of negotiating prices with products that are extremely expensive, perhaps prohibitively so for smaller universities and colleges, where these kinds of monies only come once in a lifetime.

As methodically as we describe this process, it often is anything but. Some typical problems that arise in the negotiation and procurement stages:

- The sales department of the company was unable to get its accounting department to generate a one-line invoice—or any bill at all.

- The licensing department has a different definition of "urgency" than the sales department.

- A selector has indicated to the vendor that we will assuredly buy something that we found out costs more than we thought. When we have to back out, the vendor is frustrated as are we.

- In one case, there was a large set for which the sales rep had no price negotiating authority, and it was clear the rep's manager had no idea how to price the product competitively.

- After we had encumbered the $1.6 million, we signaled the Business Office on Thursday, June 26, that we were able to spend up to another $750,000 in two chunks. They said yes.

- Because of the timing of ALA, the acquisitions head left for the meetings, and the head of cataloging, Paul Orkiszewski, a wonderful colleague and former acquisitions head librarian, stepped in to finish some large deals on the afternoon of Friday, June 27, our drop-dead date.

An analytical mind-set and a sense of humor are important qualities to solve the constant puzzles offered in the negotiation and procurement process. An analytical mind-set helps keep details organized throughout the hectic phone calls and library work. A sense of humor keeps everyone from the library colleagues and staff to the vendors in a good mood despite all of the strange situations that arise.

Cleaning Up after the Two Weeks

When we finally put through our last invoice for a quarter million dollars, there was a collective exhale throughout the acquisitions department. However, we knew that all of our work had not been finalized, and that the work of obtaining these new digital resources had just begun for other teams in the library.

For cataloging, we needed to make a list of all the new products and detail items for which we had bought MARC record sets and those that needed more individualized attention. It is best if the collections or acquisitions librarian can speak with the cataloguers ahead of time to troubleshoot any issues and ask the right questions of the vendor before the sale is made. In our case, we consulted with the head of cataloging and a lead cataloguing team member about various questions related to our purchases before we actually made the sale. During that time period, when the vendors know of your strong interest but you haven't committed to a product, librarians have the most leverage to command the attention of the technical staff at the company and ask tough questions answered about the availability and quality of MARC records and the ease of adding new collections to our catalog.

Also, consulting with acquisitions staff throughout the process is important to staff morale and a feeling of team spirit. With such a large project and a short turnaround time, it would have been easy for the lead negotiators to sequester themselves with a telephone and computer until the money had been spent. However, acquisitions team members need to understand the full scope of the issues and the work at hand. Even staff members who focus primarily on monographic acquisitions were brought into the conversation so that they knew what stress had been placed on the accounting and e-products/serials ordering staff during those two weeks. Everyone tried to maintain a good spirit, and we had an ice cream party to celebrate the hard work of the staff and the new resources.

Once everything is turned on and working, subject liaisons or departmental liaisons then pick up the ball with publicity and training opportunities for all the new products. There can be a steep learning curve with new digital collections, and it is important that subject specialists are prepared to delve into the new products and learn them as quickly as possible so that they can promote them to their faculty members, start using them in instruction sessions, point them out at the reference desk, and utilize other publicity-oriented activities to get the word out about the new expenditures.

Throughout the publicity efforts, it may be wise to balance enthusiasm and thanks (to the business affairs office or similar) for the money to purchase the collections with a certain discretion about the amount of end-of-the-year money received by the library. After all, other departments and their faculty may have had similar requests in for money that were not granted, and if the university has a large pool of end-of-year money, it may not be wise to be indiscreet about the amounts.

Final Lessons

Our conclusions from this experience led to lessons that would be applicable to vendors and to librarians.

Five Lessons for Vendors

1. Be aware of your clients' fiscal year. Call libraries early—in April for a June fiscal year calendar end—and ask about end-of-the-year money.

2. Review your client's holdings and make suggestions. Know what your clients have and what they might need. With the proliferation of information on university Web sites, it is be appropriate to look at the departmental homepage for certain disciplines within the university as well as the library's holdings or databases page.

3. Make sure that your company has strong communication links between the sales department and the licensing and invoicing departments. It is important to have good technical support as well, but the speedy turnaround time required at year's end is needed most in obtaining a correct invoice and getting the licensing details settled.

4. Ensure your availability at the fiscal year end. Check voice mail and e-mail or have a competent backup who can help with orders while you are traveling.

5. Don't leave the customer hanging after the sale. Make sure that products are turned on and without glitches and, if the university accounting rules require it, that these products work before the end of the fiscal year.

End-of-the-year money can be an opportunity for congruence among the needs of patrons, librarians, the university, and vendors. If we are all equally prepared for quick action and do not waste time, this can be the occasion for great resources. To prepare our colleagues in libraries, we considered the following suggestions to be of relevance.

Ten Lessons for Librarians

1. Do homework in early spring to prepare an itemized wish list with the cost and terms of available products. Digitized backfiles of serials and journal collections, digitized historical documents and primary sources, e-book collections, and digitized newspapers all make excellent choices for this type of one-time money expenditure.

2. Have your list prepared to send before anyone asks for it.

3. Be bold.

4. Have only one person talk to only one person. This rule may apply to the business affairs office or to the relationship between library and vendor. This tenet essentially replicates the advice of "too many cooks in the kitchen spoils the soup."

5. Know when to move on. As hard-hitting and stern as it may seem, in this situation, we are the customers, and we have all the money. Once we have committed or expressed sincere and strong interest in a product, vendors should really be working full time to meet our needs. They should be quick to respond to questions and problems and quick to provide licenses and invoices, as well as answers to crucial questions. If they cannot do this, then there are plenty of other vendors out there who are hungry for the sale and have wonderful resources that the campus also needs.

6. Be clear and firm with selectors. Don't commit to products or give unreasonable promises about what we can purchase. Unfortunately, sometimes negotiations break down or you need to be able to walk away from a deal because of difficulties with the terms or price. If the selectors understand the process and the reasons why the deal failed as an end-of-year purchase, everyone is much more satisfied with the results of the process.

7. Deal in good faith with vendor representatives. Although we strongly encourage assertive negotiating on pricing and access terms, we would never recommend leading a vendor to think that a purchase was imminent if it is not. We advocate a straightforward attitude and honesty in negotiations and conversations about products. This advice extends to the vendors as well.

8. Get permission to speak directly with the campus accounts payable, academic affairs, and the budget or controller's offices. It is too difficult in crunch time to have to speak through the director or dean of libraries. If you can be trusted to spend the money, you should be trustworthy enough and have enough authority to speak directly to the campus budget directors.

9. Stay within the auditor's rules. Don't violate guidelines or local policies just to make a sale happen. For us, this meant we could not pre-pay invoices (paying twice for a product within the same fiscal year) and we must receive—technically, having access turned on to a digital product—the product before the end of the fiscal year.

10. Be as flexible as a yogi. The constraints we place—whether it's how much money we can spend, how much advance notice we need, how much time we need to get the work done—limit the opportunities available to the library. End-of-the-year money may be the one chance that the library has to procure fantastic but prohibitively expensive research materials.

Different types of collaborative projects were presented this year at the Charleston Conference. Librarians are now finding themselves in more collaborative relationships than ever before. Several topics were addressed including analyzing articles, workflow issues, and working with vendors.

Collaboration

8,000 CITATIONS...ARE YOU CRAZY?

Susan deVries, Instructor, Halle Library, Eastern Michigan University, Ypsilanti, Michigan

Robert G. Kelly, Assistant Professor, Halle Library, Eastern Michigan University, Ypsilanti, Michigan

Paula M. Storm, Assistant Professor, Halle Library, Eastern Michigan University, Ypsilanti, Michigan

Jackie Wrosch, Assistant Professor, Halle Library, Eastern Michigan University, Ypsilanti, Michigan

Drawing upon a list of 244 number of Eastern Michigan University (EMU) faculty publications found in Web of Knowledge from 2005 to 2007 the team of Susan deVries, Bob Kelly, Paula Storm, and Jackie Wrosch extracted and analyzed the articles and their 8,643 supporting citations to determine if the library had access to the books, articles, government documents, etc., to support faculty research.

To further refine the process the team, with the assistance of professor Joe Scazzero and using Survey Monkey, developed a short set of survey questions for all the represented EMU authors to determine if and which EMU library resources they used to support their article research. We asked about their use of the University of Michigan libraries and other academic libraries in southeast Michigan. We asked them to identify the department with which they are affiliated and provide extended comments about EMU Library services and resources.

We wrapped up the information gathering with face to face interviews of highly published faculty from each of the colleges to gain an in-depth understanding of how they personally used the library and what could be done to improve its resources/services. All team members concurred that the personal interviews, aided with the survey data, revealed new information that both surveys and numeric analysis did not yield, including how faculty research affects students and library usage.

In Summary

Out of all of the 209 unique journal titles in which faculty published, EMU owned 183 titles, or 87.56%. After reviewing 95% of the 8,643 cited references, we were pleasantly surprised to learn we owned almost 70% of the references cited. 86% of these citations were journal articles, 11% books ,and 3% other—including government documents, tests, Web sites, etc.

The most frequently cited journals were in the science subject areas (68%). This could be due to the bias of the Web of Knowledge (WOK) file. Even though we included the WOK Arts & Humanities Citations, the humanities were still not well represented. We need to look at other resources to learn where the EMU humanities faculty have published.

Out of the 124 participants surveyed, we had a return rate of 28%. We were encouraged that 94% of respondents reported utilizing the EMU Halle Library for their research. Over the past few years we've enhanced our interlibrary loan service to improve its performance and 50% of all faculty responded they use this service and are pleased with the speed and electronic delivery of most items. 64% of all respondents reported using the nearby University of

Michigan libraries (10 miles away), which included collaborative research with UM faculty and funding to support specialized collections.

We gleaned from the interviews that because our faculty do use the library and are familiar with our resources, they encourage their students to utilize Halle Library materials to support their research needs and know they will receive the in-depth help for their information literacy needs. Additionally, EMU faculty do not expect the library to subscribe to those highly specialized publications that directly support their research, but are not likely to be used by EMU students.

Virtually all faculty indicated they seldom use print journals and purchasing ejournals is clearly the best option for insuring usage of journal content. When reviewing journal titles for cancellation, in addition to usage, citation analysis could be another measure for determining whether to retain or cancel a title. Conversely, looking at heavily cited titles which EMU doesn't own would provide a funding request opportunity to fill in those gaps in our collection.

Our future plans include determining if we own the remaining 5% cited articles and comparing other journal evaluation tools such as Eigenfactor.org with Web of Knowledge to see if they provide a more comprehensive assessment based on several factors vs. citations alone.

RETROSPECTIVE TITLES: VERIFICATION AND ONLINE ACCESS

Charles F. Hillen, Head of Monograph Acquisitions and Metadata Services

Ann J. Roll, Acquisitions Librarian, The Research Library at the Getty Research Institute, Los Angeles, California

Introduction

Ever increasing online access to retrospective titles has generated new challenges for acquisitions and collection development staff who are verifying orders and performing pre-order searching. Several university presses, such as the University of California Press, are offering fully-digitized titles free of charge. Other projects that are broader in scope, such as the University of Virginia's Digital Text Collections and the Internet Archive's Open-Access Text Archive, are digitizing public domain books, among other things. When faced with ordering a retrospective title, staff can search a wide range of sources of digitized materials and may discover online access. In the case of gray literature, such as conference proceedings, they often discover that online access is the only option.

A major concern is that no one is mining and aggregating this large body of scattered digital resources, which means that the pre-order search and verification process can be time-consuming. In the Research Library at the Getty Research Institute, we began to face these challenges by writing a white paper that identifies some major questions about our collecting process, how to incorporate these sources for digitized material into our ordering workflow, and how our discoveries are affecting our perception of the print collection in general. The basic premise being that if we are concerned about providing e-books to patrons for all of the many advantages they offer, we must to some degree be concerned about our retrospective print holdings that now have electronic versions that are not available in the library catalog.

Background of Institution

J. Paul Getty opened his art collection to the public in 1954, founding the J. Paul Getty Museum. In 1982, most of Mr. Getty's personal estate passed to the J. Paul Getty Trust, which was established as a cultural and philanthropic organization for the promotion of the arts. The Trust is currently manifested in four programs: The J. Paul Getty Museum, The Conservation Institute, The Foundation, and the Research Institute. The Research Institute is composed of several departments and work areas, including the Research Library, the International Bibliography of Art (formerly BHA), Avery Index to Architectural Periodicals, Art & Architecture Thesaurus (AAT), Union List of Artist Names (ULAN), Thesaurus of Geographic Names (TGN), Project for the Study of Collecting and Provenance, Exhibitions, Scholars Program, and Publications.

The Research Library was established in 1983. The collections focus on the history of art, architecture, and archaeology with relevant materials in the humanities and social sciences. The range of the collections begins with prehistory and extends to contemporary art. Online databases and materials made available to professionals and the public. The library catalog (Voyager) is available on the Web (http://library.getty.edu) and provides access to over a million secondary source volumes, including books, periodicals, and auction catalogs. The library's collections focus on western European art, but it is expanding to include Latin American, Eastern European, and Asian art. Other areas in the library include special collections that consist of rare books, prints, drawings, archival materials, maps, films, optical devices, photographs, and architectural models. There is also an Institutional Records and Archives, a Photostudy Collection and a Conservation Collection.

Challenges in the Verification Process

Collection development and patron research needs require that the collection has no date or language restrictions. The library maintains twelve approval plans covering France, Italy, Germany, Netherlands, Spain, Portugal and Brazil, Spanish-speaking Latin America, USA & UK. Staff regularly firm order Chinese, Japanese, Korean and Scandinavian titles. The young age of the library and the esoteric research needs of the scholar community make retrospective firm orders plentiful and routine across languages and countries of publication. For new titles, staff is accustomed to going straight to vendors' selection tools to place orders. However, in the case of retrospective titles they go to online second-hand booksellers or place their hopes in vendors who might accept retrospective orders and seriously pursue hard-to-find titles.

New Horizons

By way of the Research Library's involvement with what became commonly referred to as "The Sloan Project" among participants, acquisitions staff became increasingly aware that full-text retrospective titles, particularly those that are now in the public domain, are becoming digitized and made available online. "The Sloan Project" was spearheaded by The Internet Archive, which received grant funds from the Alfred P. Sloan Foundation in order to help organize, facilitate and create an open digital library. Several institutions participated in the project, including the Boston Public Library, Johns-Hopkins Libraries and the Bancroft Library of the University of California, Berkeley.

Since the sources for free-of-charge digitized full-text monographs are not, on the whole, aggregated or distributed in a cohesive way, the idea of searching in multiple discrete sources for a given title is daunting, to say the least. In order to begin incorporating searches in these types of resources into regular workflows, we created a pilot procedure in which Google Books and the Internet Archive would be the only two sources we would check. We decided to start with these two because they have the highest numbers of monographs digitized. While keeping concerns for workload, efficiency and proof of payoff in mind, we felt that staff could add searches in these resources with relative ease. In the meantime, as we discover new sources of free digitized texts, we maintain a list of sites and continue to familiarize ourselves with the types of resources each organization is offering.

Sites of Scholarly and Other Interests

- The Internet Archive: http://www.archive.org/details/texts
  All free and full text. Includes Gutenberg Project, Universal Library, American and Canadian Libraries, Children's Library and the Biodiversity Heritage Library.

- Google Books: http://books.google.com/advanced_book_search
    Choose "full view" to retrieve full text only.

- eScholarship Editions: http://www.escholarship.org/editions/search?style=eschol;
  brand=eschol;smode=advanced
    Choose "public access books" to retrieve freely accessible titles.

- The Gutenberg-e Project: http://www.gutenberg-e.org/
    Open access site. Columbia University Press collaboration with the American Historical Society. Humanities and award winners only.

- Rice University Press (Connexions): http://cnx.org/
    Books are full-text and can be read online. Open access, print-on-demand model.

- University of Virginia Free Ebook Library: http://etext.virginia.edu/ebooks/
    About 2,100 titles available to the public. Humanities only.

- University of Michigan Digital Library Texts: http://quod.lib.umich.edu/cgi/t/text/
  text-idx?xg=1;page=simple;
    Offers browsable collections, several of which contain full text books.

Conclusions

While library vendors are centralizing the purchase of e-books that are available through major distributors, there is no centralized location in which to locate **free** materials. Staff search OCLC to see if we find a record for an electronically accessible version, but where that fails we proceed with our new workflow. Vendors are unlikely to take on this task because there is nothing tangible or discrete to sell. Besides providing libraries the service of aggregating and allowing centralized searches on these discrete resources, there is little else from which an established library vendor can profit.

Where questions about payoff regarding searching for free versions of retrospective titles arise, do we choose cash flow (i.e., free access) over cost-benefit (i.e., staff time to search for free access)? We believe that the experiment is worth the trouble. It is arguable that staff time is really wasted because, for us, the gamut of research, ordering, payment, receiving, is much more time consuming and costly.

Patron and staff have always reacted positively when we have informed them that we found free online access to a requested title. Time and again we have noted that it does not seem to occur to anyone outside our department to search for free online access to retrospective titles.

We can add more sites to our verification process over time, but we will carefully assess the potential for payoff. For example, sites like Gutenberg-e do not have many titles to offer at this time. However, we feel confident that digitization projects will become more common at libraries, and we will see many more retrospective monographs become freely available online.

THE OLD GRAY MARE IS NOT WHAT SHE USED TO BE

Christine M. Stamison, Senior Customer Relations Manager, Swets, Runnemede, New Jersey

Presenters (In speaking order)

Ann Okerson, Yale University, Associate University Librarian for Collections and International Programs—Moderator

Dan Tonkery, EBSCO, VP Business Development

Christine M. Stamison, Swets, Senior Customer Relations Manager

Tina Feick, Harrassowitz, Director of Sales and Marketing for North America

Abstract

Subscription agents have made major investments in supporting e-journal subscriptions, publisher packages and consortia activities. This panel of industry experts will take a look at how agencies have changed and cover the new way of doing business.

The Current Situation for Subscription Agents

Competition in the subscription agent arena is stiffer than ever. The past ten years have seen the demise of many subscription agents, both large and small. Some industry analysts conclude one of the primary reasons for this situation was the introduction of electronic media. With this new media, agents needed to invest millions into updating their existing systems to become "Knowledge Bases" as Dan Tonkery, Vice President Business Development, so aptly explained during his presentation. Agents needed to develop new services to stay competitive. Those who could make those steep investments and could provide value in this complex online age survived and gained the edge; those who could not simply went out of business or were bought out by another company.

To stay competitive, subscription agents have been listening intently to their customers' needs and have been attempting to stay ahead of the curve in the management of electronic collections. All the while, libraries' budgets have been shrinking or have been diverted elsewhere. This has made the task of maintaining and increasing the subscription agents' market share more difficult. As "faster, better, cheaper" has become our customers' mantra subscription agents have been tasked with solving the complex electronic needs of our customers in the most efficient and cost effective way possible. In this fiscal environment, not only do libraries have to leverage their budgets to become more efficient, agents must do as well.

Simplifying the Complex eWorld

With vast investments and improvements in systems, some subscription agents are now well poised to assist both consortia and individual libraries with their electronic media needs. Over the past few years consortia have bypassed subscription agents and have negotiated directly with some of the larger publishers for entire packages of electronic content. As these deals have increased, libraries have lost the ability to receive line by line EDI (Electronic Data Interchange) invoices for the titles in the packages. Neither publishers nor consortia can provide this value added service that has benefited libraries for many years. With EDI invoicing, libraries are automatically able to load invoice information into their Integrated Library Systems (ILS) and store title by title pricing information for budget tracking purposes. When going direct for these large package deals libraries are rarely receiving the title by title cost information. For those who are getting this information from the publishers/consortia, the libraries are entering it manually into their ILS systems. At a time when it is crucial to track major expenditures, libraries are losing this functionality.

How Subscription Agents Add Value for Consortia

To reintermediate themselves with consortia, subscription agents have developed services to assist consortia (and libraries alike) manage the administration of the "Big Deal." The services include:

- Harmonizing large publisher package lists

- Simplify complex pricing models (price increase cap adherence)

- Breaking out costs for participants

- Providing EDI invoices

From the beginning of the "Big Deal" one of the most labor intensive tasks has been assuring that the title lists match. Often the list of titles that a library believes should be included in a deal does not match the list of titles the publisher believes should be included in the deal. This is what is referred to as the harmonization of lists.

Once the prices are broken out for each title, the agent then supplies each library with an EDI invoice that can be automatically uploaded into a library's ILS system. Over the years libraries have come to depend on EDI invoice loading to lower their administrative costs and to free up staff time to devote to more pressing matters.

In order for consortia to take advantage of the above benefits in the management of large publisher deals, it is important to stipulate when negotiating with the publisher that the consortia can use a subscription agent for billing and invoicing arrangements. By doing this, consortia can offer the valuable service of better tracking of electronic expenditures for its member libraries.

How Subscription Agents Add Value for Libraries

It is important to state that the services listed above under "Adding Value for Consortia" also apply to those libraries who manage their own publisher agreements. Many of the larger academic and corporate libraries prefer to negotiate packages on their own and would also benefit from outsourcing billing and invoicing to a subscription agent.

As mentioned in the beginning of my presentation, subscription agents have transformed their back-end systems into knowledgebases by adding a panoply of information. All of this new information has now been made available in subscription agents' online systems and add further value to libraries. Some of the information subscription agents are now tracking is:

- Terms and conditions of generic licenses

- Definition of site

- ILL rights of the electronic copy

- Electronic reserve rights

- Access length

- Links to publishers' licenses

This information, integrated into subscription agents' online system, speeds up the discovery of relevant information to make informed decision about electronic resources.

Apart from transforming their systems into knowledgebases, subscription agents have also introduced new services that help track and manage libraries' electronic resources. In the case of Swets, our service, eSource Manager is a cost effective remotely hosted service that comes prepopulated with a library's information and population. This service also includes:

- Ability for customization

- Ability to add a library's license

- Information that is automatically maintained

- Procedure for tracking internal workflows

As libraries' needs evolve in the electronic environment, agents will continue to invest in new and innovative services to manage libraries' collections.

Conclusion—Partnering for Success

The services mentioned above are just a few ways that subscription agents are staying ahead of the curve in this fast-paced electronic environment. It is important to stay in touch with your subscription agent and find out what new services they are providing and to make suggestions for enhancements or new services of interest to your library. Whether the customer is a member of a consortia or library, subscription agents have developed products and services that can simplify the complex nature of the electronic environment. Subscription agents are not "just periodicals" anymore; we offer a host of services that allow libraries to manage their electronic collections, and yes, even e-books! Please be sure to ask your subscription agent for a demo of their services.

When you think of the Charleston Conference you think of content development. With the tremendous growth of electronic resources, librarians find themselves looking for ways to accurately evaluate resources. Key topics essential to collection development were presented including scholarly communication, approval plans, and identifying core collections.

Content Development

KNOWLEDGE MANAGEMENT IN ACQUISITIONS

Xan Arch, Electronic Resources and Technology Librarian, Stanford University Libraries, Stanford, California

Introduction

Spending the time to create a central organized resource for Acquisitions information greatly improves the ability of users to find information efficiently. This translates into more time for staff to do their work and greater satisfaction overall. So how can we create a better platform for Acquisitions information? After looking at the landscape of knowledge management tools in the Stanford Libraries Acquisitions department, we identified **structure**, **linking**, **multimedia**, and **personality** as qualities that were needed in a new resource. Focusing on these four methods of presenting information allowed us to create a resource that is efficient and pleasing to use. As the resource evolved, we found three major categories of information to manage: **staff**, **management**, and **outreach** from Acquisitions to other groups.

To create our Acquisitions information resource, we used Confluence, an enterprise wiki platform from Atlassian. Using an enterprise-level platform allowed us to create multiple wikis within a single installation. Each wiki could have its own layout and preferences, specific to the audience. Confluence was purchased by our Digital Library department for their internal project work and after seeing how my staff struggled with finding the information they needed, I decided to adapt Confluence for Acquisitions use. I was initially reluctant to move my staff procedures to a wiki platform because I was concerned about allowing staff members to add or change procedure information. I changed my mind after learning that I could set up our wiki space as a unidirectional communication. All Stanford Library users could view the procedures, my staff could view and comment, and only I could edit the content. Knowing that I could establish stable, secure documents for my group, I was ready to get started.

Staff Information

The first wiki was a procedure repository for the Acquisitions Ordering unit, a group of nine staff supervised by an operations manager and a librarian. This group works directly with bibliographers to purchase material in all languages and formats. Each of the Ordering staff members has very specialized language and procedure skills, and most have been working in Acquisitions many years. To start, I had to think about what this group needed to know, and where that information was located.

The two major categories of information we found were procedures and meeting notes. Procedure documents were the most basic type of information we needed to manage. These documents had been housed on the library website in a long alphabetical page of links. This was not a bad resource but suffered from the difficulty of updating the website quickly. Documents became outdated and new procedures were often just emailed to staff to save time. Additionally, the alphabetical organization made it hard to find documents efficiently. Group meeting notes were stored separately in a shared folder of Word documents, on the library server. These documents were not indexed in any way besides date, so it was difficult for staff to use them for their work. Besides procedures and meeting notes, additional important categories of information were contact lists for other departments, administrative policies, links to web resources, and lists of vendors by country and type of material. We had never tried to provide a central place for these categories of information, mainly because of the difficulty of keeping the documents up-to-date. Instead, staff made their own lists or printouts, making it hard to share this information or insure that it was kept current.

After identifying what types of information we had, we had to structure the wiki. In discussions about wikis, the prevailing idea is often that wikis should evolve organically. This is certainly true for a group of colleagues working together on a project; an organic evolution promotes involvement and does not impose a structure on participants. As a wiki evolves this way, it is usually set up as a two-part structure—the homepage links to all the documents. However, as a manager, trying to create an efficient resource for staff work, I felt that structure was important to establish from the start so that information would be organized and easy to find. The two-part structure can feel cluttered and confusing so my aim was instead a three-part structure. In this three-part structure, the homepage links to category pages which then link to individual documents. The categories allow a user to navigate through the wiki like they would use a menu on a website.

With this structure in mind, I created the Ordering group home page. The home page has broad category links, such as "Ordering" and "Vendors," that lead to secondary pages with lists of procedures. I also created a few direct links to procedures from the home page as a type of "quick reference" tool. For example, while the staff will know that Electronic Orders are in the Ordering section, they are likely to use the Electronic Orders section frequently so I added a link directly from the homepage.

After creating a structure, I tackled linking. Three types of linking that were fairly basic, but important for creating this resource, were contextual linking, links to websites, and links to the procedures of other units. Contextual linking was possible in our old library webpage, but as many of our old procedures had been copied directly from paper documents, there had been no effort made to link procedures together when they referenced each other. Uploading Ordering procedures to the wiki gave us the opportunity to find these intersections and make a more networked system of documents to help staff understand the interrelationships between procedures. Links to websites and to the procedures of other staff units had not been done systematically in the past and were a way to provide a wider context to Ordering work. In evaluations of the wiki, ordering staff particularly mentioned the links to other units as a valuable way to learn about the holistic Acquisitions workflow.

The final type of linking was with tags. As mentioned earlier, the procedure documents and the meeting notes had been stored separately – one in library webspace and the other in shared folders. However, these two types of documents are very closely related. Procedures come out of discussions in meetings, and meetings are a chance to explain and elaborate on procedures. Tags helped us show these relationships in the wiki. For example, a tag for "940" (the MARC field) could be used in both a procedure and in the notes from a meeting. Looking up this label shows both of these documents together for the user.

Multimedia was the next technique we used to create the Ordering unit wiki. Like contextual linking, screenshots were possible in the existing library website, but no-one had taken the time to add these pictures to the staff procedures. With the move to the wiki, I used SnagIt (a very nice screenshot tool) to take screenshots and used these screenshots to illustrate our documentation. It was very easy to upload and place the screenshots in context with each document and the added information gave staff another way to understand a procedure. In some cases, I also used Visio to create workflow graphs or organizational charts for addition to the wiki. Screencasts were another useful media addition to the wiki. Screencasts are short videos of a procedure done on your computer. An example might be setting up an advanced search in your library database – each mouse click or menu choice can be captured. You can add audio narration or captions to explain each step. These short videos were also easy to upload and link to the wiki, giving users another format to learn a process. I used a program called Camtasia to create these screencasts for the wiki.

The last technique of presenting information for the Ordering group was personality. I added a cartoon animal to the homepage on a whim, though having a group mascot seemed somewhat silly and unnecessary. However, I found that the staff really enjoyed having a mascot and it provided an anchoring point for the wiki. As a part of a system of linked wikis, it was helpful to have a recognizable picture to show you at a glance that you were in the Ordering space. Soon after the wiki launched, we held a naming contest for the mascot, and the staff chose the name Tofu. The contest was a fun way to encourage the group to support the new wiki platform.

The second use of personality, the addition of staff-contributed content, might seem to run counter to my earlier insistence that staff not be able to update or change the wiki content. However, each of the staff in our Ordering unit has very specific knowledge of certain procedures as well as knowledge of the countries and languages they use for ordering. This is the idea of "tacit knowledge"—that individuals can have important information to contribute to a group but either not understand its importance or not know how best to express it to others. Even if I prefer that my staff does not update the wiki themselves, a platform that is easy to use and update is an opportunity to find these areas of knowledge that have not yet been explored. I asked staff to send me brief outlines of procedures that they alone did as part of their work or lists of vendors that they used for specific countries or language groups. I then mounted these on the wiki, making sure to credit the staff that created each procedure.

After we created a resource for the Ordering staff, other Acquisitions units began creating their own wikis using many of the same techniques – the anchoring picture, the broad categories linking off the homepage. The Serials Receiving wiki site was particularly interesting because of the dual ways they organized their content. The Serials group started with an alphabetical list of procedures, just like Ordering, and when they moved to the wiki, everyone was happy except for a few people who protested that they could not find anything unless it was alphabetical. So the managers in the Serials group linked the procedures two different ways within the wiki: categorically and alphabetically. Staff who preferred the alphabetic list could view procedures that way, and those who liked the new categories could view procedures like this. This illustrates the flexibility of the wiki platform to provide different ways to organize content for different viewers.

Management Information

After the Acquisitions staff units had created procedure platforms, we thought about what other information we needed to manage. The second wiki was aimed at Acquisitions managers, a group of eight people with a mix of professional librarians and paraprofessional operations managers. What kind of information do Acquisitions managers need? Some of the major categories we identified were Integrated Library System testing, high-level vendor information, and departmental statistics.

The Acquisitions managers are responsible for testing the acquisitions modules of our ILS for every upgrade. In the past, we have done this on a spreadsheet in a shared folder. This makes the end of an intense testing cycle difficult since multiple managers are trying to access the spreadsheet at the same time. So we moved Integrated Library System testing to the management wiki. This allowed us not only to let more than one user access the spreadsheet at the same time during last-minute testing, but it allowed us to create links between each ILS function and the corresponding release notes from our ILS vendor. The managers could test each function in comparison with the notes about how that function should have changed during the upgrade. This richer context for testing allowed us to be much more detailed in our feedback to our Systems department about each change in the ILS.

High-level vendor information is another important category of information to manage. This might include approval profile documents or shelf-ready processing specifications. These had been stored previously in shared folders, according to vendor, and we needed a more secure organized place for them. After moving them to the management wiki, we used tags to make the vendor information even more accessible. Whereas the staff wiki contained many documents that were interrelated, the management wiki had very different types of documents so tagging them as a group wasn't as important. Instead we used the tagging function in one section of the wiki to bring together information about a specific vendor. This was a new vendor with whom we were having weekly calls as we established our business together. As we had more calls, it became harder to remember what decisions we had made at what time. Tags brought together the calls by topic and helped us retrieve the decisions we had made with the vendor when needed.

Departmental statistics had mostly been kept by individual managers, and then emailed once a year to the head of Technical Services. The wiki provided a way to display the statistics all in one place in multiple formats including tables and graphs. The head of Technical Services can now go to a single place to see all the statistics for Acquisitions and can choose to view the month-by-month details (linked to the graphs) or compare the graphs to see the performance of different units.

Outreach to Other Groups

After the management resource, the third wiki project was outreach from Acquisitions to bibliographers. The Stanford Libraries include approximately 40 subject specialists spread out all around campus. The physical separation between the bibliographers and Acquisitions means that the flow of information has often been scattered and incomplete. Usually we have communicated with bibliographers through mass emails and trainings, and without any resource for Acquisitions information, the bibliographers came to us frequently for reminders or retrainings.

How could we provide a resource for the bibliographers that would save Acquisitions from repeating the same information and trainings and would make the bibliographers feel supported in their work? First, we needed to establish what the bibliographers needed to know. Some basic categories were Acquisitions contact information, ILS documentation, vendor database information, and fiscal data.

Acquisitions contact information is very fundamental, and we had provided a brief contact list on the library website in the past. However, the bibliographers could benefit from more detail about staff in each unit as well as who to contact for specific questions. For the

Acquisitions contact page, we used several formats to provide multiple ways to find the correct contact person. First there is a listing of the unit heads with contact information, and those are accompanied by envelope icons that lead to pages with more details. There is also a link to a listing of contact people according to the type of question. "If you need help with…" allows the bibliographer find the correct contact person for questions that might seem to involve multiple Acquisitions staff.

ILS documentation and vendor database information are types of information we were providing to bibliographers only through group trainings. While Acquisitions used these databases daily, subject specialists might use them weekly or less frequently. This meant that they forgot how to perform processes and needed reminders or more training. The wiki provided a place for detailed documentation, including screenshots and screencasts, on procedures using the library acquisition tools.

Finally, fiscal data is something that often comes initially to Acquisitions. We find out from vendors about next year's price increases or the last few years of monograph pricing. We establish the serial cancellation deadlines and know how to run the budgeting reports. We had been emailing this information to bibliographers but the wiki provided a more organized way to communicate fiscal data.

Conclusion

In summary, we found three types of information to manage in Acquisitions: staff, management, and outreach. We used four techniques to make this information easy and efficient to use: structure, linking, multimedia, and personality.

Why do this? We struggled a lot with the currency and accuracy of our procedures when we were using shared folders and a central website. This was improved by moving to a platform that could be updated quickly to keep pace with changing procedures. The ability to easily upload different information formats, such as textual, video, and audio, made the wiki a good place to reach all types of learners. The wiki provided a way to teach those staff members who prefer to follow a procedure through screenshots or a short video, rather than work their way through a step-by-step text procedure. Finally, we have found that our users are very happy with the new resource. I did a survey of the Ordering unit after the move to the wiki platform and every single person found the wiki to be a better resource that what we had previously. Meetings between our new Acquisitions Head and all 50 Acquisitions staff also revealed that staff consistently mentioned the new procedure documentation as an improvement to their work environment.

The time needed to create a new knowledge management platform for Acquisitions is well spent when you can provide a place where staff, managers, and bibliographers can find current information quickly and easily. Our wiki projects in the Stanford Libraries Acquisitions Department have given us a place to house and access our most important documents and we continue to find new uses for this space.

SCHOLARLY COMMUNICATION AND COLLECTION DEVELOPMENT LIBRARIANS: GETTING THE CONVERSATION STARTED

Karen Fischer, Collections Analysis & Planning Librarian, University of Iowa Libraries, Iowa City, Iowa

Introduction

In many academic libraries, knowledge of the issues surrounding scholarly communication is considered a skill set required by every librarian who has contact with faculty and students. In fact, these skills are now being written into job descriptions for librarians who are on the front lines with faculty. Learning about these complex issues takes time, but there are ways to facilitate the process of empowering librarians with the information they need to be knowledgeable enough to have conversations with their constituents.

The issues surrounding scholarly communication are very complex. They take time and effort to understand, let alone to be able to talk eloquently about them. Conveying the complexities of scholarly communication issues can seem daunting, so how do we to begin the conversation?

The agenda for my presentation will involve:

1) Discussing the Foundations—I will define scholarly communication and then talk about some fundamentals to get you started in thinking about setting up a program.

2) Areas of Expertise—This will provide an overview of four main areas of expertise related to scholarly communication that any librarian with contact with faculty will need.

3) Methods of Education/Training—I will discuss some methods to learn about the issues and how to share what you know with staff.

4) Challenges Ahead & Next Steps

The library alone does not have control over the outcomes of scholarly communication education efforts. The efforts of libraries to effect change on the system are only one of many factors at work. There are many players in addition to libraries, such as faculty, researchers, commercial publishers, scholarly societies, and government regulations (Newman).

Defining Scholarly Communication

Scholarly communication means the formal and informal processes through which research results and other scholarly work are disseminated to other researchers and scholars, students, policy makers and the public.

Current discussions of scholarly communication are rooted in such inter-related problems as: the consolidation within the journal publishing industry that has increased control by a few large companies; more than a decade of very high journal price increases that have decreased libraries' ability to purchase access to them and have led to dramatic reductions in scholarly monograph purchases; and continued, serious erosion of authors' rights to their work.

Stages: The Road to a Scholarly Communication Program

Before embarking on a program to educate librarians, it is helpful to have some measure to evaluate and understand progress. Joyce Ogburn, in her article "Defining and Achieving Success in the Movement to Change Scholarly Communication," nicely outlines the stages on the road to a scholarly communication program.

A program has to recruit many people to speak eloquently and take direct action on the issues – a lone voice or two is not enough. Collection managers, who have direct contact with faculty, can be considered an asset in the stages of a Scholarly Communication Program.

The first stage, Awareness, involves being conscious and having knowledge of the issues. Journal pricing is seen to be the main issue to be addressed, and librarians are the most knowledgeable players at this stage and they begin to share their concerns with others. This stage tends to be marked by complaints and limited conversations, but efforts are put toward researching and comprehending the problem.

In Understanding, the second stage, a higher order of knowledge, intelligence and appreciation of the issues is obtained. In the library, concern becomes alarm. Librarians recognize that the issues extend beyond journal prices and that authors also are integral to the structure and function of the publishing enterprise. This is the stage where many libraries start a formal scholarly communication program.

The third stage, Ownership, connotes commitment and obligation to the issues. During the ownership stage, scholars, administrators, and librarians increase in their engagement with the issues. "Scholars speak on behalf of solving the problem, and are personally and acutely cognizant of how the system functions in their discipline and across the wider scope of scholarship. . . . Ownership is marked by the recognition and acceptance that the players in scholarly communication all share responsibility and a stake in a healthy system" (Ogburn, 46).

The fourth stage, Activism, involves "goal-oriented, concerted and purposeful action" to make change. Actions are taken to make the system sustainable and to create new models. "Activists successfully recruit external allies to take action and librarians collaborate to employ common and coordinated strategies" (Ogburn, 46).

The final stage, Transformation, equates to the attainment of a profound alteration of assumptions, methods and culture. Local programs at the transformation stage are involved with rapidly evolving scholarship, and it demands collaboration by many stakeholders to achieve a shared vision. Currently there are no programs at this time that are at this stage.

As you can see from these stages, engagement from scholars becomes an integral part of achieving a marked, sustained impact on scholarly communication. Librarians must get involvement and engagement from faculty and scholars on the issues. "Scholars must be the new face of the effort to change the scholarly communication system and focus on how the present system restricts access to their research" (Stemper, 692). Collection management librarians need to understand in-depth what matters to faculty, so that the issues around scholarly communication can be framed in terms they understand and care about.

What Matters to Researchers and Scholars?

Efforts to change the system and reach out to faculty will not work if you do not understand what matters most to academics. Effective strategies with faculty include discovering their concerns, interests and motivations and this in turn may encourage them to support scholarly communication transformation.

In March 2008 the Joint Information Systems Committee (JISC) published a report titled, "Key Concerns within the Scholarly Communication Process." The Executive Summary of the report nicely outlines four main areas of concern: accessibility, cost, rights, and quality. Noted below are a few key points that help us to understand what researchers are most concerned about.

Accessibility

- Availability does not equal accessibility. Researchers' top concern about scholarly communication is that they cannot access all the content they wish to access.

- Researchers remain poorly informed about open access. Awareness is growing but still only slowly and many misconceptions remain.

- Researchers are eager to maximize their own impact and reputation but do not understand what means and opportunities are available to them.

Cost

- There is considerable uncertainty and lack of informed reflection on the issue of payment of article processing charges for publishing in open access journals. Researchers tend to believe that all OA journals require payment (when fewer than half do) and tend to dismiss this avenue for disseminating their work on the basis of that misconception.

- The cost of using copyright-protected materials is inhibiting and distorting scholarship in some areas of the arts and humanities.

Rights

- Researchers remain rather confused about copyright. They are aware of it but are not fully informed about operational details or implications.

- Researchers are not clear about how to manage their own rights in their work or about how to present their outputs in forms that can easily be re-used.

- They are interested in the notion of retaining the rights in their own work but are not sure how to go about this.

Quality (peer review)

- Peer review is considered to be the gold standard although researchers' thinking on this is not consistent.

- The assessment systems (such as ISI's Journal Citation Reports) in place for research are based on few indicators and have skewed researchers' publishing behavior.

Becoming knowledgeable in the areas that matter to faculty is an important inroad to being an advocate. To this end, reviewing why scholars publish is part of understanding what they care about. Scholars publish for many reasons. Some of the common reasons are to make an impact and have an effect on their field of study, to build a reputation, to engage with other scholars, to fulfill institutional expectations (get tenure, promotion, etc.), for professional advancement (another position, grants), and to make money or become famous. Keep in mind that much of what matters to faculty also matters to graduate students. Reaching out to graduate students is important too, since many of them will be the scholars of the future.

Areas of Expertise

The four areas of expertise that I will address today are: author rights/copyright, the economics of publishing, alternative publishing, and repositories. I will touch on key points of each of these to give you an idea of the content that could be included in a scholarly communication program.

Author Rights and Copyright

Author rights and copyright will likely be the most complex issue to be addressed when talking about scholarly communication. It serves as the foundation for all the other issues, and the topic will probably matter the most to faculty.

"All rights reserved" is the norm in today's environment; the complete regulation of the use of creative works is more common than not. Because the environment for publishing is growing increasingly complex, it is more important than ever to manage copyright in ways that serve author interests and those of the scholarly community. Authors need to know the following essentials about their copyrights:

- The author or creator of an original work automatically has copyright for it, which gives them exclusive control of how the work is reproduced, distributed or performed.

- Copyright is a bundle of rights that can be transferred, in part or in full, from the author to a publisher. Almost all rights in bundle can be given away or sold. The bundle includes:

  The right to: (1) to *reproduce* the work; (2) to *prepare derivative works*; (3) to *distribute* copies; (4) to *perform* publicly; (5) and to *display* publicly;

- Faculty, graduate students and researchers own the copyright to their journal articles and books, *unless the sign away their rights.*

One good option for authors is to retain all rights but transfer to the publisher the single right of first publication, rather than completely transferring the copyright bundle as scholarly journal publishers often request.

So, why should authors retain their rights? First, retaining rights allows authors to share their research more widely. They can control how their work is distributed and used, including future uses not yet anticipated. Second, authors have the opportunity to maximize their work's potential reach and impact by minimizing barriers between their work and their potential readers. More readers equal more impact. Studies show that making your work more accessible increases readership and citations. And third, authors may reuse their work for updates or derivatives.

The essential rights an author should retain allows them to: 1) use their own work in teaching and scholarship, 2) reproduce, perform, or display their work as they wish, 3) distribute their work to students and colleagues, 4) use their work in presentations and later publications, 5) authorize non-commercial uses of work, and 5) to deposit their work in open online archive or on a web site.

Knowing how to retain rights is an important so that we may help faculty do this. The negotiability of publication agreements is becoming increasingly more common, and many publishers have responded by making their agreements more author-friendly. Authors should read and edit the existing publishing agreement and remove any "exclusive" language. Or, they can change the publisher's copyright agreement by attaching an author's addendum.

An author's addendum is an easy way to address author needs without authors having to edit the legalese on an existing agreement. It serves as a tool for educating faculty about their options and the negotiability of agreements. Many publishers are willing to negotiate publication terms; submitting an addendum is important, even if initially unsuccessful, as publishers are likely to consider policy changes in response to requests from faculty authors. Additionally, it is becoming more common for publishers to have an alternative license which allows the author to retain some (or all) of the rights an author wants. Publishers may accept new terms even if they reject an addendum.

The Creative Commons (CC) and SHERPA provide free tools that can be very helpful for authors. Creative Commons (http://creativecommons.org/) has tools that allow authors, scientists, artists, and educators easily mark their creative work with the freedoms they want it to carry. CC helps authors make their own license; this can be particularly useful when copyrighting something not published in a traditional manner, but it works well with traditional scholarly works and some publisher use this license. The Public Library of Science and Rockefeller University Press are two examples of publishers who use a CC license for all their publications. The SHERPA project is a consortium of UK institutions with active interest in the establishment of open access institutional repositories. RoMEO (http://www.sherpa.ac.uk/romeo/) is an online tool where you can view the self-archiving and copyright policies of a publisher, as well as many examples of publisher agreements. There are currently 414 publishers listed.

The Economics of Publishing

The second area of expertise is the economics of publishing. Most collection managers are familiar with what has been happening in the world of publishing and the drastic price increases that libraries have endured for over two decades. However, it is likely that non-collection managers who serve in roles as liaisons may need some training on this topic. In the interest of time and because I know that you all understand these concepts well, I will just briefly talk about this topic—mostly to illustrate a few ways of presenting the information to maximize its impact.

We know that the volume of Information is increasing exponentially. World production of scholarly communication is estimated to have doubled in the past 20 years, yet the average research library subscribed to 6% fewer journals and purchased 26% fewer monographs in that same time period.

Prices are increasing exponentially as well. This graph from ARL, which has been modified, illustrates some startling facts.

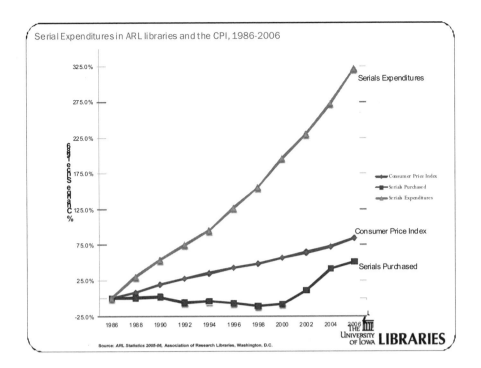

Serial Expenditures in ARL libraries and the CPI, 1986-2006

Source: *ARL Statistics 2005-06*, Association of Research Libraries, Washington, D.C.

Statistics collected by ARL show that in the past 18 years serials expenditures for ARL libraries have increased over 275%, the number of serials purchased has increased only 50%, and the consumer price index (CPI) increased about 73%. This illustrates the reduced buying power for libraries. The volume of information available has skyrocketed and library budgets have not been keeping pace with rate of inflation.

Showing faculty this ARL graph or examples of "sticker shock" can help convey the message of a library's reduced buying power. Most faculty members have no idea what libraries pay for of an institutional subscription to a single expensive journal or a package deal.

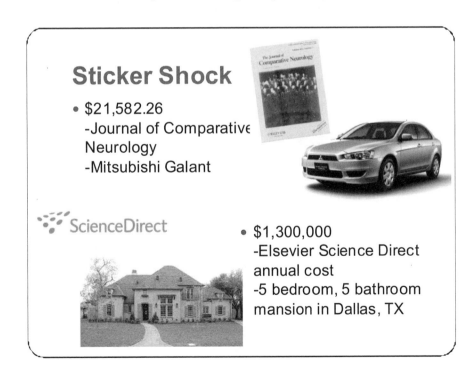

Sticker Shock

- $21,582.26
  -Journal of Comparative Neurology
  -Mitsubishi Galant

- $1,300,000
  -Elsevier Science Direct annual cost
  -5 bedroom, 5 bathroom mansion in Dallas, TX

Understanding the ramifications of purchasing bundled or aggregated content is important too. The advantages of bundled content is that you get more content, it can be a more efficient way to obtain content (one license agreement, one order), and it helps to limit inflation through price cap deals with publishers. The disadvantages are a loss of control over selection decisions, a larger portion of the budget goes to fewer publishers, and it can have an effect on new journals entry into the market.

The University of Iowa Libraries spends more than 50% of its budget on electronic resources. The graph below shows how our expenditures on electronic journals are divided by publisher. It is readily apparent that a few large publishers are dominating the market.

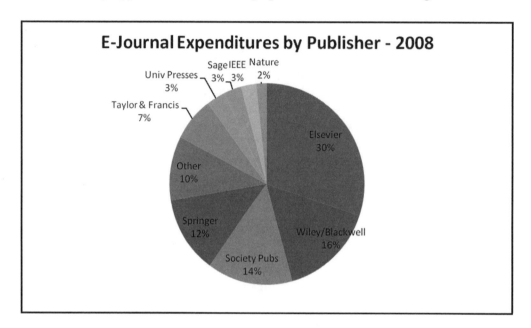

As collection development librarians know, expenditures on electronic resources impacts monographs. Due to shrinking demand and rising costs of publishing, the market for books has been reduced; scholarly books today sell 200-400 copies compared with 1500 copies a decade ago. Additionally, research shows a strong correlation between mergers and rates of inflation in journal prices. Mergers increase the price of academic journals. All these economic changes have forced librarians (and others) to start looking at alternatives to traditional publishing models.

Alternative Publishing

New publishing models attempt to make scholarly information more broadly available while sustaining the advantages of traditional publishing, such as peer review and the availability of articles through indexing and abstracting services. There are costs associated with journal publishing, no matter what model is used for access to content. For traditionally published journals, funding is generated by subscription charges, while funding for open access journals and other alternatives often comes from author charges or the funding subsidies. The third area of expertise, alternative publishing, encompasses open access and other alternative publishing models, such as the new role of libraries as publishers.

Open access generally means that scholarly articles are freely available to everyone on the internet, regardless of affiliation, and that the copyright is retained by the author. For those of you who have attended the Charleston Conference over the past five years, we've heard a lot about open access. I'm not going to spend much time on this now, but be aware that it is an area with which all liaisons should be extremely familiar. Several studies indicate that articles that are freely available have as much or even more research impact as other articles. An OA choice may also make a difference in how often an article is read or cited.

There are real challenges to OA publishing, as well as many misconceptions. Two main challenges are the sustainability of OA publishers and journal viability. With many new journals coming on to the market at the same time, competition is fierce. Additionally, understanding and overcoming misconceptions (such as OA always means the author pays or, OA will destroy peer review) are part of the process of becoming knowledgeable about open access.

The hybrid journal model includes a mixture of fee and free access and the author has the choice to pay for open access to his/her article. The portion of publishers offering OA options has grown from 9%-30% in 2008 alone. The SHERPA website provides a list of all the publishers offering an OA option. With a hybrid OA model, confusion can result from difficulty in determining what is free and what is not within a single journal issue. This becomes especially problematic for libraries that use of link resolvers.

ARL published a study of publishing services provided by member libraries (http://www.arl.org/resources/pubs/reports/). Key findings of the study show that publishing services are rapidly becoming a norm for research libraries, particularly journal publishing, and that the numbers of titles research libraries are publishing represent a very thin slice of the scholarly publishing pie.

One good example of a library as publisher is the University of Michigan Libraries Scholarly Publishing Office (SPO). The SPO provides an array of sustainable publishing services to their community. They keep costs low and the methods sustainable by leveraging the resources and expertise of the Library to offer a core set of services for digital publishing and partnering with others to extend these services when necessary.

Digital repositories are another component of alternative publishing. Repositories will be discussed next, and in-depth, because all librarians should have a good grasp of what the benefits (and challenges) are for repositories, and specifically institutional repositories.

The choice of where to publish can make it easier for scholars and their colleagues to read and make use of their work, and the alternative models discussed are important elements to increasing readership and accessibility.

Digital Repositories

Digital repositories are the final area of expertise. From the standpoint of scholarly communication discussions, librarians should have a basic understanding of the purpose of repositories (institutional or disciplinary).

Purpose of digital repositories is: to create a place for author self-archiving of peer-reviewed publications; to archive non-standard scholarly products (working papers, technical reports, data sets); to collect, disseminate, and provides persistent and reliable access to the research and scholarship of faculty, staff, and students; and to support new uses of digital media for scholarship.

There are two main types of repositories. Institutional repositories are digital archives of intellectual products created by the faculty, staff, and students of an institution and accessible to end users both within and without the institution. Disciplinary repositories are used to facilitate sharing and storage of research materials within a certain subject area. These repositories have high rates of participation in their fields. Repositories exist in many disciplines.

The University of Illinois at Urbana-Champaign's Center for Informatics Research in Science and Scholarship (with support from the Mellon Foundation) conducted a one-year study of advances in institutional repository development. The report, titled "Identifying Factors of Success in CIC Institutional Repository Development," indicates that librarians have a key role in the success of an IR. Liaison librarians are part of the "essential human infrastructure of IR development" (Palmer, 3).

The report shows that in IR development, librarians worked in existing liaison roles to inform planning and policy decisions, to identify potential early adopters, and to communicate the mission of the repository to faculty.

Many libraries and campuses across the nation have are in the process of implementing an institutional repository. Challenges in these endeavors have been identified, and some of those challenges are:

- Engaging faculty and students in IR content submission

- Complicated publisher policies on what can be deposited

- Copyright issues

- Faculty reservations about trends in open access (and misconceptions)

- Faculty from different disciplines perceive and value IR services differently

We are facing many of these challenges at Iowa. As the liaison to the School of Library and Information Science (SLIS) at the University of Iowa, I discussed with faculty the launch of our institutional repository, called Iowa Research Online (IRO). I approached SLIS about serving as an early adopter; the department would benefit by having faculty pages built for them by library staff, and the libraries would benefit by getting content into IRO and having a department to showcase to around campus to promote it. I was very surprised to find that they were a reluctant group, and generally felt that there was going to be "one more thing" they'd have to do.

Palmer writes in her report, "Perhaps most important to the viability of IRs, however, were the faculty who found that the IR could solve a particular information problem they faced in the everyday practice of scholarship." As you develop a program to educate your own staff and faculty about the benefits of an IR, think about ways to frame your institutional repository to solve information needs of your faculty.

Methods of Training

The final portion of this presentation will highlight methods to be employed in a scholarly communication program to help you get the conversation started with your collection managers, and to enable you to bring forth the issues discussed up to this point.

1. **Attend the ARL/ACRL Institute on Scholarly Communication.** The Association of College and Research Libraries and the Association of Research Libraries jointly sponsor the institute to promote the development of library-led outreach on scholarly communication issues. The institute's signature event is an immersive learning expe-

rience that prepares participants as local experts within their libraries and provides a structure for developing a program plan for scholarly communication outreach that is customized for each participant's institution. Many attendees have found this to be a valuable experience.

2. **Create a public website.** A website serves as a resource for your own librarians on topics related to scholarly communication, as well as a public place for librarians to show faculty and for faculty to find on their own. Some example websites are:

> MIT Libraries - http://info-libraries.mit.edu/scholarly/
>
> University of Minnesota Libraries - http://www.lib.umn.edu/scholcom/
>
> University of California Libraries - http://osc.universityofcalifornia.edu/
>
> University of Iowa Libraries - http://www.lib.uiowa.edu/scholarly/index.html

3. **Develop a Departmental Assessment Instrument (also called an "environmental scan").** This idea originated from the Institute on Scholarly Communication and has been further developed and refined by the University of Minnesota Libraries. It is a survey tool used by collection managers and departmental liaisons. Its purpose is an information seeking exercise which helps selectors get to know their department in depth, opens the door to discussions with faculty on topics such as OA, author rights and archiving, and lastly, helps identify content for your institutional repository.

In preparation for the Institute on Scholarly Communication, you attempt this exercise. I completed one of these for political science, which included a discussion with the past-chair of the department. I was very surprised to learn about his perceptions of online only journals (that they were of less value and has less vigorous peer-review), of OA (that they had no peer review), and about tenure requirements (publications in online-only journals count for less), and author rights (he assumed that he had retained the rights to his work all these years). Our conversation opened the door to a topic he had never thought much about before.

Part one of the assessment instrument involves identifying disciplinary repositories and OA journals in a certain discipline, and listing primary societies, any OA mandates they have, and the journals they publish (and their copyright and self-archiving policies). Part two involves discovering major grant activities in the department, identifying faculty who are publishing in OA and journals those who deposit in repositories, recording the tenure requirements concerning alternative publishing venues, and identifying journals and books published within the department.

Examples of Minnesota's instruments can be viewed at:

> https://wiki.lib.umn.edu/ScholarlyCommunication/SurveyPartOne
>
> https://wiki.lib.umn.edu/ScholarlyCommunication/ScanPartTwo

4. **Develop talking points and slide banks.** Talking points serve as a quick reference guide and can be used as a handout on relevant topics for librarians or patrons. Developing PowerPoint slides on specific topics, which librarians can modify as needed, can serves as a slide bank for librarians who may use these to present the topics to faculty or graduate students. At the University of Iowa, we have created four different PowerPoints based on the four areas of expertise identified in this presentation. In the slides we have provided subject specific information librarians may use depending on who their audience may be.

5. **Present forums or workshops to library staff.** A general forum introducing the broad topic of scholarly communication is a good way to get the conversation started. Or, invite a guest speaker to present on a scholarly communication topic. Having an expert from outside the library puts into perspective a topic's importance and can be very inspiring. After a general session, delving more deeply into specific topics is useful and this approach has been well received at Iowa. For example, a 90-minute copyright/author rights session might include the what, why, and how of author rights, reading and understanding actual publishing agreements, becoming familiar with author addenda, and introducing the resources within the Creative Commons and SHERPA. A workshop on the NIH Public Access Policy could involve going over the NIH FAQ, a demonstration on how to deposit an article, and other important factors that an NIH-funded author should know. A session on institutional repositories might include the selling points on benefits of a repository, details on tools the repository provides, how to deposit an article, and advice on how to talk to faculty about your IR.

6. **Develop brochures.** Brochures highlighting your library's scholarly communication website and the services your library provides regarding these areas adds support to your scholarly communication program. Most importantly, it gives liaisons materials to share with faculty and can assist them when an opportunity arises to talk to faculty or graduate students. Brochures on copyright and the NIH Public Access Policy can provide a good resource for authors, and give the library an opportunity to showcase any related services.

7. **Publish a newsletter or blog on scholarly communication.** At the University of Iowa we publish two newsletters, one for whole campus and one specifically for the health sciences campus (Transitions: (http://blog.lib.uiowa.edu/transitions/) and Hardin Scholarly Communication News: (http://blog.lib.uiowa.edu/scholar/). The newsletters, published about 4 times a year, are in a blog format and are intended for faculty and librarians and the news items are distilled and summarized. Keeping appraised of developments in scholarly communication can be daunting; a newsletter or blog helps to highlight the most important or interesting stories that are related to academia. Some excellent sources of news are:

   - LJ Academic Newswire
   - Peter Suber's Open Access News (http://www.earlham.edu/~peters/fos/fosblog.html)
   - Scholarly Communications @ Duke (http://library.duke.edu/blogs/scholcomm/)
   - Other blogs: UIUC Libraries, MIT, Scholarly Kitchen (SSP)
   - Chronicle of Higher Education

Challenges Ahead and Next Steps

There are challenges ahead. Some of these are:

- The journals market is rapidly evolving and changing and as is area of open access and alternative publishing. Because of this, it demands much of our attention to keep appraised of new developments.

- The community of scholars and researchers remains uninformed and naïve about many issues that loom large in this period of transition and reinvention regarding scholarly communication.

- It is increasingly important that a much broader group becomes engaged in the dialogue around a number of key scholarly communication issues and concerns. Assisting our collection development librarians to become well versed in scholarly communication and helping them find ways to relate this to what scholars care most about will help in broadening this discussion.

- There is overwhelming agreement in the library community that the most effective way to engage scholars and researchers in change in the scholarly communication system is thorough one-on-one conversations.

Being educated on author rights, the economics of publishing, alternative publishing, and institutional repositories will give librarians confidence to talk intelligently when they have the opportunity for one-on-one conversations faculty or graduate students. The ultimate goal is to make the discussion of scholarly communication scholar-centric, not library-centric (Hahn). Ogburn stresses that an integral part of going down the road to scholarly communication program is faculty involvement. Understanding what matters to faculty is fundamental to effecting change.

Works Cited

Carole L. Palmer, et al. *Identifying Factors of Success in CIC Institutional Repository Development - Final Report*. New York, NY: Andrew W. Mellon Foundation, 2008. http://hdl.handle.net/2142/8981

Hahn, K. L. "Talk about Talking about New Models of Scholarly Communication." *Journal of Electronic Publishing* 11.1 (2008).

Newman, Kathleen A., et al. *SPEC Kit 299: Scholarly Communication Education Initiatives*. Washington, D.C.: Association of Research Libraries, 2007.

Ogburn, Joyce L. "Defining and Achieving Success in the Movement to Change Scholarly Communication." *Library Resources & Technical Services* 52.2 (2008): 44-53.

Stemper, J., et al. "Scholarly Communication: Turning Crisis into Opportunity." *C&RL News* 67.11 (2006).

Swan, Alma. *Key Concerns within the Scholarly Communication Process: Report to the JISC Scholarly Communications Group*. Key Perspectives Ltd, 2008. http://www.jisc.ac.uk/media/documents/aboutus/workinggroups/topconcernsreport.doc

Van Orsdel, Lee C. "The State of Scholarly Communications: An Environmental Scan of Emerging Issues, Pitfalls, and Possibilities." *The Serials Librarian* 52.1/2 (2007): 191-209.

APPROVAL PLANS AND THE SMALLER LIBRARY

Steve Hyndman, Sr. Collection Development Manager, YPB, Contoocook, NH

Dr. Elaine Yontz, Professor- MLIS Program, Valdosta State University, Valdosta, Georgia

Jack Fisher, Acquisitions Librarian, Valdosta State University, Valdosta, Georgia

The session "Approval Plans and the Smaller Library" was held at the concurrent sessions on Friday, November 7. The speakers for the session were Steve Hyndman, Senior Collection Development Manager at YBP, Elaine Yontz, Professor of Library and Information Science at Valdosta State University, and Jack Fisher, Acquisitions Librarian at Valdosta State University. The presenters felt that all too often, approval plans are perceived as being utilized only at large and well-funded institutions but approval plans can work for smaller libraries too. The use of approval plans in smaller academic libraries was discussed from the perspectives of the vendor, professor-selector, and the acquisitions librarian. Approval plans that are tailored for a small budget and focused on discrete subject areas can speed up the receipt of new materials, save library staff time, and improve the collection.

Steve Hyndman spoke first and pointed out some basic facts about approval plans. They are an efficient way to bring new books into the collection by targeting publishers and subject-specific areas and then combining that with non-subject aspects to purchasing, such as cost or format. Steve also pointed out that an approval plan should have several goals.

- Providing books to strengthen a specific subject area

- Provide coverage in the absence of a subject selector

- Bring the number of titles selected to a manageable number by utilizing core lists, awards lists, and key reviews

Approval plans work in two ways. Books that meet the profile created by the vendor and librarian are automatically shipped. Returns are possible, usually with some restrictions. Slip notification plans send paper copy bibliographic information and these serve as an alerting or notification service of new titles for potential ordering. Vendors now also make it possible to have virtual approval or slips plans through their online ordering systems. Virtual slips can also be made available with reviews for additional fees.

Steve illustrated the use of an approval plan by Goddard Library at Clark University in Worcester, Massachusetts, an institution of less than 2,500 undergraduates and offering 31 undergraduate degrees. They created a Library of Congress classification profile for their U.S. and world history collection that brings in about 400 books per year.

Dr. Elaine Yontz, professor of Library and Information Science at Valdosta State University spoke about her experience creating an approval plan from scratch in support of the new degree program. Through her knowledge of publishers in the field of library science, an analysis of the course syllabi and an understanding of potential research needs of the library science students and faculty she and the vendor created a publisher/subject area profile that has met the needs of building the collection.

- The plan makes it possible to take minimal time to manually select titles.

- The plan skims the best titles that probably would have been manually chosen anyway.

- The plan gets important new titles into the collection quickly.

- The plan uses only a portion of the department's allocation allowing for book selection outside the profile.

- The plan utilizes paper slips to broaden the selection beyond the books that are automatically sent.

Jack Fisher, Acquisitions Librarian at Valdosta State University, an institution of just slightly over 10,000 full-time students, spoke about the implications of the approval plan on the acquisitions department. Odum Library had not had any approval plans because they were considered cost prohibitive. Several departments were chosen to experiment with an approval plan to see how they might be integrated into the workflow and budget. As mentioned above, the Master of Library and Information Science Department was chosen because it was a new program in need of collection development and the department liaison, Dr. Yontz, knew from previous places of employment that an approval plan could be effective even with a limited budget. The Early Childhood Education Department was also selected because they were interested in ordering children's awards books but found the process of manually determining all the awards titles to order took too much time and they frequently missed important titles. The library also wanted to make its browsing book collection more current so they wanted to receive New York Times bestsellers in a timelier manner. The three profiles were created, books are shipped, and the titles are available in the catalog for patrons shortly after they arrive in the library. The Early Childhood Education Department spends less than one-fourth of their allocation on the awards books and the Library Science Department spends slightly less than one-half their allocation. In addition to approval books the Library Science Department uses a combination of vendor slips and manually selected titles to spend the remainder of their allocation.

The only difficulty the acquisitions department has encountered is the spending timeline for the university. All ordering must be completed and items received three months before the end of the fiscal year. Funds may be encumbered for items expected to be received by the library during those three months but determining an exact figure is difficult. It is possible now, since the plans have been running for several years, to get a fairly close figure to reserve for approval shipments during those three months.

Those in attendance at the session were presented with a comprehensive view of approval plans by the fact that a vendor representative and a subject area selector and an acquisitions librarian from a small academic library were present at the session. Just as in a real life situation, these three collaborate to develop a profile or plan that meets the needs of the library and the department. Each pointed out the benefits to a small academic library of using an approval plan such as saving time for the selector, currency of the collection, and ease of workflow for the acquisitions department.

A brief bibliography from the presentation:

Jacoby, Beth E. (2008). Status of approval plans in college libraries. *College & research libraries*, 69(3), 227-240.

> Based on a survey, included in the appendix, this article details the current status of approval plans in academic libraries. Other aspects of library purchasing of monographs are included such as budget information and how libraries are dealing with electronic books. This article updates information from 2003. This is a very significant work and worthy of your time.

Fenner, Audrey (2004). The approval plan: selection aid, selection substitute. *The acquisitions librarian*, 16(31/32), 227-240.

Fenner's article is a must read for those thinking about approval plans or not familiar with this purchasing method. Very basic information is presented in an easy to read style. Though it might be considered a little old or too fundamental by those experienced with approval plans it would be very helpful to someone new to the field or considering this purchasing option.

Wilkinson, Frances C. & Lewis, Linda K. The complete guide to acquisitions management. Libraries Unlimited, 2003, 68-69.

These two pages of this textbook present some basic information about approval plans and list some important questions to ask when considering this method.

BIBLIOGRAPHIC CONTROL AND THE LIBRARY OF CONGRESS

Deanna Marcum, Associate Librarian for Library Services, Library of Congress, Washington, District of Columbia

Summarized by Heather Miller, Director for Technical Services and Systems, University Libraries, SUNY Albany, Albany, New York

Presented at the Charleston Conference, November 7, 2008

Good morning and thank you for this opportunity to address The Charleston Conference. My plan is to speak briefly about the current state of bibliographic description and then let you ask whatever questions are on your minds.

As you know, the Working Group on the Future of Bibliographic Control was established by the Library of Congress to examine the future of bibliographic description in the 21st century. The group consisted of information professionals representing the American Association of Law Libraries, the American Library Association, the Association of Research Libraries, the Special Libraries Association, Google, Microsoft Corporation and the Program for Cooperative Cataloging. At-large members represented the Coalition for Networked Information and OCLC. It was chaired by Dr. Joe-Maria Griffiths, Dean of the School of Library and Information Science at the University of North Carolina at Chapel Hill. The group's charge was to:

- Present findings on how bibliographic control and other descriptive practices can effectively support management of and access to library materials in the evolving information and technology environment

- Recommend ways in which the library community can collectively move toward achieving this vision

- Advise the Library of Congress on its role and priorities

When I received the Report of the Working Group I reviewed it carefully. Additionally, I sought assistance from the Management Team of our Acquisitions and Bibliographic Access Directorate, from an internal working group that has been giving thought to bibliographic control as part of our Library Services unit's strategic planning efforts, and from Thomas Mann, the LC reference librarian who has been most vocal in criticizing changes proposed in our system of bibliographic control. The report and LC's response to it are on LC's website (http://www.loc.gov/bibliographic-future/news/index.html).

The Library of Congress needs to position itself to work in a new, networked, collaborative environment and is thus paying close attention to the recommendations. Some of them include: paying more attention to LC's special collections, making catalog records and content of unique materials available; sharing production of catalog records for more widely held materials; and finding new ways to collaborate and broaden LC's reach to the user. The report also recommended suspending work on Resource Description and Access (RDA), a new standard for resource description and access intended to work smoothly in the digital environment, being developed by LC and global partners. This was highly controversial and, in fact, LC and other libraries will be testing RDA. The test methodology in still being designed and will be available on the web.

Questions and Answers

Is the Library of Congress the national library? By practice, yes; by statute, no. Congressional views of LC vary. LC has strong interest in providing services to the library community. We do this out of tradition, but are not funded for it.

What counts as a catalogable item for this discussion? At LC, the focus has been on creating catalog records that other institutions will use. LC's own collections number some 138 million items. There are only about 30 million catalog records for them. LC needs to find ways to get information from finding aids into the catalog.

What about foreign language materials? LC is particularly concerned about foreign language materials which constitute sixty percent of the collection, in 450 languages. This is an important continuing focus at LC.

The quality of LC's cataloging seems to be declining. *We do not think our quality is declining* staff *has a* commitment to "gold standard" cataloging, but considering all of LC's needs and services provided and all the materials we have not yet cataloged, it is not proper for LC to be defined by just one activity. *We provide different levels of cataloging for different types of materials.*

Do we need to embrace bringing catalog records from amazon.com and get away from perfect records? As good as the catalog records are, 89% of users of the LC online catalog come from Google. My main concern is providing sufficient access points.

Is there a strategy to ensure that catalog records are created for all books that are published? Yes, the Program for Cooperative Cataloging (PCC) which also is examining standards and how to broaden its base. Its website is: http://www.loc.gov/catdir/pcc/2001pcc.html.

Quality control is a concern. How can a small staff deal with it, if LC does not? There are enough institutions able to contribute to enable PCC to broaden its base without negative impact on small libraries.

Re the special collections of the Library of Congress: better descriptions would be outstanding, but the numbers are so big that it will not be done in a generation. How can it be done? It is indeed a gargantuan task! A team of technical experts is looking at the possibility of extracting data from finding aids. They are looking first at the roughly 25 million music records, rare books and the Asian Divisions.

A NEW DECAMERON: CHARACTERS AND TALES IN THE BLACKWELL COLLECTIONS BODLEIAN LIBRARY AND MERTON COLLEGE

Rita Ricketts, Blackwell's Historian, Bodleian Visiting Scholar, Kellogg College, University of Oxford, Oxford, United Kingdom

Prologue

"There is a special aura of adventure…You may begin in a one-room office and branch out all over the world……………………yet stay more-or-less in one place"[i]

This paper looks inside the Blackwell Collections, lodged or to be lodged at The Bodleian Library and Merton College, University of Oxford. Settling in the Collections was the first stage, followed by an examination of the actual papers and books themselves. Perhaps one of the most revealing ways to think about these Collections is to see them as a "new" Decameron: a series of stories used as a device to explain not only the history of Blackwell's, booksellers and publishers, and its association with reading and writing folk around the world, but also its characters: their life and times and interactions with their readers, customers and each other.[ii] The Collections reveal a portion of cultural, social, political and economic history within a moment of time, roughly 1840-1960. But they are just one small *local* contribution to the much greater work being carried out at the Bodleian. Implicitly the study is a celebration of over 150 years of the relationship Blackwell's has had the privilege to enjoy with its closest neighbour, the Bodleian, as well as universities and libraries worldwide. The first known contact outside of Oxford, and the UK, was in 1846. A bill survives, dated 11 January 1853, for the production by the Oxford Chronicle of 250 catalogues for Benjamin Harris Blackwell, bookseller, numbering twelve pages.[iii] Somehow these catalogues found their way to other centres of learning across the world: an invoice dated May 30, 1853 for books to the value of £4.14s, was sent to a Mr John Gooch of Pennsylvania.

Although the Blackwell Collections chart the course of the firm's success, from its halting beginnings in 1846 to the end of Sir Basil Blackwell's time in Broad Street, they also reveal Blackwell's inseparability from the people, time and place that made it. In preserving their tales, the Blackwell Collections brings to life a tantalising cast of characters: from young boy-apprentices, war poets, early feminists, bookseller diarists and unworldly typographers, to the grandees of politics and academia. In the presentation made at the Charleston Conference, an attempt was made to show the variety of tales "told" by this New Decameron of characters and how they came to be preserved. That they should be preserved was the wish of Julian Blackwell, anxious to preserve the memory of his great grandfather, Benjamin Harris, his grandfather, Benjamin Henry, and his father, Sir Basil.[iv] Bringing his father's papers, and the company's archives, out of the old squash court where they had been hiding, we avidly read through them. They themselves seemed to beg an audience lest, as Goethe said, *"We lay* (them) *aside never to read them again, and at last we destroy them out of discretion, and so disappears the most beautiful, the most immediate breath of life, irrecoverable for ourselves and for others."* Thus, after some discussion with the Warden, and Librarians, of Merton, it was agreed that the Blackwell's archive should have a final, and safe, resting place, joining the collection of rare books that Sir Basil Blackwell had amassed for his old College during his lifetime.[v]

Once their preservation had been assured, the content was too irresistible just to be put in archive boxes, and I was, willy-nilly to be their medium, their "ghost writer." However daunting a task, I would be employed by very agreeable ghosts, ones who wouldn't lie down until their adventures, many of which had been passed on orally, were written down. Many of their stories were, of course, written down, and were in front of me, contained in the copious—and very diverse—writings, drafts, letters, articles, speeches and musings of Blackwellian characters, principally Sir Basil. Basil Blackwell had always intended to write his own account, even though he wasn't sure if it would be of interest to others.[vi] In the address to the congregation of the University of Oxford, on the occasion of Sir Basil Blackwell's admission to the Doctor of Civil law, June 27, 1979, the Public Orator referred to the idea, "put forward by that true Blackwellian, William (Rex) King," for a "Boswell" to "come forth and undertake the pleasing task of doing justice to the life and character of Benjamin Henry Blackwell."[vii] What is scarcely known is that it was Benjamin Henry Blackwell who pioneered the publishing side of things, as well as establishing the famous Broad Street shop in Oxford. Serendipitously Wiley Blackwell have graciously handed over the publishing files, which are to be lodged at the Bodleian with the generous help and support of Sarah Thomas, Bodley's Librarian, and Richard Ovenden. Research on these papers will be a small contribution to the work of the Centre for the Study of the Book.

The earliest, recorded, call for a written record of the Blackwells had come from the famous author, Dorothy L Sayers, who had cut her own literary teeth in the Blackwell's workrooms. Leafing through her early poems, I was re-introduced to the iconic Blackwell Series *"Adventurers All"*: *A Series of Young Poets Unknown to Fame*. The Blackwells played Ulysses, as commanded by Tennyson; they were brave enough to take the risk of launching poets, at their own expense: "Come my friends, tis not too late, to seek a newer world. It may be that the gulfs will wash us down. It may be we shall touch the happy isles. Yet our purpose holds: To sail beyond the sunset." Unable to resist this call, I, too, set out to try to produce a "history," setting the Blackwell tales in an economic, social and political, as well as literary, matrix.[viii] At first I thought my travels would take me no further than my desk. Given the quality of Sir Basil's accounts, there was no need for a Boswell, and I had "all of the equipment necessary: a pair of scissors and a pot of glue"; more accurately a word processor that did a very good "cut and paste job." But it wasn't really that simple. I soon realised, what every professional biographer already knows, that the scribe gets in the way of material, and the material gets in the way of the scribe.

In John Worthen's preface to *The Gang: Coleridge, the Hutchinsons and the Wordsworths*, he warns of the difficulties of the job: "We write biographies of individuals as islands; we live as part of the mainland" and we cannot possible tell "the whole truth about individuals." In her recent book, *My East End*, Gilda O'Neill tells us that "much of what we call history …the factual representation of the past, is as much to do with opinion, faith, dogma as any philosophical or religious system of belief." Blackwell's "history," as revealed in the archive, like hers, is interspersed with written and oral accounts "where the participants, the characters in the book," have "explained the meaning of the past ……….and thus the meaning of the present" for themselves. Explaining the past and present according to their own lights was indeed a preoccupation of the Blackwells, just as much as the writers they encouraged. But where to begin their tales, and how to choose one, from among the many, for the purposes of this conference paper? Taking up the gauntlet thrown down by D L Sayers's, this paper, or first day story if Boccaccio is to be faithfully followed, will single out her story and introduce other women writers who made their way onto the Blackwell lists when the publishing firm was in its infancy. It also serves to show how the Blackwells initially made their way in the publishing world through poetry; and how many writers "unknown to fame" came for their muses. And D L Sayers was one such.

First Day

Here begins the first day of the (Blackwell New) *Decameron, wherein…the author explains the circumstances in which certain persons…make their appearance*

Blackwell's did in fact produce its own Decameron, and both Basil Blackwell, almost contemporaries at Oxford, were contributors. This present story, of Dorothy L Sayers and her association with Blackwells, reveals a slice of history: cultural, social, political and economic, within a moment of time, roughly 1914-20.[ix] Her Zeitgeist was the Great War, and it enabled her, the men being away at the front, to break new ground. This paper focuses on the idea of DLS as a "warrior." In securing a foothold in the publishing world as a trainee editor, she helped to bring women's poetry to the fore with a radical opposition to the "Georgian" stronghold, and in her art she gently waged a "fight" against the horrors of war.[x] Although she was never at the Front, DLS, like her contemporaries Edith Sitwell and Vera Brittain for example, could be seen as a "war poet."[xi] DLS poems were not however overtly about war, unlike for example Vera Brittain's famous *Perhaps*. Nor was her experience quite so heartbreakingly immediate as Brittain's.[xii] While Brittain went off to nurse the troops, DLS saw *poetry* as her "war work": not in the Front line, but in the imagination.[xiii] Her poetry, like Wilfred Owen's, was empathetic: "in the pity" (of war). This idea of women warriors had suggested *itself* when working on the Blackwell archives. And the uncovering of this aspect of DLS's work, together with that of Sitwell and Brittain against the backdrop of the Blackwells, provided a way of "reading" into the work of other, non Blackwell, twentieth century women writers, Sylvia Plath for example. Plath's own "war work" had diverse strands, and alongside the preoccupations which underpinned her development as a poet: being an exile, a wife and mother, was her deep-seated fear and loathing of war. But unlike Plath, DLS, Edith Sitwell (who continued to write "war poetry" during the Second World War) and Brittain were survivors: poetry was their catharsis. They saw it as a counter balance in the healing power of faith in God combined with the beauty and richness of nature.[xiv]

Women Warriors

"Now from the grave wake poetry again,
O sacred Muses I have served so long"[xv]

"The Poetry of Search"

Famous for her detective stories, The Man Born to be King and her translations of Dante, we do not normally think of DLS as a poet, still less a war poet. But poet she was and would have liked to have been known as thus.[xvi] In her introduction to Hone's *Extracts from the Poetry of Dorothy L Sayers*, Barbara Reynolds writes that DLS "began as a poet …(and) she always remained one, even in her prose works."[xvii] Hone adds that DLS would have been taken more seriously if she had gone on with her career as a poet![xviii] It was through poetry that she searched around for her place in the literary community. And it was through poetry that she wore out, and tried out, her feelings about war.[xix] DLS began writing poetry at school and this tendency heightened during her adolescence.[xx] Many of her poems are lost, others were printed in journals; some were circulated privately and sometimes given as presents to friends. The theme of war creeps into her work as early as 1908; DLS writes in her complex poems *Lyrics of War* and *The Prisoner of War*.[xxi] Her earliest collection of poems, Op. 1, B.H. Blackwell, published in 1916 is full of a general sense of loss (for leaving Oxford where she had been so happy) and has haunting references to the First World War.[xxii]

War and a sense of death are indeed palpable in DLS's 1916 collection: *Hymn in contemplation of sudden death*, of those who do not die "*at the time planned*," epitaph for a young man when "*God smote England in her dalliance*," songs that "*break my heart*," songs "*so fantastical … departing from our dead youth's funeral*," her song of harvest "*when the leaves are growing old … For me you weep, for me you sigh, For me I think that you will die -.*" She writes of the "*sour smell of hemlock…on the breath…the foretaste of death.*" Of "*a tall pleasure-house … resting on the restless quicksand.*" She harks back to other wars: to those "*that were gay … in the hour Sir Tristan lay dying*," to "*Troy… to see in fancy the appalling light Of Ilion in fire', where 'all that is left unsaid.' *" The immediacy of her preoccupation with war can be heard clearly in *Last Song*:

> *Look long. Tomorrow we shall stand*
> *Thronged in the dreadful street,*
> *And bloody hands of men o'erborne*
> *Will clutch us by the feet*[xxiii]

In her letters DLS writes of this being forcefully brought home to her on the streets of Oxford where "The sight of a poor Australian youth – once, no doubt, sane and strong – gibbering and moping like a brainless ape in the High St has brought home to me the horrors of war and of its eternal devilishness more powerfully than the hundreds of crippled men about the streets." And in her poem *Socks* (1915) DLS is so sensitive to war that the very mention of the word "socks" translates into a vivid imagining of those lying dead in the trenches. Two years later in her second collection this distress intensified in her Carol for Oxford:

> WHEN all the Saints that are in Heaven keep Christmas at the board,
> Our Lady Mary calls a health before her Son our Lord,
> Says: "Let us sing the fairest town that is in all Your earthly crown;
> Nowell, Nowell, Nowell, Nowell
> To the Bells of Oxenford!"
>
> Then saith the Holy Trinity: "There be We well adored;"
> Saith John to Mary Maudleyn, "There we walk across the sward;"
> And All the Souls that lived on earth lift up their voice to swell that mirth:
> "Nowell, Nowell, Nowell, Nowell
> To the Bells of Oxenford!"
>
> King Jesus saith: "That will I well, thereof rest you assured,
> For I have a dwelling fair and Church with aisles so broad;
> So let us drink at Christmas time to all that dwell by Great Tom chime:
> Nowell, Nowell, Nowell, Nowell
> To the Bells of Oxenford!"[xxiv]

This latter collection was produced while DLS was actually in the employment of the Blackwells. In fact this employment may well have come about because the Blackwells had published her first collection, having already noticed her work in a previous volume of Oxford Poetry. Benjamin Henry Blackwell was known for his determination "to remove from the work of young poets the reproach of insolvency." His choice was "to be confined to such work as would seem to deserve publicity. It is hoped that these adventurers may justly claim the attention of those intellects which, in resisting the enervating influence of the novel, look for something more permanent in the arduous pursuit of poetry."[xxv] That Mr. Blackwell, and his son Basil, esteemed her work enough to publish it prompted her father, the Rev. Henry Sayers, to contact them.[xxvi] Seeing how much his daughter missed Oxford, how unhappy she was as a teacher in Hull and how frustrated she was at not being able to continue with her writing in a serious way, DLS's father wrote to Mr. (Benjamin Henry) Blackwell to see if he could, for a sum, place his daughter. By this time the reigns of publishing were being passed to Basil Blackwell and it was to him that DLS was to report. Interviewing her in his father's workroom, Basil was confronted with a "tall, very slim young woman, dressed in a formal blue serge costume with informal yellow stockings."[xxvii]

As a result of the interview, it was agreed that DLS should be employed as a "pupil" editorial assistant to Basil Blackwell, starting at Easter 1917.[xxviii] He soon discovered they had much in common; he too had intimations of being a poet and writer. Nonetheless, Basil Blackwell was ambivalent about the idea of an educated woman in the workplace. As an undergraduate, just a few years before DLS went up to Somerville, Basil hardly known any female students. "Female undergraduates," he recalled, "were remote mysterious creatures and chaperones were de rigueur"; as they were in DLS days at Somerville.[xxix] One of his friends, on the same staircase, confessed to never having spoken to a girl during his time at Merton. Basil remembered that "a few girls, not accorded matriculation at the time, came to lectures in pairs and, in one case I recall, chaperoned by a nun. Only one of them in the Greats School took any care of her appearance; we rejoiced in her elegance and grace and discovered her name from a scrutiny of her bicycle. Verily Phoebe W. had her reward; she married her history tutor."[xxx] For Basil, this was "a proper ending for a clever girl." And it was with this attitude DLS had to contend! For his part, Basil Blackwell soon realised that DLS was more interested in gaining a further entrée into publishing than in the detailed and meticulous work required of a trainee editor. No wonder then that Basil wrestled with her while she was in her editorial role.

For three years the relationship held until Basil Blackwell dispensed with her editorial talents with a mixture of relief and reluctance, describing her employment as "like harnessing a race-horse to a plough."[xxxi] But her influence was not in doubt. Despite a fair dose of chauvinism, which Basil's classical scholar wife and his clutch of clever daughters failed to subdue, he acknowledged her role in opening the doors for women writers. Certainly DLS was to "became more memorable for her literary fame, than her editorial gifts."[xxxii] Whatever Basil Blackwell's ambivalence about DLS's editorial talent, the three years she was in harness saw a rush of output from the infant publishing house. Many of the writers featured in the poetry series were women: 1916 (Wheels) Edith Sitwell, Vera Brittain, Nancy Cunard, Helen Rootham; 1917 editions, Lucy Hawkins, Marian Ramie, Emma Gurney Salter, Doreen Wallace, Beautrice Llewellyn Thomas, Marion Pryce, Vera and Margaret Larminie and in 1918 Eleanor Deane Hill, Susan Miles. Soon after her departure came Dorothea Still's *Poems of Motherhood* and Gladys Mary Hazel's *The House*. So all was square it seems: DLS was launched on her own writing career and Blackwell's lists were almost bursting with women poets, giving Basil a wider entrée.

No wonder then that DLS called for a Blackwell history to be written! Some have even suggested, Graham Green's wife for example, that DLS immortalised Basil Blackwell, using him as her model for the famous detective Lord Peter Wimsey. As evidence we could point to Basil's enthusiasm for bell-ringing and DLS had earned herself quite a reputation for parody while still a student at Somerville.*xxiii* What ever the truth of this idea, it is clear that their short-lived but productive professional partnership spawned a life-long friendship.*xxiv* It was a friendship based on their mutual love of Oxford, of cats and most of all poetry. But it also found expression in the direct experience of war they shared: the agony they felt for their University friends and work colleagues who died "as cattle" as they worked side by side in Broad Street.*xxv* The memory of this suffering and the loss was later recorded in many of the notes and unpublished writings of Basil Blackwell. Their preoccupation and torment was shared by other, Blackwell, women poets, Edith Sitwell for example; in the Blackwell *Wheels* cycles her selections bewailed the variety of human suffering produced by modern civilisation. But, Basil Blackwell later observed, Governments didn't learn.

Less than thirty years later Basil Blackwell, DLS and so many of their associates witnessed the advent of even more deadly, nuclear, warfare. They harked back to far-off Garsington days when Basil Blackwell had sat at the feet of Bertrand Russell, and heard his gloomy prognostications. Later, when an aged Russell was in full flood in his "ban the bomb," CND, mode, Sir Basil had written dismally of the "potentiality of contraries" in the physical world that had "reached its apogee in the atomic bomb." Reflecting on these themes in old age, Basil Blackwell was drawn to the work of other writers in the English tradition who were intensely disturbed by war. On his lectern he always had open the work of Barbara Tuckman whose writing catalogued "man's inhumanity to man." While Basil Blackwell's thinking went back in time to the "war" writers he had personally supported, the idea of women in this role, not as front line journalists but as poets, seemed to resonate forwards. And his tradition of Oxford poets, like DLS and Edith Sitwell, continues. It is here again right under our noses in the new writing heard in Blackwell's. Across the road, at the Bodleian, reading from Andrew McNeillie's Archipelago, a now white-haloed Seamus Heaney issued a direct challenge to his audience. He behoved the assembly to think deeply and take responsibility for what is happening to our physical, mental and spiritual world. In the room, his appeal was aimed directly at you and me; you couldn't duck.

Basil Blackwell had tried not to duck from personal responsibility, although his eyesight ruled him out of active service in the Great War and age in the Second. Just before the Second World War, lying in the bath reflecting on the ascendancy of Nazism and Fascism, he was deeply suspicious of the rhetoric of appeasement, "I got the idea that Hitler and Mussolini were not only telling lies but also drawing false conclusions." Basil recounted how his own brand of "spiritual appeasement" recommended itself as a way to combat them "by appealing to the essence of Christianity." His strategy was to have "the Pope or some other Christian leader take charge of the broadcasting stations throughout the world and recite the Lord's Prayer to the worldwide audience." Unfortunately, Basil's, peaceful, strategy was pre-empted: "Before I could put this idea to the Vatican or to Canterbury, Germany had invaded Poland."*xxxvi* He was not surprised that, as an individual, he had no chance to play a part in the greater scheme of things; although he, like Vera Brittain served a fire-watcher. DLS's way of coping was similar to Basil's. Before and during the Second World War, she immersed herself in her Christian work and writing. By this time, unlike the period when she had been happily working in Oxford, at Blackwells, during the First World War, her sense of loss was layered over with more personal and deeply hidden experiences.

DLS's heightened sense of personal suffering, exacerbated by the Second World War, led her straight back to where she started: to poetry, or as Hone argues, to resurrect "poetry in her prose writing." At the same time Edith Sitwell, her contemporary from the Blackwell stable, produced one of her most famous "war" poems:

Still falls the Rain...

...

In the Field of Blood where the small hopes breed and the human brain
Nurtures its greed, that worm with the brow of Cain.[xxxvii]

DLS's "war work," however, led her into new pastures. Broadcasting on the BBC during the war, she did much to shape the future of religious programmes. Serendipitously, and nearly seventy years later, the spirit underlying these messages to the British people took physical shape. In her exquisite and agonising film, New Zealander Sandra Lahire shows how Plath's personal agonies were heightened by the experience of living through war. Over her head, Lahire graphically depicts, Plath felt burning the burning of electrotherapy, which re-minded her of the gassing of the Jews, the McCarthy period in American history, Korea, and the nuclear near-miss in Cuba. And as Plath sunk into despair, Vietnam loomed. DLS died in 1957, Plath in 1964, Sitwell in 1964 and Brittain in 1970. Basil Blackwell, however, stayed the course into ripe old age: he died in 1984 at the age of 94. But his consciousness of war did not diminish: "I seldom enter my beloved College," he wrote, "without a pang, for the names of so many of my contemporaries are engraved on the memorial to those killed."

All the Blackwells had witnessed the ill effects of "man's inhumanity to man," from Balaclava, to the Somme, from Dunkirk to Hiroshima, and, later, in the killing fields of Vietnam. Perhaps this genetic memory propelled Basil Blackwell to publish poets who were similarly attuned? But what would they have felt, I wondered, about the more recent nationalistic and ethnic wars in Central and Eastern Europe? Sir Basil had supported European, political and economic, co-operation, as an insurance against this worse kind of narrow, nationalism. It is due perhaps to Dorothy L Sayers and her insistence on a "history," that we know anything of what they thought? It is due to her that the Blackwells ever seriously thought of preserving the stories of their life and time.[xxxviii] Perhaps she knew that such small collections would remind us of the privations and lunacy of war, as well as preserving the names of many "unknown to fame" lest, as Goethe said, *"We lay aside never to read them again, and at last we destroy them out of discretion, and so disappears the most beautiful, the most immediate breath of life, irrecoverable for ourselves and for others."*

The Bodleian and Merton collections provide rich pickings and we go on searching them:

Muse, daughter of Memory and Zeus,
Where to start this story is yours to choose.

Notes

[i] Literally all over the world – this quote comes from The Auckland Star 9 June 1956.

[ii] Basil Blackwell did indeed commission the New Decameron, where he is portrayed as the Master Printer and where he too contributed a Tale.

[iii] Benjamin Harris Blackwell was the first Oxford; Blackwell, setting up his little book shop in St Clements, just over Magdalen Bridge, in 1846.

[iv] Benjamin Harris had died young and it was his son who opened the famous Broad Street shop in Oxford in 1879.

[v] See Reid, Ricketts and Walworth, A Guide to the Merton Blackwell Collection, Merton College, University of Oxford, 2004.

[vi] Ian Norrie, The Bookseller, May 26 1979.

[vii] This plea had been recorded in the diaries of Rex King, written between July and August, 1920, and later recorded in Blackwell's "BroadSheet," May 1948.

[viii] Rita Ricketts, *Adventurers All*, Blackwell, Oxford, 2002.

[ix] DLS, surprisingly, was not the first woman to have had a volume accepted by Blackwell. At number nine in the series, she was following closely in the footsteps of Elizabeth Rendall, Ester Lillian Duff and with other women appearing in Oxford Poetry.

[x] Others too, such as Helen Rootham, Iris Tree, Nancy Cunard who, together with Edith Sitwell, saw themselves as a "radical opposition" to the "coalition government" of the Georgians (Poets).

[xi] Both V. Brittain and E. Sitwell were published by B H Blackwell.

[xii] Brittain lost both her lover and brother - see P Berry and M Bostridge, Vera Brittain, A Life, Virago, 2001.

[xiii] See Wilfred Owen: Preface to Edition, *Poets of the Great War*. Harold B. Lee Library, Brigham Young University. It was Edith Sitwell indeed who put together the work of Wilfred Owen, see *Wheels* 1919 published by B H Blackwell where seven of his poems were published.

[xiv] See Edith Sitwell, 1942 *Still Falls the Rain* and *The Raids*, 1940, *Night and Dawn*.

[xv] From DLS's translation of Il Purgatorio, i, vii-viii.

[xvi] DLS's most prolific period was in Oxford 1915-21 even though during this period she taught in Hull and another year in Normandy as bilingual educational assoc of Eric Whelpton, Extracts from the Poetry of Dorothy L Sayers, Ed. Ralph E. Hone, The Dorothy L Sayers Society 1996 p 3.

[xvii] Ibid., p xi. In her introduction Barbara Reynolds argues that DLS's muse reawakened in 1929 with her translation of the Anglo-Norman poem *Tristan*, and in 1937 when she was invited to write a verse drama for Canterbury Cathedral, p xii. See also *The English War* published by the Times L Supp 1940 anthologised by C Day Lewis, Stephen Spender, Laurie Lee, etc.: *Ariel Reconnaissance* and *Target Area*.

[xviii] Ibid., p. 1.

[xix] See Barbara Reynolds introduction in *Extracts from the Poetry of Dorothy L Sayers*, Ed. Ralph E. Hone, The Dorothy L Sayers Society, 1996, p. xiii. Reynolds argues that this "poetry of search" became the "poetry of statement," in DLS's more mature years, see for example *The House of Zeal*, 1937 and *The Devil to Pay*, 1939.

[xx] Her son wrote (John Anthony Fleming) that she kept numerous exercise books full of childhood poetry, see extracts from the *Poetry of Dorothy L Sayers*, Ed. Ralph E. Hone, The Dorothy L Sayers Society 1996, p. 3.

[xxi] Ibid. Hone p. 3.

[xxii] Opus 1 was No 9 in the Adventurers All series, B H Blackwell 1916.

[xxiii] DLS: The Last Song, Op. 1, 1916, p 46.

[xxiv] Catholic Tales and Christian Songs, 1918 Basil Blackwell.

[xxv] Basil Blackwell's own notes on his father's life and work; see also end piece note in Adventurers All Series, B H Blackwell, Oxford and Rita Rickets, Adventurers All, Blackwell's, 2002.

[xxvi] Dorothy Leigh Sayers, born Oxford, 13.7.1893, only child of Rev. Henry Sayers who was at the time headmaster of Christ Church Cathedral School.

[xxvii] Op Cit Adventurers All.

[xxviii] Son of Benjamin Henry, see letters of DLS 29.4.1917, Bodleian Library.

[xxix] See DLS papers in the Bodleian MS ENG MISC c698 and her parody of the poems of E L Duff and T W Earp in Oxford Poetry 1915, the same volume that contained Tolkien's first published work: a poem entitled *Goblin Feet*.

[xxx] This account of his life at Merton was written by Sir Basil for Postmaster (Merton) in 1971 and reprinted in Broad Sheet in 1984.

[xxxi] Basil Blackwell's notes.

[xxxii] Basil Blackwell's notes, May 1956, Merton Blackwell Collection.

[xxxiii] DLS papers Bodleian MS ENG MISC c 698.

[xxxiv] Benjamin Henry Blackwell died in 1924.

[xxxv] Books for the Blackwells provided a "unity" in a disunited world. And during the Second World War Blackwell's sent thousands of books to the troops and to the POW camps.

[xxxvi] Interview Basil Blackwell with Ved Metha op cit p 15.

[xxxvii] 1942.

[xxxviii] "Harnessing a race-horse to a plough," Dorothy L Sayers at Blackwell's, Talk to the Dorothy L Sayers Society, St Anne's, Soho, London Saturday 3 November 2007, A contribution to the commemoration of Dorothy L Sayers' on the 50th Anniversary of her death

DEVELOPING A MULTIFACETED APPROACH TO IDENTIFY A CORE UNDERGRADUATE BROWSING COLLECTION

Doug Way, Collection Development Librarian, Grand Valley State University, Allendale, Michigan

Sarah Beaubien, Arts and Humanities Librarian, Grand Valley State University, Allendale, Michigan

Julie Garrison, Director of Research and Instruction, Grand Valley State University, Allendale, Michigan

Abstract

In planning for a new library that will include a limited number of open stacks, Grand Valley State University librarians were asked to identify what materials should be reserved for the browsable shelves. To accomplish this, librarians considered user behavior by discipline, material types, shelving options and the role of core collections. This paper will discuss these issues as well as differences in how library resources are located and the impact of new discovery tools, such as Innovative Interface's Encore, Bowker's Syndetics, and Google's Book Search on redefining browsability. The paper will also include a discussion of resources used in this process, such as the results from our recent LibQual study, WorldCat Collection Analysis' Circulation Analysis and Bowker Book Analysis reports.

Introduction

The Grand Valley State University Libraries are currently in the early planning stages for a new library on the main campus that is estimated to begin construction in 2010. In planning for a building that will have approximately 150,000 square feet of usable space, there has been significant debate regarding how to best maximize user space and accommodate library collections. Because much of this space will be dedicated to user activities such as computing, group project space, presentation practice, multimedia equipment and quiet study areas the library is acting under the assumption that open stacks will be limited and an on-site retrieval system will be necessary. The question of how best to manage a collection split between browsing shelves and an active collection, housed in an automated retrieval system, remained unclear. With that in mind, an Open Stacks task force was formed to evaluate all shelving options and make recommendations as to the most appropriate distribution of titles in open shelving and the retrieval system.

Background

Founded in 1960, Grand Valley State University is a young comprehensive public university. Its first student enrollment in 1963 was 224. In the past 50 years, it has grown to a size of approximately 24,000 students. The main campus is located almost midway between downtown Grand Rapids and Lake Michigan, in the town of Allendale, Michigan.

The Zumberge Library opened on the Allendale campus in 1969 and was built to accommodate an enrollment of 6,000 students. The Zumberge Library serves an estimated population of 16,000 students today. The current structure has approximately 50,460 square feet of usable space and contains over 250,000 items in open stacks. This figure does not include print periodicals or special collections and archives. Due to space constraints, approximately 100,000 volumes of low circulating materials were moved to an offsite storage facility in 2004.

A second University campus, which opened in the year 2000, is located approximately 15 miles east of Allendale, in downtown Grand Rapids, Michigan. This campus has buildings distributed throughout the downtown area. The main campus primarily offers liberal arts programs, while the downtown campus focuses primarily on graduate and professional education programs.

Due to the geographic and programmatic differences in the campuses, the library collections are divided and housed with regard to the major programs offered on each campus. To accommodate the needs of downtown students and faculty, the Steelcase Library opened in 2000 with a fully operational automatic storage and retrieval system to house library materials in its limited footprint. It primarily contains materials relevant to business, education, engineering, and criminal justice. In 2004, a second facility, The Frey Learning Center, opened in another part of downtown, in the Cook-DeVos Center for Health Sciences building, and focuses solely on serving the University's health sciences programs.

Open Stacks Task Force Considerations

The Open Stacks task force was a cross-functional group made up of liaison librarians whose departments heavily rely on print materials and others immersed in collection development issues in a variety of ways. This group was tasked with examining scenarios for developing the open stacks collection in a new library facility. Some of the factors considered were: user behavior, disciplinary differences, collection use, anticipated collection growth, including a large scale humanities retrospective project, expectations for the future of print reference materials, anticipated continued print journal collections, standard collection lists, and the impact of new discovery tools on browsing and findability. In addition, the task force gave careful consideration to the Libraries' recent LibQual survey comments and a literature review.

LibQual

The GVSU Libraries conducted the LibQual survey in the fall of 2007. Though it is primarily designed to measure user satisfaction with library services, many comments regarding collections and the library as a physical space were reflected in our user comments. A total of 2,752 surveys (229 faculty, 283 graduate students, 108 staff, and 2132 undergraduate) were received. Of 229 faculty responders, 36 submitted comments in the survey. Of this number, 64% were from individuals in Humanities disciplines. There was a general, and sometimes strongly worded, theme amongst these comments: "we want books on open shelves because browsing is key for our research."

Literature Review

The ITHAKA Report: "Ithaka's 2006 Studies of Key Stakeholders in the Digital Transformation in Higher Education", presents the compiled and analyzed results of surveys conducted in 2000, 2003, and 2006 of faculty attitudes toward the academic library. Its findings, in large part, reflect the LibQual comments received and our own anecdotal evidence about library use. That is to say, humanists still see the library and librarian's role as having continued importance. They still want to browse the stacks. Scientists and social scientists, meanwhile, are becoming less reliant on the library for information and services.

Others have reported similar findings. According to Levine-Clark, "…humanists conduct research differently than do those in other disciplines, relying more on…browsing the shelves" than their colleagues in the sciences, social sciences and professional programs (Levine-Clark 2008). Many of our long-held assumptions about humanists' research behaviors are reinforced by recent surveys and studies of the research process in humanities disciplines. While it is important to consider traditional research patterns and the preferences of arts and humanities scholars, it is also necessary to recognize that these behaviors are changing. Some humanities scholars are employing technological search tools in addition to, and often in place of, physically browsing library shelves. For example, a 2001 study of scholarly research in the humanities conducted by the Digital Library Federation found that most humanities scholars "reported browsing in the library to be of value to them in their work." However, one scholar said, "I have found going on the Web to be not only useful in locating sources, but . . . equivalent to just roaming around the stacks and looking for titles of books and stumbling upon things that you never knew you'd find" (Brockman, et al. 2001). Thus, our Open Stacks task force worked to accommodate the current research needs in various disciplines, with the understanding that these behaviors will likely evolve over time.

Tools and Resources for Collections Analysis

In examining the open stacks issue, the task force visited a number of questions and topics, ranging from the role of core collections and lists to questions of collection usage and growth. General circulation data were taken into consideration, as was circulation within specific subject areas. Special attention was paid to the use of titles in the library's remote storage facility, as well as whether the age of a book had an impact on circulation. To examine these questions, a number of different tools and resources were used, including Bowker Book Analysis, WorldCat Collection Analysis and internal data retrieved from the library's integrated library system.

Bowker Book Analysis

The open stacks task force used Bowker Book Analysis to consider whether *Resources for College Libraries* (RCL) should make up the core of this open stacks collection. Bowker Book Analysis is a tool that allows libraries to compare their holdings to RCL, a standard bibliography of approximately 60,000 standard works that intend to serve as the core liberal arts college library collection. At GVSU, Bowker Book Analysis has been used extensively in program reviews and for examining the needs of new programs.

As with any tool, there are advantages and disadvantages, and Bowker Book Analysis was no exception. On the one hand, RCL is a standard tool and the library had been using it extensively with a great deal of success and credibility. Moreover, Bowker Book Analysis provides a wide variety of options for analyzing and identifying different aspects of the collection. At the same time, the task force was unsure whether titles for every subject should be treated equally. Working with the assumption that in certain subject areas, such as in the humanities, the monograph was more important than it was in others, and that in other fields, such as the sciences, the currency of information was of the utmost importance, the task force questioned whether the use a core list such as RCL was the correct determinant for developing a browsing collection. In addition, the initial analyses using this tool showed that there were large gaps in the library's holdings of these standard works. Not only were sizeable numbers of core titles not held by the library, the holdings of core titles were not consistent across all subjects. In some subject areas the library had a high percentage of the core titles, while in other areas the library had few, if any titles. As a result, the task force decided against the use of RCL or any other standard lists for use in developing the library's core browsing collection.

WorldCat Collection Analysis (WCA)

Another tool used by the task force on this project was WorldCat Collection Analysis (WCA), and in particular, WCA's Circulation Analysis functionality. This feature allowed the task force to examine the last five years worth of circulation data, which was uploaded to WCA. The use of circulation data was considered very important. The task force had preconceived notions and beliefs, as well as feedback from faculty, on how the library's collections were used and how this use varied by discipline. Circulation data allowed the task force to determine if these ideas matched the reality of what the library's users were actually doing, while also examining what should happen with different parts of the library's collections. Ideally there would have been other resources available, such as browsing or shelving statistics, however the library had not collected those consistently in the past and the task force was limited to relying on those statistics that were available.

One of the areas the task force wanted to examine was the circulation data for the materials in the library's remote storage facility. These materials would be moved into the new library facility and the task force needed to determine whether those materials should be considered for inclusion on open shelving. Using the WCA Circulation Analysis, the task force was able to determine that circulation was highest in the History and Language, Linguistics & Literature categories, which had three times the number of checkouts of any other subject area (See Figure 1). Still, in these areas and all of the other subject areas, the task force determined that the total number of checkouts, and the percentage of the total checkouts they accounted for, was too low to be considered for open shelving.

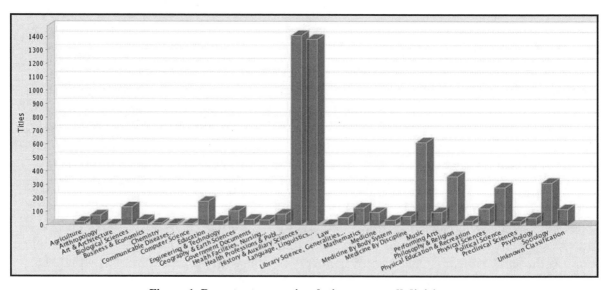

Figure 1. Remote storage circulation across all divisions.

Another question considered by the task force was what percentage of the collection circulated and perhaps more importantly, what percentage of each subject area circulated. The WCA's Circulation Analysis allowed the task force to not only see what percent of the collection and each subject area circulated, but also to easily see whether there were any portions of the collection that circulated at a low rate. It was hoped that it would be possible to identify larger areas of collections, in particular in the humanities, which circulated at a low rate and may be able to be moved into the ASRS. Unfortunately, the task force was not able to identify any significantly large subsets that circulated at a low rate. Instead it found that often when an area with a lower circulation rate was identified, the total number of volumes was also low. The task force felt it was not worth targeting these areas since putting them into the ASRS could recapture only a small amount of shelf space.

One final example of a question examined by the task force using WCA's Circulation Analysis considered the impact of a book's age on its circulation. The task force had a preconception that in the humanities the age of a book was much less important than it was in the sciences or social sciences, and when it examined the data this was exactly what it found. In the humanities, circulation was slightly higher in the most recent 20 years, but over longer periods of time, it was fairly even. At the same time, newer titles in the sciences generally circulated at a much higher rate than older titles. The same was true in the social sciences, although, not as pronounced as in the sciences. Figure 2 illustrates this by showing the circulation by publication date in three fields: Philosophy and Religion, Sociology, and Medicine. However, there were exceptions. The task force found that in Chemistry more titles published in the 1960s circulated than titles that were published since 2000. Despite this exception, the task force was able to confirm its general assumptions about the differences in the circulation patterns of books in the humanities, sciences and social sciences.

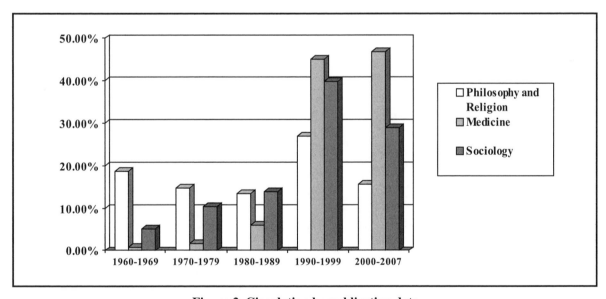

Figure 2. Circulation by publication date.

While the task force extensively used WCA's Circulation Analysis, it did acknowledge that the tool and circulation analyses have their limitations. The analyses do not take into consideration browsing and in-house use of materials, nor do they account for the use of e-books. At GVSU there are now more e-books in the library's collection than print books and in some subject areas, such as Computer Science, almost all titles currently acquired are e-books. Yet the impact of the increasing acquisition of e-books was not taken into account in this analysis, nor was the impact of the increasing use of e-books on the circulation of print titles.

Internal Data

The final source of information the task force used in its work was internal data from the library's integrated library system. This included data on the collections, such as the library's holdings by publication date, as well as holdings by Library of Congress (LC) Classification. It also included acquisitions data. The task force used the holdings by LC classification to compare the information obtained from WCA. Because WCA used a conspectus that was not a clean match to all the subject areas in the LC system, the task force wanted to confirm that the numbers were comparable so that decisions could be based on the WCA data. After examining the fields of interest the committee decided that these numbers could be relied upon for analysis. Acquisitions data were used to examine trends in the library's collection growth, which showed that in spite of receiving only inflationary increases over the past five years, the library has been increasing the number of titles acquired every year. Holdings by publication date and acquisition data were also used to determine how many books in the sciences and social sciences could fit on open shelves. The task force eventually decided to keep the last five years' acquisitions on open shelves.

Discovery Tools

Like so many other libraries, as the task force considered how to support the students of the future, considering how new discovery tools will impact their interaction with library materials was a factor. Systems such as Endeca, Encore, Evergreen, and others are offering simpler, more user friendly interfaces for discovering library materials without the need for shelf browsing. The task force recognized that many faculty continue to place great importance on browsing the shelf for discovery in the humanities fields. Balancing this stated faculty desire with the knowledge that GVSU libraries are investing significant funds in electronic resources, especially electronic journals and increasingly electronic books and media, that will never be discovered by walking through library stacks, the task force had the difficult job of weighing traditional sentiment against the complex realities of the current and future library collections. In addition, significant staff and budget resources are spent in acquiring and improving the customer interaction with these online resources. This shift in collections strategy and new innovations in discovery tools will impact browsing and, the task force assumed, will minimize this attachment to physically scan shelves to find the range of needed materials.

These new tools, currently being coined "next generation discovery tools," come in both proprietary and open source packages. They tend to be striving toward simpler interfaces and a better online user experience. They look more familiar, with more similarities to Internet search engine interfaces than traditional catalog interfaces. They accept keywords and natural language queries that are able to achieve better results than traditional catalogs. A "did you mean" feature generally leads the user to the appropriate result if a word is mistyped or is out of order. As a result, the user has a greater opportunity of success in finding what is needed from the outset, interacting with the online catalog, before ever making it to the library's book stacks.

Features, such as faceted searching and tag clouds, offer users new ways of taking very broad searches and refining them to get to a more specific result. Users can quickly see the options for drilling down on the same page as the search results, again hopefully making the potential for successfully finding a range of needed information more likely. Facets may include browsing a call number range, or as in the case of Evergreen, clicking on the shelf browser from within an individual record to see what else is available "near" the selected content. So, when a user finds one book of interest, he or she is introduced to the shelf around that book through the online environment.

Other features such as the ability to set up RSS feeds to keep current on new acquisitions and to retrieve search results based on enriched content such as book jackets, tables of contents, reviews, and summaries are also being integrated into many of these new library catalogs. Interaction and participation with the catalog through user recommendations tagging, and opinions are also functions being tried in next-generation catalogs.

These catalogs are going beyond book content, and beginning to explore intuitive ways of offering a great expansion of content to the user. For instance, Worldcat Local incorporates federated searching to include articles in search results, searches for resources beyond the local university into Ohiolink, and retrieves holdings from the entire Worldcat database to help users identify the material they need, no matter where it is located.

Conclusions

Ultimately, the taskforce recommended housing 150,000 to 175,000 titles in an open, core browsing collection. This number includes all currently held humanities titles, titles acquired in the retrospective humanities project, juvenile literature, and materials for all liberal arts disciplines acquired in the most recent five years. Also included in open shelving, but not accounted for in the numbers, are small specialized collections such as popular reading, reference, new books, etc. This plan assumes that all titles currently held in the offsite storage facility will be placed in the automated retrieval system, along with most Government Documents, and bound periodicals. Current periodicals will be placed in open shelving.

There is a growing realization that catalogs will continue to remain relevant and central to the library's future. None of the next-generation catalog options create a whole package at this point in time, but that is likely to change. They are in various stages of development, but all are getting better with each new version or iteration. Functionality will continue to remain key. The catalogs that are easy for users to manipulate and offer libraries flexibility are mostly likely to thrive. Those that continue to be too closed and proprietary are unlikely to gain market share. Users will continue to change the way they interact with libraries and experience "browsing" in new ways that have yet to be imagined. These will be driving forces as libraries move forward.

Bibliography

Breeding, Marshall. 2007. AquaBrowser. *Library Technology Reports* 43(4): 15-18, http://search.ebscohost.com/login.aspx?direct=true&db=lxh&AN=26074117 &site=ehost-live&scope=site.

———. 2007. Encore. *Library Technology Reports* 43(4): 23-27, http://search.ebscohost.com/login.aspx?direct=true&db=lxh&AN=26074119 &site=ehost-live&scope=site.

——. 2007. Endeca. *Library Technology Reports* 43(4): 19-22, http://search.ebscohost.com/login.aspx?direct=true&db=lxh&AN=26074118&site=ehost-live&scope=site.

——. 2007. Introduction. *Library Technology Reports* 43(4): 5-14, http://search.ebscohost.com/login.aspx?direct=true&db=lxh&AN=26074116&site=ehost-live&scope=site.

——. 2007. Next-generation flavor in integrated online catalogs. *Library Technology Reports* 43(4): 38-41, http://search.ebscohost.com/login.aspx?direct=true&db=lxh&AN=26074122&site=ehost-live&scope=site.

——. 2007. Primo. *Library Technology Reports* 43(4): 28-32, http://search.ebscohost.com/login.aspx?direct=true&db=lxh&AN=26074120&site=ehost-live&scope=site.

——. 2007. WorldCat local. *Library Technology Reports* 43(4): 33-37, http://search.ebscohost.com/login.aspx?direct=true&db=lxh&AN=26074121&site=ehost-live&scope=site.

Brockman, William S., Neumann, Laura, Palmer, Carole L. and Tidline, Tonyia J. Scholarly work in the humanities and the evolving information environment. Digital Library Federation. 2001. Available from http://www.diglib.org/pubs/dlf095/dlf095.htm#top (accessed September 23, 2008).

Housewright, Ross, and Schonfeld, Roger. Ithaka's 2006 studies of key stakeholders in the digital transformation in higher education. Ithaka. Available from http://www.ithaka.org/research/Ithakas 2006 Studies of Key Stakeholders in the Digital Transformation in Higher Education.pdf (accessed October 10, 2008).

Kim, Taeock, and Paula J. Popma. Out of sight but not out of mind: Preparing for an automated retrieval system. *Library Administration & Management* 21(4) (Fall 2007): 189-92.

Levine-Clark, Michael. 2008. "Electronic books and the humanities: A survey at the university of Denver". *Collection Building* 27(4) (11): 176-, http://search.ebscohost.com/login.aspx?direct=true&db=lxh&AN=35590341&site=ehost-live&scope=site.

Ogburn, Joyce. 2008. University of Utah installs automated retrieval center. *American Libraries* 39(5) (May): 73.

The Charleston Conference appears to be one of the best places to talk about material formats. The talks included some about e-books, e-journals, different ways to digitally preserve e-journals, and microfilm.

Format

DR. ZHOU AND BEYOND: FROM THE "SMART GUESSER" TO CONTENT SYSTEMS

Mary Frances Marx, Reference/Instruction Librarian, Southeastern Louisiana State University, Hammond, Louisiana

E-books, metadata, overlap/redundancies, confidentiality/privacy, analysis products, resource sharing, intersecting trends, data mining, holdings patterns/holdings trends, digitization decisions!!!, user behavior, **rapid, rapid** change, rising costs, open access, publishing models, Technology, Technology, rapid, rapid change. Whew! Is it any wonder that with all we have to think about, and to keep us busy, in the present, we hardly have time to think about where we are going??

Back at the beginning…by beginning, I mean the 1970s or thereabouts, it wasn't necessarily so. There were visionaries in our profession who saw the future with a little more clarity than some of us did, the technological future of libraries. They thought about it, wrote about it, and were keenly interested in knowing about the discoveries that were being made in the technological environment, as they related to libraries, and were reported in the literature. FW Lancaster and Yuan Zhou were two such visionaries, and reading some of their work can take us back to 1982 and 1994, to an understanding of what expectations were at that time, particularly with Dr. Zhou in Collection Development. There is enjoyment in looking back, but there is also knowledge to be gained.

The sources that I am using are Lancaster's *Libraries and Librarians in an Age of Electronics* (1982) and Dr. Zhou's tremendous 1994 article, "From Smart Guesser to Smart Navigator: Changes in Collection Development for Research Libraries in a Network Environment."

FW Lancaster

Lancaster sees the future of libraries as intrinsically tied to the future of publishing, but perhaps not publishing as it is known in 1982. He has been interested in information transfer in a paperless mode, since he worked in the 1970s as a consultant for the CIA, which had already conceptualized a paperless system of information distribution. This led him to believe that print on paper would eventually give way to electronics. He describes this evolution as taking place in four publishing phases:

1. **Paper only**. Has existed for 500 years, and we are not out of it yet.

2. **Dual mode**. Began in the early 1960s. Refers to the existence of 2 parallel forms: machine readable and print on paper. **Photocomposition** is increasingly important. In 1982, many publications are photocomposed (i.e., Index Medicus).

3. **New Electronic only**. This phase parallels with the second. Completely new publications are in machine readable form. Never issued in print on paper.

4. **Conversion from paper**. In 1982, has reached no significant level, but Lancaster believes it is inevitable for several reasons, all economic. The cost of producing and distributing publications on paper continues to increase, but he believes that the costs of doing so electronically would continually decline. (Oh boy!) Some print/electronic competition already exists in the marketplace, and libraries are already seen to be dropping subscriptions to some indexing/abstracting services.

The "Electrobook"

To Lancaster, 1978 was a landmark year due to the new electronic forms that emerged. A magazine featuring recreational material and issued as a tape cassette for use on a home computer was one, and another was a type of "electronic reference book," for which he coined the term, "electrobook." In the form of a hand held microprocessor, it resembled a pocket calculator. By 1982, bilingual dictionaries based on what Lancaster called "memory capsules" had been issued in this form, and though expensive at around $200, he thought that as the capsules became smaller, costs would drop, and other reference books could be issued in this format. Texas Instruments had produced an electrobook dictionary with voice output. Perhaps one day the entire *Oxford English Dictionary* could be issued on a single capsule plugged into a hand-held device. These and video disks might be considered the "books" of the future, of the electronic era.

Electronic Journals

In 1982, scholarly journals have been influenced less by electronics than other forms have been. A prototype, developed by the Electronic Information Exchange System in 1979, was not successful. Still, there is optimism about the long term future of electronic journals.

The question for Lancaster, then, is no longer "Will the complete evolution to electronic communication occur?" but when will it occur? Will print on paper have disappeared by the year 2000? His forecasts rely somewhat on a Delphi study on the future of electronic publishing, but somewhat on his own highly informed intuition.

1. Conversion to paperless, according to the study, will lag behind economic and technological feasibility, as participants in the study believe that that feasibility has already been reached. In terms of libraries though, Lancaster says, developments will occur more rapidly than librarians can participate.

2. He believes it unlikely that novels or popular magazines will be read online. The novel, in fact, may give way to something like dramatic presentations on videodisk.

3. Electronic applications such as word processing, email, computer conferencing, interactive television and online data base searching, etc., will be brought together into a completely paperless communication network.

4. Terminals will "creep" into homes in ways, such as, "distributed by the telephone company."

So what is his overall conclusion? That the move away from paper will greatly improve access to information.

Dr. Zhou

By 1994, Dr. Zhou is telling us, of course, that the powerful communications system envisioned by Lancaster is in use throughout library services. Collection development, however, has experienced fewer changes through technology, except for acquisitions. Computer proficiency is not emphasized for bibliographers. He does not believe that this situation can last. Information technology, after all, is an agent of change. His 3 stage model of how collection development in the academic research library would evolve is very similar to Lancaster's phases of publishing. Movement is from traditional formats and acquiring to a combination of traditional and non-traditional to completely electronic, a 3 stage process. In each, agreeing with Lancaster, he sees a shift from ownership to access, but this "smart guesser" also believes that "none of these three phases will entirely replace the other two….they will co-exist for a long time, each serving as the principal pattern at a given period."

Let's look at the model:

Phase I: The Smart Guesser

- Based on <u>paper</u> files and <u>manual</u> processes; embodies all of the materials collected in libraries, with the exception of computer based items.

- Needs to respond to the present and future needs of the local community, thus selectors must be well educated **guessers** with: a solid knowledge of the publishing industry, full understanding of their institution's goals and commitments, knowledge of their user group, expertise in a subject area, and usually, facility in a foreign language and an additional advanced degree, other than the MLS.

Phase II: A Better Way

- Last link of the collection development chain, **identification**, **evaluation**, **selection** and **acquisition**, are automated. Ideal for automation, because they are repetitive and labor-intensive chores.

- 1984-1994 strategies developed to automate this process included: in-house acquisitions programs, acquisitions software, time-sharing acquisitions programs and installing an acquisitions module in an integrated system…the best solution.

- Electronic facilitating of other parts of collection development will take place: (Welsch, 1989) presented the "selector's workstation" idea. Components included online library catalogs, worldwide bibliographic databases, online access to selection tools and a system for faculty consultation. Also, a sophisticated data analysis system will be needed (much like the OCLC collection analysis system that we have today). The basic concept of selector's workstation is available in 1994.

In Phase II, Dr. Zhou emphasizes needs that he sees in order to migrate to fully automated collection development:

- The need exists to make publication information available to selectors' workstations. In 1994, Yankee Book Peddler, for example, has an online approval service capable of offering standard search processes through the Internet or direct dialing. Zhou believes that more selection tools and publication information will be available in time.

- Access to reviews for evaluation is needed. CARL, for one, has loaded <u>CHOICE </u>for this purpose. Dr. Zhou says, "As research libraries collections become increasingly interdependent, within the network environment, …information on others (cooperative partners)….becomes more important to selectors." He posits that online catalogs of regional library networks "could become powerful tools in cooperative collection development," if system upgrading and timely data input are followed by each member. While the Internet offers access to many research collections, there are problems in 1994. Slow response time, system drops, and the lack of a standardized interface are three of those.

- Most importantly, there is a need for training. The workforce must develop its electronic skills, for a successful transition to computer-facilitated modes to take place. Members must understand that an integrated selectors' workstation will require those skill, but it will also offer a better way of accomplishing requisite tasks.

Phase III: All Electronic; Is This a Radical Change?!

- In Phase III, formats are electronic; they can be viewed at a computer terminal, and the acquisitions process is computer facilitated.

- Formats are online and offline. Libraries own the offline products, but purchase rights to online products. In a third class are products that may be licensed to a library, consortium or regional network for later use.

- Expert selectors become increasingly vital to the academic research community. Widespread full-text full-image publication of primary source material is already underway in 1994. Dr. Zhou recognizes that as products exist simultaneously in online, offline and print formats, overlap will become a concern, and may be a financial burden to libraries. Expertise will be needed for intelligent selection decisions.

Dr. Zhou's conclusion: Computer technology, which will continually improve, will change the future of collection development.

Movement among the 3 phases of the model will be continual, until phase 3 moves to center stage, and phase 1 and 2 will be largely off the stage. At this point, movement will cease. However, collection development activities, as we now understand them, will not remain static, but they may decline, as Lancaster predicted in 1982. Access, rather than ownership, will be the dominant practice, and in this, Dr. Zhou is again agreeing with Lancaster. Librarians' roles will change, but with the acquisition of new skills as information selectors, they will be empowered to perform in their roles in a way never before experienced.

2008

And here we are in 2008. We have Collection Management systems. Blackwell's, for example, gives us the ability to find publication information on our desktops that Dr. Zhou said we must have to be fully automated. We have title lists, reviews, bibliographic information, table of contents, dust jacket summaries, and on and on. We can place an order in 2 clicks of a mouse. Approval books, standing orders and firm orders are all displayed in Collection Manager. For those libraries that don't have a Collection Management system, CHOICE makes life easy for the liaison selector by providing reviews online matched to a selector's profile, and an ordering service. Furthermore, we can compare our entire collection to those of peer libraries, using one of the collection analysis systems presently available. Taking all of this into consideration, let's look at some questions for discussion:

Are we in Dr. Zhou's Phase III? He was so wise to see that movement between phases would last for a long time. Where are we now in this model? Is electronic development moving, as Lancaster thought it would, faster than librarians can take advantage of it?

Are we being properly trained to use all of the functions available to us, or are we just being overwhelmed? To put this more personally, how do you feel about your own situation?

Do we have, finally, a situation more of access than ownership? What are your hopes for the future of Collection Development? A truly paperless future?

MICROFILM AS A PRIMARY AND SECONDARY SOURCE

Tinker Massey, Serials Librarian, Embry-Riddle Aeronautical University Libraries, Daytona Beach, Florida

Microfilm was developed in this country primarily to help the government convert print documents into a smaller format to save space, and to pass secret documents covertly. It was the thirties and many things were happening that were a prelude to WWII. In those days, the film was developed on an acetate base that was guaranteed to last 50 years. This kind of film was produced until the mid to late seventies, so there is some film that is beginning its deterioration process, and some that is well into the decay. In the late seventies a more stable product was produced on a polyester base that will last for approximately three hundred years. The present day product has been continuously produced on this base for many years and companies will help you convert your acetate products to polyester for a small fee.

In academic libraries especially, we find microfilm being used as a primary source of journals, newspapers, and some documents, especially as a preservation source for older materials. It is standard practice to film current titles and issues as they appear in libraries, so that the print format can be replaced by microfilm for longer life. Many academic libraries do not even purchase the original print, but opt for the microfilm either six months or a year after the original production. The advantages are better reproduction, better preservation, no gaps in issues or other materials, and minimal costs for housing. Recently, Interlibrary Loan alerted me to a situation where a faculty member and her research team were ordering all the articles from a specific journal. Since there is a regulation about how many of these articles can be ordered from each issue, we were asked to purchase the journal title. That specific title was too expensive for us to purchase, so we investigated buying the product on film. The faculty member was very excited. In two weeks, I was able to purchase five years of the journal title and have them on the shelf for their use. The price for five years of the film was equivalent to one year of the print. They are happy and using the material very often. Now they request only the current year's articles they need. We saved a lot of money. We have placed the title on a microfilm standing order, and will receive it every year.

Libraries also purchase microfilm as a secondary or back-up source for journals, newspapers, and documents. Our library tries to have at least two sources of our titles, so that no matter what the local problems are, we have a method for retrieving the information. If the internet or databases go down, we still have the microfilm to back us up. Likewise, if print sources are stolen or damaged, we still have the microfilm to view. We lose very few reels of film compared to print issues, and replacement is far easier. Since a lot of reference work is for students and faculty around the world (off campus), we find that scanning the film for electronic delivery is a primary option and easier than the print source. There is minimal equipment required and better reproduction through a faster delivery system. Here again, we are able to save more money and time, as well as personnel.

Previously, we mentioned the deterioration of acetate film. The first characteristic is the smell of vinegar. When I began my present job three years ago, I took a tour of the microfilm and discovered that specific smell and reported to the administration that we would have to replace the film. I subsequently discovered that NAPC (National Archives Publishing Company) offered a program of replacement at $18.50 per reel plus shipping. The procedure was a little cumbersome, but we worked together, finding the fastest and most efficient method for this system. Turn around time is two weeks from send out to return of the polyester product. We split up the total reels into about twelve shipments and completed the conversion of all of our acetate in just one year. We were lucky the need coincided with a good money year. Our shelving units are in an archway structure near the front doors of our library. I purchased drying packets for placement in the units, so that we can reduce the moisture level. We are in the process of wrapping each reel of film with an acid free strip so that air pockets do not develop and create areas where moisture and warmth will create mold. As I create an inventory of the film, I am adding preservation information about the format and production year for future librarians. This new process should give us all the information we need to deal with the preservation. The university has instituted automatic readouts for heat and humidity, and we will build/buy a unit that will allow us to clean the film and fiche over the years as needed.

We have a format developed for saving space, which still continues to be very useful as a means to save information over long periods of time. It has proven to be easy to use, easy to preserve, less costly to keep and purchase, and more dependable for the library and patrons. It has a lifespan of three hundred years and is easy to replace if necessary, as well as duplicate for fast delivery. What could be better?

PRESERVATION REALLY WORKS—REPORTING ON A TRIGGER EVENT

Clive Parry, Director, Sales and Marketing, SAGE, London, United Kingdom

Jayne Marks, Vice President, Journals, SAGE, Los Angeles, California

Eileen Fenton, Executive Director, Portico, Princeton, New Jersey

Abstract

Publishers have been working with various preservation organizations for some time, including CLOCKSS and Portico, to deposit copies of their e-journals. It is rightly important to librarians that they can be reassured of long-term access to the content that they have purchased. And this is particularly important for any librarian considering moving to online only. But until SAGE closed a journal and it was "triggered" or made available via the archives, no one was really sure if these preservation systems would work. This paper reports on the trigger event that released a journal to the archives and how the market has responded.

Introduction

In December 2007, *Graft Organ and Cell Transplantation*, published by SAGE from January 2001 to March 2003, was the first journal to become available from a dark archive managed by a preservation program. Until recently, while several major publishers had entered into agreements with one or more preservation partners, there was nothing to test the capabilities of these programs. We therefore decided to use Graft as a test case to demonstrate the effectiveness of different preservation programs, while at the same time providing a long-term access solution for this closed title.

Why Archive?

The majority of readers of scholarly content now search for, and access, their content online. Libraries and publishers agree that online-only journal access is also more cost-effective and more environmentally friendly. Yet despite all of this, many librarians remain concerned about the long-term availability of online journals in the future, and this holds them back from moving their collections to online-only.

But should we worry about digital preservation? Experience suggests that the concerns librarians have are not unfounded. Take for example the demise of the floppy disk for data storage. Unless we take steps to future-proof our digitized content, and ensure that its long-term accessibility is well managed, we do take the risk of it one day vanishing or—worse—becoming unreadable.

This is why digital preservation initiatives must have an economically sustainable model that will be able to support data, even as content formats change over time. The Council on Library and Information Resources (CLIR) has also made recommendations for publishers, libraries, and archiving programmes to ensure e-journal preservation. These include that publishers work with at least one preservation partner; communicate preservation arrangements clearly, including in license agreements; and grant sufficient rights to permit preservation activities. Libraries are also guided to support at least one preservation initiative, regardless of library size; urge the publishers they work with to participate with their preferred preservation partners, and to communicate openly about their decision-making process. In addition they recommend the archives themselves be transparent and auditable; communicate their holdings details; and assure that content once committed remains in the archive permanently.

SAGE has committed to a robust preservation strategy. We believe that we have a responsibility to ensure scholarly content and research materials, both archived and digitally born materials, remain accessible to future scholars, researchers, and students. It is critically important for us to preserve our content so that our readers—and authors—have confidence that the content will still be accessible in the future.

In developing a preservation strategy SAGE considered the various preservation initiatives available: national archives such as the Dutch National library (KB) and the British Library; institutional repositories; community-based archives; and product solution archives. We evaluated each program, considering strategies for future technologies; geographic area; and expertise. We felt it important that we use both government supported and other programs, selecting Portico, CLOCKSS and the KB for our investment. All three programs are well regarded and SAGE has made long-term commitments to them.

The Process

For each of the programs that we joined, details of our digital availability, samples of our journal content, and details of the content format had to be provided. Once these stages were complete, all backfile content had to be sent to the providers for loading. As we publish more than 500 journals, this was a long and resource-heavy exercise. The files were then managed by each preservation program to ensure that as future formats become available, the content could still be accessible.

The Trigger Procedure

Triggers are identified as an occurrence causing a particular title to no longer be available from either its publisher, or through any other commercial source. Specific occurrences include:

- A publisher stops operations

- A publisher ceases to publish a title

- A publisher no longer offers back issues

- Complete failure of a publisher's delivery platform

Graft was a title that SAGE had discontinued. Although we could have kept the published content on our own platform, we decided to use this as an opportunity to test our preservation programs, and requested that the journal be triggered by Portico, CLOCKSS and the KB.

Portico took the lead, making the journal available first, CLOCKSS following shortly after; the Dutch KB version is still pending.

As this was the first journal that any preservation program triggered, there were inevitably teething problems: one that we encountered was in the handling of DOIs. Under regulations from CrossRef at that time, multiple resolution of DOIs was not possible. As the first to release the content, SAGE assigned these to Portico for re-depositing to CrossRef. This meant that only Portico's version of the content was initially linked to from CrossRef.

Further difficulties arose for those articles that had no DOIs—who should assign these and how? No precedent had been set for doing this, and as a result CrossRef has now established a working group (with SAGE involvement) to determine the best solution for these and other problems. The working group will establish a method for other preservation services to take advantage of the DOI work that Portico has done.

Market Reaction

While inevitably there has been some negative feedback regarding the closure of a journal, the majority of feedback from librarians has been positive. We now have concrete evidence that preservation in dark archives works, and librarians can use this example to help justify to library committees the time and investment spent on these initiatives.

The DOIs will remain active for the content, ensuring readers do not experience disruption and authors know that their work is safe and available. Most importantly, SAGE's actions have ensured that users have perpetual access for a journal when it would have otherwise been obsolete.

Since *Graft* was released, we have also now taken steps to trigger a second title, *Autobiography*. This was a print journal that ceased publication without ever having an online presence. We took the decision to firstly digitize the content, and then deposit the content to the same services. The journal can now be accessed via Portico and CLOCKSS' websites.

The success of both these trigger events gives us confidence that preservation initiatives work, and we hope that these examples will help to give librarians confidence in the future of e-only journals access.

WE WANT MORE E-BOOKS! LESSONS LEARNED FROM SEVEN YEARS OF EMBEDDING ELECTRONIC BOOKS INTO A UK UNIVERSITY LIBRARY COLLECTION

Kate Price, E-Strategy & Resources Manager, University of Surrey, Guildford, United Kingdom

Introduction

This paper will first introduce the University of Surrey, then move on to explain the history of e-books at the university. The means by which e-books have been acquired and made available over this time are addressed, along with an examination of some of the issues that were faced along the way. Moving into the present, data from the first JISC National E-Books Observatory are used to compare the use of e-books at the University of Surrey with the national picture. Some perspectives on the use of online information by academics and students emanating from the results of the survey, alongside other recent research, are also considered. Finally, some thoughts on the future of e-books are presented.

The University of Surrey

The University of Surrey is located in Guildford, a market town some 30 miles south west of London. The University was incorporated in 1966, at first concentrating on engineering and technical disciplines, but now with more than 30 research groupings and over 14,000 students.

The university is research intensive, with 32% of students currently studying at postgraduate level. A further 11%, mainly in health care, are studying for professional qualifications. Major focuses are still in science and engineering, with international recognition for work on micro- and nano-satellites, but there are also thriving schools of business and law, health and social care, human sciences and performing arts. The university has an international outlook, with students from 140 countries studying on campus, and close relationships with institutions in North and South America, China and Russia.

The History of E-books at Surrey

Going back as early as the mid 1980s, reference-type e-books (such as the *Oxford English Dictionary*) were to be found in CD-ROM format, first mounted on standalone computers in the University Library and then accessible via the university's computer network. When the World Wide Web appeared in the mid-nineties, the Library began to link to e-books available through initiatives such as Project Gutenberg. However, online e-journals rapidly outpaced e-books. E-journals were both more widely available in, and more enthusiastically adopted by, the science and engineering disciplines, which are the stock in trade of the university.

Eventually, in the late 1990s and early 2000s, e-books in relevant subject areas began to emerge in the academic publishing market, and Library staff began to consider whether they would be useful, and, if so, how they should be made available. Funding was obtained to explore these issues on a pilot project basis, and it was decided to subscribe to one package and a set of 100 individual e-books focussing on civil engineering (CRC EngNetBase, and a range of NetLibrary titles). Early handheld e-book reader devices were also available at that time, but they were considered difficult and expensive to obtain. Also, since internet-based e-journals had already set the precedent, it was felt that this mode of access was likely to be widely accepted by academics and students. Links to the individual e-book titles purchased were painstakingly added to static web pages, promotion and training was carried out, usage was monitored, and feedback was obtained from users through a variety of means.

The outcomes of the project were positive – e-books were well received in civil engineering (Green, 2003), and subsequently became part of the Library's usual portfolio of resources across most subject areas. Whilst checking through reading lists and bibliographies, Academic Liaison Librarians were encouraged to identify titles which could also be purchased in e-book format via NetLibrary, particularly where these were deemed to be "essential reading". The requests were passed to the Acquisitions team, which placed the orders directly with NetLibrary.

In parallel with this, online reference titles and packages began to replace both CD-ROMs and printed reference resources. Thus the OED, KnowUK (a package of well-known reference works such as Whitaker's Almanac) and Xrefer+ became available, and the print books on the Quick Reference shelves were dramatically reduced in extent. By the mid 2000s, the listing of individual e-books titles had been abandoned, and only package level links were listed on the Library website. As part of the acquisitions process, NetLibrary books were routinely catalogued by hand. However, e-books within packages were not yet being catalogued, which meant that unless readers knew which package to look within, they were largely unaware of the content that was available to them online, despite such promotional efforts as posters and give-aways.

In 2005, a major opportunity was created with the upgrade of the Library Management System, Talis. Before this, it had not been possible to import catalogue records from outside the system's own co-operative union catalogue (TalisBase), which had been a major barrier to the inclusion of e-book records in the catalogue. Now, an import module was made available, and the cataloguing team began to make use of the MARC records that are often made available as part of an e-book subscription or purchase.

E-book cataloguing has been a process of trial and error due to a lack of relevant guidance from existing standards, and the level of cataloguing possible has been dictated to some extent by the staffing available (roughly 1.5 professionally qualified cataloguers and 0.6 library assistant). Early decisions, such as the attempt to include print and e-versions of the same book on one record, have had to be re-thought as the workload became too great. Also, it has not been possible, due to the limitations of the import manager, to include extensive notes on how to access individual e-books, although direct links are included. MARC records provided by e-book vendors can also be inaccurate, for example often including irrelevant details such as the physical dimensions of a virtual book!

However, the frustrations inherent in not being able to provide the most accurate and functional catalogue records possible have been outweighed by the fact that the individual titles are now very much more visible to the end user. For example, if searching for a book title given on a reading list, readers will see both the record for the print version and the record for the electronic version appearing side by side on the catalogue, and library staff are able to easily point out the e-book if the print versions are on loan or otherwise unavailable. An example screenshot from Surrey's catalogue can be found in Figure 1 on the next page.

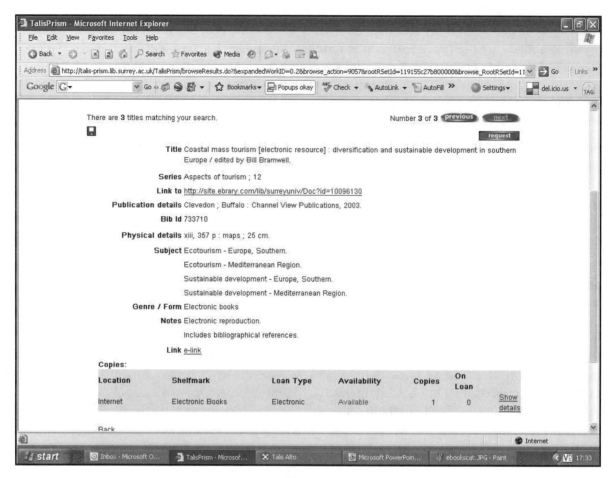

Figure 1

Currently, there is a compromise situation where e-book records are added, even if imperfect, onto the LMS as quickly as possible. This has meant several different streams of work – importing individual records where e-books are purchased one by one, creating templates for packages where no records are available to import, and ensuring that updates are regularly imported for packages where there is a monthly, annual, or ad hoc update (which can encompass both additions and withdrawals of titles). A more detailed study of e-book cataloguing at Surrey and the issues involved can be found in Gravett (2006).

By 2008, the Library had subscribed to a wide range of e-book packages and purchased many hundreds of individual titles, covering all disciplines taught and researched at the University. A new supplier, Myilibrary, had been introduced for the purchase of individual e-books, largely so that orders could be placed using EDI (Electronic Data Interchange), as with orders for print books. E-books were being used to rapidly develop collections in areas that the university was beginning to teach, for example English Literature. By mid 2008, over 60,000 e-books were available, and there were almost 120,000 downloads / section views per year. Library staff in the Academic Liaison, Acquisitions and Cataloguing teams were by now, well used to dealing with e-books as part of the day-to-day workflow.

However, a major issue of workload remained, and still does to this day. The Library still deals with an acquisition rate of 10,000-12,000 print books per year, as the university continues to expand and add new subject areas. Library staffing at Surrey has always been lean (having 33 more students per library staff member than other UK universities with a similar profile – SCONUL, 2008), and there has been continued downward pressure on staffing budgets for several years, although senior management has successfully argued for more funding for information resources. There is no team or staff member in the Library dedicated solely to electronic resources, as the philosophy is a whole team approach, which ensures that the knowledge and skills required to deal with e-information are spread and used widely. Training, constant encouragement, careful recruitment, and the flexibility and willingness to learn of existing staff members have underpinned this approach, although staff still find dealing with e-resources on top of their existing print-related workload very challenging indeed.

So, by 2008, e-books were integrated into the selection, ordering and cataloguing processes at Surrey, and usage statistics seemed healthy. However, in common with many other libraries, Library staff were aware of problems that readers were encountering in finding and using the e-books that they wanted for their study and research. It was therefore extremely useful to be able to join the JISC National eBooks Observatory (NeBO), a major UK research project, which aimed to use surveys and deep log analysis to examine how e-books were actually being used in the academic environment, in order to inform the development of e-books by publishers and vendors. Much more information about this ongoing project is available via the NeBO website (JISC, 2007-). However, the next section of this paper concentrates particularly on the results of the first online survey of readers to be carried out during the project.

E-book Use at Surrey

Over 20,000 readers from 127 UK Higher Education institutions completed the first NeBO survey, held in early 2008. Of these, 510 were from Surrey (a completion rate three times the national average, and comparable with the much more complex LibQual+ survey held at Surrey in 2007). The survey results were collated and circulated by the NeBO research team (JISC National E-Books Observatory 2008a), and institutions were able to see their local results as well as the national results, which gave us a valuable insight into e-book use at Surrey, as compared to the national picture (JISC National E-Books Observatory, 2008b).

As can be seen in Figure 2 below, Surrey students are in some ways different to the average. Surrey students have used e-books more, are more highly dependent on Library-provided e-resources, are less highly dependent on virtual learning environments, and are more likely to visit the Library online daily or weekly. It would be tempting to think that this high use of library-provided e-resources was due to the skill of library staff in promoting them, but it may just as well be due to the high proportion of post-graduate students (more likely to be aware of library resources through longer and more in-depth study) who attend Surrey.

In other ways, Surrey students are actually very similar in profile to the UK average [Figure 3]. They are highly dependent on Internet resources, still visit the Library in person daily or weekly, go to the Library primarily to borrow books and are a bit or very dissatisfied with print book availability. It is this dissatisfaction with print book availability (not enough copies on the shelf), common to the users of almost every UK HE library, which is of great concern to librarians, and which has to some extent driven the take up of e-books.

Surrey Students:

Have used e-books more
UK: 62.7%   Surrey: 71.4%

Are more highly dependent on Library-provided e-resources
UK: 45.4%   Surrey: 56.3%

Are less highly dependent on VLEs
UK: 37.5%   Surrey: 24.2%

Are more likely to visit the Library online daily/weekly:
UK: 67.4%   Surrey: 80.4%

Figure 2

Surrey students (and UK students):

Are highly dependent on Internet resources
UK: 52.4%   Surrey: 50.3%

Still visit the Library in person daily/weekly
UK: 70.5%   Surrey: 69.6%

Go there primarily to borrow books
UK: 87%   Surrey: 87.3%

Are a bit/very dissatisfied with printed book availability
UK: 21.8%   Surrey: 22.4%

Figure 3

Moving on to the specifics of e-book use, the figures below demonstrate that Surrey students (broadly in line with the UK average) tend to read the contents from the screen rather than print them out [Figure 4]. They also spend very little time per session reading, with nearly a third spending 10 minutes or less per session (somewhat quicker than the national average of 23% spending 10 minutes or less per session) [Figure 5]. Surrey students also have a very strong tendency to dip in and out of chapters rather than read a whole chapter, let alone a whole book [Figure 6]. Is this behaviour inherent in the reader him/herself, or is it to some extent a product of the way that e-books are presented? We will examine this question below.

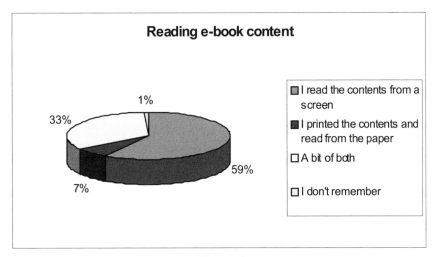

Figure 4

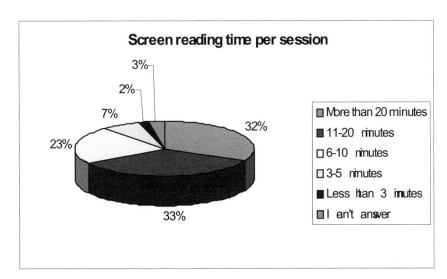

Figure 5

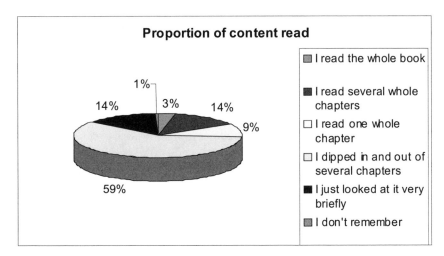

Figure 6

The findings of the first NeBO survey echo strongly the findings of the recent report "Information behaviour of the researcher of the future: a CIBER briefing paper" (CIBER, 2008). This major piece of research, dubbed the "Google Generation" report, which included an extensive review of the previous research as well as deep log analysis of actual academic use of some specific internet resources, aimed to find out whether there are real generational differences between the "Digital Natives" who grew up with the Internet, and those who came to it in later life.

The Google Generation report found that users tended towards horizontal information seeking behaviour ("bouncing" between websites), short viewing times ("power browsing"), and squirreling behaviour (saving things for later). They spent as much time attempting to navigate to useful information as they did viewing it once they found it, and they tried to ensure the authority of the information through swiftly cross-checking it with other trusted information or relying on the fact that it was provided by a known brand.

Further perspectives on readers' experiences using online material can be found in the free text comments that respondents were encouraged to add when completing the NeBO survey. Analysing the Surrey results revealed that of the 92 comments about e-books that were left after weeding out all of the comments about other types of resources, 14 comments were broadly positive, and the rest dealt with a variety of difficulties that readers had encountered (see Figure 7 for an overview).

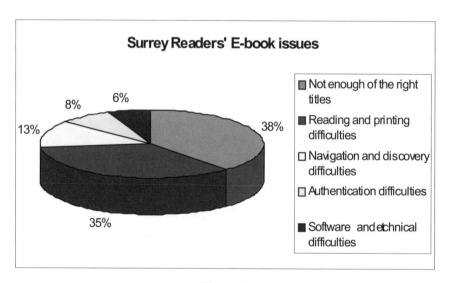

Figure 7

The positive comments all dealt with the fact that e-books were available when print books were inaccessible (e.g., "I have found access to online resources very helpful as I live quite a long way from campus and find it difficult to pop in to pick up books if I need them out of lecture hours") . Interestingly, and not very good news for publishers, is the fact that not a single comment was made about the additional features of e-books that are much promoted, such as the ability to annotate text or keep personal libraries. This is not really so surprising, when it is understood that readers need to access content across a variety of different platforms in order to satisfy their needs, and these additional features are not portable across platform barriers.

Of the remaining comments, the most common concerned the topic of not having enough of the right titles available (hence the title of this paper). Indicative comments include:

> "More books online!!!"

> "It would be great if all the popular text books are available as e-books."

> "There are often only 1 or 2 copies available of newer texts – there could definitely be opportunity to extend the range of e-books!"

Readers have noticed that the number of e-books available is still only a small proportion of the full range of books that is published; text books (which are often the largest revenue earners for academic publishers) are very often not available; and often the availability of e-books, where it exists, lags behind the publication of the printed version by months or years, all of which results in frustration for the reader (as well as the librarian).

Nearly as many comments dealt with difficulties in reading and printing. Often these comments were long and impassioned, with a few of the shorter ones reproduced below:

> "Existing copyright laws are frustrating as printing off text from e-books makes it easier to read than reading vast amounts of text online."

> "Looking at the screen hurts my eyes and gives me a headache after a short period of time and my concentration goes rapidly."

> "It is quite difficult to physically read things while on the computer screen. When I have needed books, I usually print the main part(s) I need and ignore the rest."

> "I don't really see why I wouldn't be allowed to print more than 10 pages or so... that is just silly."

The remainder of the comments deal with technical issues such as the limited number of simultaneous accesses for some titles, problems with passwords, difficulties in finding e-books, the need for specific plugins, and incompatibility with operating systems such as Linux. As one reader comments: "They are a work in progress."

Perspectives on Online Information Use

The common factor in both the Google Generation report and the NeBO survey (incidentally, both carried out by the CIBER research group at University College London), is that readers appear to be scraping the surface of the information available. It should be of deep concern to anyone working in education that readers may not be assimilating and interrogating information in enough depth to be able to then create new and original knowledge.

It is tempting to attribute this to a youthful inability to concentrate and persevere when encountering difficulties. Anyone working in education (perhaps even anyone over the age of 30) is familiar with the idea that those belonging to the younger generation have shorter attention spans and want immediate gratification in all things. However, what is intriguing about both the Google Generation report and the NeBO survey is that the information seeking behaviours listed above (short viewing times, bouncing quickly between websites and so on) are common to all ages, right up to retirement age.

In some ways this is unsurprising. Human psychology works on the principle of least effort. It has been observed for over 20 years that people will tend to use the most convenient search method in the least exacting mode possible and to stop trying to find information when they have found something that is "good enough" (Mann 1987). In other words, when someone is faced with a chore they do not enjoy (and, to non-librarians, information seeking is just such a chore), they will tend to take the easiest path possible, and to give up quickly when they encounter barriers.

What is disturbing is that with e-books in particular, there appear to be so many barriers in the way of easy use that readers, although on one hand they find e-books very convenient if they can get hold of them (and want more of them because of this), are on the other hand perhaps finding it very difficult to make the best use of the information within. Hence the large number of comments from Surrey students about the difficulties in printing and reading in the results of the NeBO survey.

Taking Down the Barriers

There would appear to be many possible ways for both libraries and publishers to begin dismantling these barriers, and thus allowing academics and students to concentrate more fully on exploiting the fantastic ideas contained within the scholarly works to be found online. Some ideas are listed briefly below:

Libraries

Content

- Pursue an aggressive acquisition policy for e-books.

- Let suppliers know which titles readers are demanding.

- Accept that, for some titles, higher payment or different payment models may be necessary.

Discoverability

- Catalogue as many titles as possible.

- Implement best of breed search tools, to ease navigation.

- Import enriched records if possible.

Skills

- Assist readers via leaflets, web guides, face-to-face training and real-time troubleshooting.

- Focus formal information skills learning on information recognition and handling instead of step-by-step guides to using specific platforms.

Publishers

Currency and range

- Publish e-book and print book titles simultaneously.

- Find a business model for textbooks which suits both parties (library reference copy linked to student purchase copy?)

Usability

- Remember that some books are written to be read all the way through, and make it easier for this to happen.

- Do not lock down reader activities so tightly – consider lockouts only when major transgressions occur (as with e-journals).

Connectivity and Standardisation

- Enhance descriptive metadata for books and book chapters, and make these fields accessible to Federated Search engines.

- Enhance linking from bibliographies ("CrossRef for books") .

- Look towards standardising features and practices in a similar way to e-journals.

Conclusion: The Future For E-books

The take-up of e-books seems to have been very slow, compared to that of e-journals. We can see that in the journal environment, there was a feedback loop that was started by some publishers and librarians identifying the potential of e-journals, working hard to make them viable, and then academics and students taking them up and creating further demand, which then in turn a much wider group of publishers and librarians sought to satisfy. This feedback loop is starting to take effect with e-books too, although the commercial pressures on publishers have been somewhat different in the book environment. We may yet see a flip-over point where the e-version of a book is seen as the standard version of a text, with the print version being a sort of stand-by, as is now the case in many major research libraries with journals.

There has also been much interest recently in handheld e-book readers (such as the Sony Reader and the Amazon Kindle). These have proven popular with consumers of general literature due to the large amount of text that can be contained and easily accessed by a neat handheld device, and may perhaps become part of the apparatus of student life in the future. However, if that student already has a laptop computer onto which he/she can download academic texts, transfer ideas from them into word-processed assignments, also import clips from YouTube, and then e-mail the whole lot back to their lecturer for assessment via a wireless network, it is quite difficult to see why they should be induced to purchase an e-book reader as well. But, perhaps the cool factor will come into play and it will become a must-have item.

Finally, there is no doubt that there is now a very real demand for e-books from readers, particularly in the academic environment, as can be seen from the results of the NeBO survey. However, more in-depth research is required into how readers actually use the information within. Perhaps more easily observable behaviour such as bouncing quickly between chapters/websites obscures other more private actions such as going back to saved information and reading it in more depth later on? The NeBO deep log analysis (still ongoing) and case studies will perhaps provide some further insights, and will help publishers and librarians create an e-book product that is both desirable and highly usable for the reader. The best is yet to come!

References

CIBER (2008). *Information behaviour of the researcher of the future: a CIBER briefing paper.* British Library & JISC, London.

Gravett, K. (2006). The cataloguing of e-books at the University of Surrey. *Serials.* 19 (3), pp. 202-207.

Green, K. (2003). Introducing e-books at the University of Surrey. *SCONUL Newsletter.* 29 (Summer/Autumn), pp. 54-56.

JISC National E-Books Observatory (2007-). *Project website* [online]. JISC, London. Available from: http://www.jiscebooksproject.org/.

JISC National E-Books Observatory (2008a). *Findings from the first user survey* [online]. JISC, London. Available from: http://www.jiscebooksproject.org/wp-content/e-books-project-first-user-survey-a4-final-version.pdf.

JISC National E-Books Observatory (2008b). *JISC User survey January 2008 (local results for University of Surrey).* Unpublished.

LISU (2008). *SCONUL annual library statistics 2006-07.* LISU, Loughborough.

Mann, T. (1987). *A guide to library research methods.* Oxford University Press, New York.

This year we had several talks on the topic of library management. Key topics that were covered included the role of the library in a Googlized world, managing workflows in technical services, merging two library systems, and merging collections.

Management

THE ROLE OF THE LIBRARY IN A FULLY GOOGLIZED WORLD

Nancy L. Eaton, Dean of University Libraries and Scholarly Communications, The Pennsylvania State University, University Park, Pennsylvania

Rick Luce, Vice Provost and Director of Libraries, Emory University, Atlanta, Georgia

Joyce Ogburn, University Librarian and Director, J. Willard Marriott Library, University of Utah, Salt Lake City, Utah

Rick Anderson (moderator), Associate Director for Scholarly Resources & Collections, J. Willard Marriott Library, University of Utah, Salt Lake City, Utah

Three distinguished and forward-thinking library directors came together as a panel to respond to the following hypothetical scenario:

> *It's the year 2020. Google has digitized effectively all of the books, journals and newspapers in the major research libraries of the Western world, and has improved its search engine to such a degree that all the content is easily searchable and any user can find any book, chapter, or article she wishes in seconds. Furthermore, Google has entered into agreements with all affected publishers that make it possible for anyone to view and download up to 30 pages of any book or journal issue for free, and purchase additional pages at half a cent per page. Currently-enrolled students and faculty from kindergarten through graduate school get unlimited free access, underwritten by advertising. Question: What does the library do now?*

For **Rick Luce**, this scenario offered an opportunity to reflect imaginatively on the ways that the library profession had "risen to the challenges" of the dozen years leading up to 2020:

- 2009: A sharply weakened economy exacts a heavy toll on U.S. libraries; spending on serials finally peaks as libraries begin to make budgetary adjustments. Calls for new serials pricing models largely fall on deaf ears. Some institutions begin to reposition their spending on content after concluding that the need for budgetary adjustments are not a one-year phenomenon.

- 2010: Education reform continues to be a powerful current in American politics, and educational institutions at all levels struggle with new accountability measures coupled with calls for better models of assessing and evaluating cost vs. performance. Libraries are highly divided in the practice of seriously investing resources to develop the internal capabilities to assess and continuously improve their organization. Conference attendance peaks and libraries begin creatively looking for substitute mechanisms to offset the cost of sending large numbers of staff around the country to attend conferences, while attending to professional development needs. One impact is a consolidation of membership organizations.

- 2012: The PATRIOT Act is repealed, and the first heavy wave of librarian retirements hits the profession. The ripple effect impacts libraries at all levels, correspondingly there is greater urgency in the calls leadership development and recruiting entry-level professionals.

- 2014: Copyright law is modified to reflect recently emerged cultural and technological realities. Most conferences and meetings are held by means of high definition video conferencing, and many libraries now feature fully integrated sophisticated HD/Video Teleconferencing Centers with multiple cameras and supporting multiple locations simultaneously.

- 2016: Anti-trust issues having been resolved to allow libraries to take concerted collective action supporting multi-library content licensing. Libraries are now banding together in the next generation of consortia as a matter of course. New and innovative content purchasing models have emerged.

- 2018: Google slips and the first instance of Google systematically violating privacy is uncovered, which is characterized as practicing "evil." Some institutions begin to re-examine their symbiotic relationships with commercial entities. The expenditures required to support the library's electrical needs are now as high as their content budgets once were. Library buildings are now power plug-in centers featuring state-of-the-art liquid-paper readers and 3-D virtual reality browsers. Responding to calls to fund green initiatives, investments for new facilities are redirected to retrofitting old facilities, while the need for collaborative group work spaces leads to large-scale conversion of book stacks in many libraries without distinct collections.

- 2020: The total number of full-scale libraries has noticeably decreased, but those that remain are thriving, with better-paid staff whose expertise is in high demand. Libraries distinguish themselves by focusing on particular knowledge domains:

  Science libraries support e-science and embed their staff within the researcher populations they serve, working on metadata problems as well as workflow design and execution;

  Social science libraries specialize in stewardship of localized data sets, GIS data, and similar large-scale curatorial projects;

  Humanities libraries focus on e-research and digital scholarship, and provide advanced digital classroom learning environments inside the library.

  Special collections have experienced a renaissance – now that their unique collections are easily discoverable online, they are attracting visitors from around the world.

In 2020, Luce sees traditional library organizational structures as having given way to new, hybridized staffing models; those with and without traditional library training work together, crossing multi-institutional boundaries. Librarians act as "middleware," creating coherence and facilitating connections between researchers within and across disciplines. They staff "collaboratories" where students and researchers come together to use advanced tools and leverage each other's ideas and talents. They provide expertise in organizing information workflows and constructing useful metadata schemes.

Luce sees the library in 2020 as being busier than ever. Its business practices have evolved to create a culture of assessment and continuous improvement, while those libraries that failed to do so having effectively gone out of business. Successful libraries are now laboratories that mirror the evolving methods and techniques of modern scholarship. Libraries set their services apart from publicly-available generic offerings by tailoring their services to local needs and creating unique hybrid knowledge products aimed specifically at their user populations, and by embracing the task of caring for massive, locally-created research data sets. These have, in large part, become the new "special collections" area for research libraries.

Nancy Eaton began her response by reflecting on the fact that Google had only a few days earlier entered into a settlement with publishers that, if approved, would open the door to something very much like the scenario envisioned for this program. What, she asked, would be the implications of having most of the books, journals and newspapers ever published become searchable online, with the full text available to read online and with ancillary products like printing, downloading, and print-on-demand either free or for-fee?

She began by pointing out that this scenario is not very different from what libraries do with electronic journals. Most journals are now available online. Books are just catching up, both in the form of new e-books from publishers and of the long tail of mass digitization of retrospective titles. And like journals, they are beginning to be offered as aggregated licensed databases, which is what Google is now proposing in its court settlement. In reflecting on what it means to have books online, Eaton quoted from a recent article by Sara Lloyd, "A Book Publisher's Manifesto for the Twenty-first Century: How Traditional Publishers Can Position Themselves in the Changing Media Flows of a Networked Era,"[i]

> We will need to think of "the book" as a core or base structure but perhaps one with more porous edges than it has had before. We will need to work out how to position the book at the center of a network rather than how to distribute it to the end of a chain. We will need to recognize that readers are also writers and opinion formers and that those operate online within and across networks. We will need to understand that parts of books reference parts of other books and that now the network of meaning can be woven together digitally in a very real way, between content published and hosted by entirely separate entitles. Perhaps most radically, we will have to consider whether a primary focus on text is enough in a world of multimedia mash-ups.

Lloyd's warning to publishers is that they need to stop thinking of books as a product at the end of a chain, but should instead think of them as content in the middle of a networked environment. However, making the book available electronically on the Web is not sufficient unto itself. Having books available online is only one aspect of teaching, learning, and research. As Chris Borgman points out in a recent *Educause Review* article, "Supporting the 'Scholarship' in E-Scholarship,"

> Retrieving whole books, articles, and other documents is no longer sufficient for scholarly research. Faculty and students want to mine documents or other textual works – whether for molecules, materials, or mavens, depending on their field of study. Rarely do people read documents linearly, even on paper. They read abstracts, conclusions, and bibliographies; they look for tables, figures, and diagrams. What is new in the digital environment? Information can be extracted in smaller units, mashed up, and recombined—preferably with attribution to the original sources. Faculty and students alike need assistance in learning how to think with these tools and services if they are to ask truly new questions with them.[ii]

So long as libraries are viewed as repositories of books and journals, Eaton believes, we limit our future, just as publishers who view the book as an object do. However, libraries have been more than repositories for a very long time – since the 1960s, when they began to incorporate automation and new roles within teaching and learning.

Clearly, networking and information technology are changing the library's roles and operations in dramatic ways. Eaton observes that it is increasingly acknowledged that certain functions or activities are moving to the network level, certain functions or activities are better done in collaboration by multiple institutions, and other functions or activities are done best at the local level. The challenge for libraries is to tease out this emerging hierarchy and to realign our workflows and our expertise to operate at the right levels. Eaton believes that the emerging hierarchy will look something like this:

HIERARCHY OF LIBRARY FUNCTIONS AND SERVICES

Network level:
      Cooperative cataloging (e.g., OCLC)
      Search and discovery (e.g., Google)
      Access to remote collections (licensed e-collections) including Google Books
      e-science or networked science (e.g., astronomy)

Regional collaborative efforts:
      CIC shared digital repositories (data, video, etc.) and e-preservation
      Hathi Trust
      Infrastructure: Supercomputing Centers & Internet nodes

Local focus:
      Library as place
            Collections (both physical and electronic access)
            Subject-based libraries
            Learning Commons
            IT and media laboratories
      Campus and library IT infrastructure
            Networks
            Web architecture
            Integrated library systems
            Email, calendars, budget systems
            Local e-repositories and e-preservation
      Direct library services:
            Reference (face-to-face, phone, email, chat, IM)
            Circulation of materials
            Web content developed by the library
            Course-related instruction sessions
            Information and digital literacy programs
            Department liaisons
            Consultation as "informationist" (e.g., NSF data grant proposals)

Returning specifically to the Google Books Project and the scenario the panelists were asked to address, Eaton then examined some opportunities that she believes Google's mass digitization of print books will actually generate for libraries:

REVIEWING AND SIMPLIFYING LIBRARY WORKFLOW

Continued move to Network level
> OCLC Local replaces the local online catalog
> Google searches are linked directly to library catalogs and content

Google content availability (10 to 20 million titles)
> E-reserves are linked to e-content (eliminating local scanning and uploading)
> ILL requests fall dramatically due to free availability of digital versions
> Course management systems link directly to e-content

While the scenario was silent on the business models that will have to be in place to provide a stable online collection over time, Eaton observed that the probability of mass digitization of library collections is very high and will provide libraries with the opportunity to continue to evolve their service models according to tiered approaches like those suggested above. She closed with four summary "take-away" points:

- There will be continued movement to the network level for services and collections, but plenty of work will remain to be done at regional and local levels;

- We should heed the admonitions of Sara Lloyd and Chris Borgman regarding repurposing of content – making digital content available is not enough;

- There will be great opportunties to reduce or eliminate back-room processing, e.g., e-reserves, ILL, course management systems;

- The Google database, though very large and important, is still just one database among many, and for the foreseeable future will be more important to the humanities and social sciences than to the hard sciences, which rely much more heavily on the journal literature.

Joyce Ogburn also took the tack of looking back over "a decade of change" and reflecting on the myriad ways that libraries had responded to the seismic shifts in the information landscape. In her telling, there had been some very impressive developments indeed. Her comments follow, in her own words:

It is hard to believe it is now 2020 and I am retiring this month. What a pleasure to wrap up my career here in Charleston, the conference where I gave my first presentation on licensing in 1989. We have come a long way. I have been asked to review the last decade, and reflect on what libraries have become and how they enrich the vast world of knowledge construction, sharing, and preservation.

Who would have guessed ten years ago that Google would live up to its promise to organize and deliver so much knowledge? Vast amounts of content are now widely available one way or another and, in some cases, fairly inexpensively, and is also now discoverable through many channels.

But on to my task, which is to review the highlights and significant developments in librarianship, scholarship and the knowledge industry that led us to where we are today.

In 2010, academic libraries were shifting the balance more concertedly from consumption of information to its creation, but we were still swinging back and forth depending on the state of the subject fields, the ways in which interdisciplinary efforts were evolving and morphing, how quickly we could work out new relationships with publishers, and also how much we chose to publish ourselves. And we continued the trend to put plenty of new things on the Internet – not necessarily true publications, but at the very least large amounts of primary source material that we had digitized.

We also began, slowly but surely, to embed information about our rich and unique resources into social networks, alongside commercial and group-created online tools. OCLC Worldcat was "wikified" in 2010, and in the process the control of Wikicat's content resided both with libraries and publishers. This alliance took charge of enhancing the content and the editorial functions. Through this open and collaborative system both groups added vast amounts of expert information about publications and collections that became available to be reused and referred to in many places, and for many purposes. Collectively we had made more concerted steps to take our presence and our collections to the world in as many discoverable ways as we could identify and sustain.

A significant development occurred in 2011 when the Independent Peer Review Board was established to make it possible for scholars and organizations to have work of any kind peer reviewed and certified. This initiative has gone a long way toward allowing independent articles, reports, web sites, blogs, and other publications be validated for their scholarly value. This process has removed a barrier to both the dissemination and the vetting of scholarship both inside and outside of formal publishing streams. This Board put the process of peer review under the control of scholars, who establish standards and protocols themselves. The scholarly societies took a strong hand in founding and nurturing this service and are still the main managers and stakeholders in its success. Their revenue streams of publishing have in part been replaced or at least supplemented by funding that derives from this service, thus relieving the pressure of charging for all of their publications. From the start, the governing board has been run by an elected group of researchers, librarians, and publishers to ensure that the service and its costs are sustainable and economical.

The *PR* symbol that was invented by the IPR Board began to be applied to scholarly products to indicate that they have been peer reviewed, either by the Board or another agency. This has been a huge boon to those who teach information literacy and help students and researchers assess the credibility of resources. I wish we had had the *PR* symbol a long time ago. We would have obviated some misperceptions about OA journals and peer review back in the early days of electronic publishing.

In 2012 a new law was formulated to add to Ranganathan's five laws – "information that is used will be preserved." This law has been tested time and again but we still have debates about its validity, debates that hinge on the definition of "use." The chicken-and-egg nature of this new law still confounds us and the cost of information seems to have no bearing on the likelihood that it will be used and thus preserved. What has been preserved seems still to be as much a product of accident as of design.

The "long tail" effect and the pervasiveness of niche markets have persisted to this day, but the tail has stretched and the digital information of which it was composed has thinned due to lack of preservation. Even prior to 2012 much of the long tail was readable only by machines, since computers had long since become the primary consumers and processors of information – which further complicated the concept of "use."

Around 2013 librarians found renewed purpose when they recognized that our field had changed enough to become a new, more dynamic, potent and inclusive discipline; it subsequently became known as the Knowledge and Information Arts and Sciences (KIAS). KIAS came to integrate programs and collections that cover the history, documentation, recording, and visualization of knowledge and communication. Further, it incorporated the study of the impact that these have had on human culture, the history of ideas, and expression of human thought. This includes the arts and technologies that have been used in the creation and dissemination of knowledge over millennia. This new field demanded a more expansive view of our work and required us to abandon our preoccupation with information and its conflation with knowledge. Libraries have become the vehicle for delivery, teaching, mastery, and preservation of the KIAS.

I remember vividly the public policy wars of 2008, which divided the publishing community and the librarians, with authors caught somewhere in the middle. The protectionist stance that we all took suddenly broke down in 2014 when two things happened. First, librarians and publishers mended their rift as many service providers changed their focus to the provision of tools rather than content; second, authors quietly revolutionized their work around new premises.

The generation that swapped files, shared music, lived on the web, and started the Freeculture movement finished graduate school, became our new faculty, and embraced their own style of open access, which became the norm and fundamentally shaped expectations for research and teaching. This cohort was insistent on teamwork, across institutions and disciplines, facilitated by social technology and grounded in the easy availability and mutability of scholarly works and primary source materials. Its members chose to be judged on the success of the group and embraced enabling technologies that freely distributed their work, in an open process, as it was being imagined, shaped, crafted, tested, and explicated. They forged a strong partnership with librarians in creating a new ethic and a new economy of sharing. Thanks to them the products of scholarship are now findable, understandable, and usable by a very wide audience of scholars, schoolteachers, and the public. In the hope of creating an educated public, the faculty created a new tenure process that embraced the concept of popular writing as a major contributor both to the public good and to sound scholarship. There has been a resurgence of public science and writing for a lay audience.

In 2015 Web 2.0 finally blossomed into Web 3.0 with a semantic, ubiquitous structure that was especially suitable for academic pursuits. To further encourage the open sharing of their work and to tailor technology to their needs, scholars turned Information Technology into Knowledge Technology (KT). This new hybrid grew out of the synergies between knowledge management and cyberinfrastructure, both of which supported the mission-based assets of research and teaching. KT is interoperable, contextual, semantic, interpretive, integrative, evaluative, synthetic, and extractive. We also envisioned that knowledge technology could be self-organizing, could incorporate feedback and learning capabilities, and could perhaps even be self-preserving. Documents and intellectual products were to be made "smart" and "social" so as to interact with each other, and to be more independent of their creators – in effect living within a social network for things. With KT in place a wonderfully integrated environment for scholarship grew, with amazing analytical and manipulative tools.

Advances in knowledge technology hastened the ability to sort and filter through information noise, allowing us to get at most of the information products we really wanted. The new informal academic Internet that was part of this new technological construct paved the way for advancing research and discovery.

At about this same time we promulgated new models of digital preservation. As one of our key preservation initiatives, repository audits and certifications that were pioneered by the Center for Research Libraries became routine and began to be conducted by machines to validate the integrity of the content. Humans, though, designed the systems, evaluate the results, make recommendations and determine outcomes. Librarians used this approach to provide more assurance of the preservation of electronic records and materials that were in hands of many people or organizations.

Although the public policy wars were settled, in 2020 the copyright wars have still not been resolved. In 2016, dominant 20th century entertainment corporations still held sway over laws that locked up content as tight as a drum, but they lost their impact on our culture because they made it so difficult – almost comically so – to reference, use or in any way incorporate the products of their artistic legacy into teaching and learning, or new entertainment. We lost great companies because leaders were fearful of risk and overly protective of their past. Others in the entertainment industry promulgated their "property" with abandon, and in so doing became the dominant and admired companies, while losing none of their popularity or revenue growth. This movement paralleled that of scholars increasingly making their work available through creative commons licenses or similar means.

With the growth of OA resources, our new field of KIAS and the strengthening of knowledge technology, we turned our professional practice toward more fully understanding and supporting complex knowledge systems that are tuned to communities and fields of expertise that may or may not fit familiar categories. Clearly constructing a worldview and conceptualizing oneself within it is not a neat or well-understood process. Taxonomies and perspectives can differ widely, depending on where individuals draw lines in their minds. As scholars moved more fluidly between microdisciplines and research partnerships we have had to adjust to our thinking and our own systems to keep up with this behavior.

Earlier in the decade many of us started moving away from large print collections of commonly available resources to build digital collections that spanned many forms and types of content, including the acquisition and curation of complex web sites and enormous data sets. Not only did we redeploy our staffs, we redirected our budgets to focus on the unique and endangered stuff of special collections writ large and conceived on a massive scale. By 2018 the balance was firmly tipped, and libraries were beginning to see their primary role as that of *pushing out* content, along with its contextual envelopes. The sheer connectedness of people and scholarly knowledge became utterly astounding.

After finally figuring out how to define and measure new forms of scholarship – and coming to agreement on this was not easy – in 2019 it was estimated that the amount of new digital and open access data and scholarship being created surpassed the amount of new controlled-access publications. Interestingly enough, libraries still manage only a portion of scholarship and primary sources. But still, we manage a lot and influence the development of much more.

In 2020 it is wonderful that Google can deliver books and journals at a low cost, made possible in large part because of the movement toward public and open access and the efforts of scholars to create dynamic new systems of communication. Google's current model is laudable, but it reflects only the surface of the substance of constructing, sharing, and preserving knowledge. What we have built behind the scenes is a complex, interwoven, open system of data, software, and ideas presented in text, images, charts, spreadsheets, and more. And the Google model represents a diminishing piece of the scholarly pie.

With our redefined discipline, librarians have armed themselves with new skills to participate fully in scholarship that permits access to massive amounts of data and articles for data mining, making it possible to tease out trends, conduct meta-analysis, and perform large-scale textual and numerical studies of a vast amount of rich scholarship. Scientists and humanists alike can now scour the literature to discover new knowledge, determine new medical treatments and gain new insights into the human condition. Under the old system, access was provided in isolated buckets that did not permit this kind of work. Systems have now blossomed that support large-scale analyses that cross disciplinary boundaries and that reveal hidden kernels of relevance as well as the deeply important overlaps that characterize interdisciplinary research. Librarians are adding content, layers of service, and contextual information. We are advancing new information policies and perspectives. We are running multimedia and visualization labs, recording studios, text conversion and mining operations, publishing and editing arms, metadata services, repository audits, digital formatting and curation centers, and copyright offices. We have formed partnerships to facilitate high performance computing, analysis, evaluation, distribution, and remix services. We broker access to a host of resources and tools, and participate in a wide array of organizations that serve scholars. The digital scholarship that is supplementing and surpassing formal textual publication is the librarian's domain.

Today we have an incredible array of resources, systems, services, and technologies at our disposal. I can't begin to characterize the whole spectrum of changes that spanned my career.

Some things have not changed. As humans we desire to explore, learn, express, create, perform, record, and share our creativity and discoveries. This desire is unquenchable and people will continue to reinvent methods and systems to make these things happen and will knock down barriers that get in the way.

I look forward to 2030 with great eagerness and excitement, although I won't be in the profession any longer. I expect the up-and-coming generations of librarians to invent, undoubtedly, an even more interesting and compelling story for themselves and our users than the one I shared with you today. Let it be so.

Notes

1. *Library Trends*, vol. 57, no. 1 (Summer 2008).
2. *Educause Review*, vol. 43, no. 6 (November/December 2008).

A TALE OF TWO LIBRARIES: THE MERGING OF THE MEDICAL UNIVERSITY OF OHIO LIBRARY DATABASE WITH THE UNIVERSITY OF TOLEDO LIBRARIES DATABASE

Laura Kinner, Director of Technical Services, The University of Toledo, Toledo, Ohio

ABSTRACT

The Medical University of Ohio and The University of Toledo were merged on July 1, 2006. After nine months of hard work, the merging of their integrated library systems was completed on March 31, 2007. In addition to the successful merging of the ILSs, the Technical Services staffs of both libraries were combined.

This paper discusses the activities involved and the stages developed in order to merge the libraries' integrated library systems as well as the technical services staff of both libraries with as little pain or disruption to services as possible. These merging activities included but were not limited to: preparation of documentation for distribution to key team members, such as the systems librarian, head of bibliographic control and the access services assistant; development of a 6 month planning stage prior to work being done in either integrated library system in order to minimize potential manual record cleanup; the actual merging of the integrated library systems and the Technical Services staffs and finally, the re-structuring of the Technical Services Department for the University Libraries of The University of Toledo that incorporated the policies and procedures of a medical library with those of a traditional academic library.

INTRODUCTION

The Medical College of Ohio Library had its beginnings in 1967 at a hospital in South Toledo, Ohio. The Medical College of Ohio (MCO) consisted of the Medical Center, The College of Medicine, College of Nursing, College of Graduate Studies, plus its library. The Medical College of Ohio changed its name to the Medical University of Ohio (MUO) in 2004. The Raymon Mulford Library was built in 1975 and housed 165,000 volumes (books, media and serials) all related to the field of medicine and health sciences. The Library staff consisted of: Library Director, Assistant Director, 3 Reference Librarians, Systems Librarian and a Bibliographic Control Librarian, plus 12 support staff members.

The University of Toledo (UT) was founded in 1872 in West Toledo. It has grown to consist of 9 degree granting colleges at the bachelor, masters and doctorate levels. The William S. Carlson Library, built in 1973, houses over 3 million volumes (books, media, and serials) all supporting the curriculum of UT. The library staff consisted of The Dean of the University Libraries, The Assistant Dean, Director of Technical Services, Director of Special Collections, 11 Reference Librarians and 4 Technical Services Librarians, plus 28 support staff members.

The Presidents of The Medical University of Ohio and The University of Toledo began the planning for the merger of the 2 institutions in 2005. The plans became public in December 2006, when it was announced that the President of the Medical University of Ohio would be the new president of The University of Toledo. The plans became action in January 2006, when the president-elect began the transition process of merging the Universities. The new president set a goal for all of the colleges and other administrative offices of the Universities to have the basic structures in place for a merged University by July 1, 2006.

To this end many workgroups were organized for the various areas across both Universities to develop strategies and workflows. Since The University of Toledo is a state public university the state legislature of Ohio had to approve this merger. This was accomplished in March 2006 when we officially became The University of Toledo.

PLANNING AND WORKGROUPS

The Academic Technology Resources and Services workgroup was formed in March 2006. The goal of this workgroup was to review and make recommendations that would integrate technology systems to support instruction and research. The initial focus of our charge was on the integration of systems that were duplicated between the two universities. We were to develop tactical plans and associated budgets for the integration of course management systems and library systems into common platforms; to examine the migration of data and provide timelines and budget estimates for this activity. All of this information was due on April 12, 2006 but no later than May 4, 2006.

This larger group was separated into the next level of work groups. Ours was the Library Integration Workgroup which consisted of: the Dean of the University Libraries, Senior

Vice Provost of Academic Affairs, Dean of the College of Nursing, Director of Academic Computing, Director of Distance and eLearning, Coordinator of Technical Services, Associate Director of CCI, Director of Academic & Student Support Services, Director of the Center for Teaching and Learning and an Assistant Professor of Curriculum and Instruction.

This group was further subdivided into implementation and merger teams. The Library merger team consisted of the Coordinator of Technical Services (Main campus), the Head of Bibliographic Control (Health Science Campus), Coordinator of Access Services (Health Science Campus) and the soon to be hired Coordinator of Library Systems; other team members were to be added as deemed necessary.

Our goal was to provide seamless access to information resources, collections and services for students and faculty to all University of Toledo libraries. We were charged with examining the possibilities in regard to merging the respective library staffs, collections, budgets and integrated library systems. We decided at the outset that the Medical Library would retain its librarians and support staff. The Head of Bibliographic Control and the Cataloging Assistant would be moved to the Main Library's Technical Services Department and integrated into that workflow.

The Medical Library would retain its books, media and journal collections. The only changes in the collections were with the print serial and the electronic resources subscriptions. The print serials subscriptions were examined for duplications between the libraries. Since the Medical Library specializes in medicine and health sciences it was decided to cancel the duplicate print subscriptions to the main library journals.

The major task in the merging of the libraries was the integrated library systems. We decided to do a cost benefit analysis of the libraries' ILS systems. It was fortunate both libraries used the same ILS vendor for their integrated library systems; however, the Medical Library was 5 years behind the Main Campus library in loading software releases and other updates.

This analysis helped us to determine that the Main campus server had the most recent hardware (installed March 2006) with the most recent updates of the ILS vendors' software and would therefore be the target server. Hence, we would be migrating data from the Medical Library server to the Main library server.

We developed several timelines broken down into 3 month segments to accomplish the migrating of the data and the merging of the technical services library staffs.

MIGRATING DATA

Since we had the same ILS vendor software, the Coordinator of Technical Services put together a notebook of all of the timelines, email or other written communications and the tables and codes used in both systems. It was decided not to use mapping or translation tables for each code group but to change codes or other structure elements so the data migration would be smooth with very little disruption in information access for the students, faculty and staff of the merged University. The work on the updating, adding and removing of codes to system tables and records in both systems was completed in July 2006.

Additional team members were added in August 2006: Coordinator of Serials (Main Campus) and Coordinator of Library Systems (Main Campus). The new Coordinator of Library Systems had as a first task to add codes to our holdings, patron, and item record tables and to update the circulation tables. When those were in place the Coordinator of Serials and the Head of Bibliographic Control determined that it would be better not to migrate the serials holdings information.

It was decided to add a basic bibliographic record template and a serials holdings template with the appropriate default codes for the serial holdings records into the Main system. The Holdings information would be copied and pasted into the template for each serial title. This worked was completed in 3.5 months.

The target library database already was indexing the National Library of Medicine (NLM) subject headings. We had to add an index for the NLM call numbers from our ILS vendor. We had planned for this in our earlier analysis of the data.

We decided not to transfer any Acquisitions information. We would close out the fiscal year on the Medical Library database and start the new fiscal year on the merged database. We printed out the order record information for serial titles and kept them in a notebook, as these were paid in the FY2008 we added any additional order information to the new serial order records.

We had the Medical Library extend a grace period for returning circulated materials. We kept the non-merged system available for the returning of materials, until May 2007.

The preparation work was completed by the end of December 2006. We worked with our ILS vendor and our consortium (OhioLINK), especially on the changes we had made in many of our codes which impacted loaning materials and on the date to begin loading records.

It took us 2.5 days to load the data and verify the accuracy of the data. We froze cataloging for all of the libraries for this time. Since, the length of time was short it was not a hardship. We completed our data migration on March 31, 2007.

I would recommend to everyone to do as much work as possible up front in both the source database and the target database before merging library catalogs. This makes the work much smoother and you can move onto being one library.

AFTER MIGRATION

We worked on authentication software/proxy software to confirm access to all of the electronic resources now available to the Health Science Campus and to those resources now available to the Main Campus.

ONGOING CHALLENGES

Collections:

• De-duplication of remote storage of bound journal volumes

[Accomplished the 2nd year]

11,000+ bound volumes were de-duped from remote storage.

• Collection evaluation projects for HSC have been undertaken under the

supervision of the Coordinator of Collection Development at Main with direct

responsibility under the Assistant Director at HSC.

Staff:

• Different Unions – still not resolved

• Technical Services underwent 3 separate re-organizations, last one just completed.

1st one added HSC librarian and staff member to the current organization.

2nd one addressed staff changes

3rd one addressed staff attrition due to retirement

Budgets:

• Library budgets remain separate

• First year: Purchasing, receiving and processing of HSC library materials

(monographs and media) were separate from MAIN library materials.

Serials/journals were checked in by Main staff and sent to HSC

• Second year: Ordering, receiving and processing of HSC library materials have been integrated with Main Library materials.

Acquisitions' spending is separated into Main and HSC and maintained in the local ILS.

Invoices are received at Main and posted in local ILS then forwarded to HSC library for processing for payment. Their accounts at accounts payable are still separate. In this manner, we are tracking the acquisitions budget for both libraries in the local

ILS. Every now and then an invoice is paid at HSC and not posted in Main, but with monthly reports going to the Director of the HSC library, this is becoming less and less of an issue.

All in all, I think this was a successful merger and continues to be a good partnership.

BIBLIOGRAPHY

Alan, Robert (2002). "The Serials data migration dilemma." *Technical Services Quarterly* 20, no.2: 29-38.

Cervane, Frank (2007). "ILS migration in the 21st century: Some new things to think about this time around." *Computers in Libraries* 27, no.7: 6-8, 60-62.

Chester, Barnard (2006). "Data Migration 101." *AIIM E-DOC* 20, no.1: 10.

Copeland, Nora S., James F. Farmer, and Patricia A. Smith (1997). "Data migration: a brief primer." *Colorado Libraries* 23, no.4: 22-24.

Strange, Michael (2006). "Avoiding data migration delays." *Computerworld* 40, no.48: 24.

A FAR, FAR BETTER PLACE: ADAPTING TO CHANGES IN TECHNICAL SERVICES

Laura Kinner, Director of Technical Services, The University of Toledo, Toledo, Ohio

Alice Crosetto, Coordinator, Collection Development, The University of Toledo, Toledo, Ohio

Lucy Duhon, Coordinator of Electronic Resources/Serials Librarian, The University of Toledo, Toledo, Ohio

Technical Services is traditionally the first place to adapt to change in libraries – all libraries—public, school, academic. Saying that today's Technical Services is in flux is an understatement. But before we look at the challenges and changing situations, before we cast our eyes to the future, let us look back for a few minutes. What is Technical Services—what concepts and activities constitute Technical Services? Are we that mysterious? Do our fellow librarians wonder we do in the backroom?

THE PAST

If we think about the earliest libraries, the first individual who acquired an item, and made the conscious choice to maintain the item for sharing, the first individual who placed these items on the shelves in some order—that's our beginning. Julius Caesar had an individual who collected items for his public library. Documentation identifies the individual who was charged with arranging books in one of the libraries set up by Augustus. Can we say that Technical Services librarians were actually the first librarians?

In the best of times and in the worst of times, individuals have been collecting, and arranging resources in libraries. Yet it seems that recent years have been the worst of times—staff dynamics affected by societal norms, technology explosions, and budget reductions. All of these have brought about changes in Technical Services. One of the most evident changes is in the labeling and identifying of Technical Services. An examination of a dozen academic libraries in Ohio illustrates this. State-funded, private, small, or large—no two academic libraries have the same configuration of these activities which are traditionally called Technical Services. Note that only five maintain the use of the term, "Technical Services," all twelve have acquisitions and cataloging sections, only four have a Systems component, and staffing represents a diverse mixing of faculty librarians, non-faculty librarians, librarians with administrative appointments, and paraprofessionals.

This plethora of appellations seems to be reflected in Roger Brisson's declaration that, "For the past several decades technical services operations have witnessed a steady increase in the complexity of their policies, procedures, and workflows."

Once we adjust to new configurations in work functions, we look towards management, and how the managerial structure has evolved. Traditionally, management was hierarchical. Kenneth Carpenter reports that librarianship has traditionally been a woman's profession - possibly, even more so in Technical Services. But note the one distinction. Most of the upper management was composed of elite males, while females remained the subordinates. In addition, the overall power was concentrated in the hands of the head librarian—remember, predominantly male. This in turn, inhibited the display of individual initiative which meant that the subordinate female remained just that— subordinate. More and more management has morphed into a semi-hierarchical configuration with most librarians and staff realizing that collaboration in a team environment permits win/win situations and work places for all.

While the list of technological changes is too numerous to share here, I want to mention just a couple: Remember when catalog cards were hand-written. Once the typewriter was established as an indispensable means, the cards were manually typed—then electrically. After years of typing cards, finally the vendors began offering professionally produced cards—I was happy with that new change. But much to the dismay of many a librarian, one day the cards had to go—yes, even the shelf list was sent to the dumpster. We were online!

Technology that once was limited to Technical Services has been spread into other areas of the library. Having the catalog online has created a resource that is used in instruction, as well as research. One of the best examples of this has been OCLC. What once started as our Ohio College Library Catalog is now one of the best databases for a wide range of activities: research, assessment of items & collections, location of resources—on the global level.

As all of these changes were taking place, another change was happening in libraries everywhere. The actual librarians were changing; new generations of librarians were appearing and in doing so, making changes of their own. When we examine the generations and their characteristics, we must acknowledge that understanding the differences in the generations is paramount. As Julie and Eric Cooper state, "As new technologies become more pervasive and library infrastructures more complicated, librarians must understand the similarities and difference of our colleagues in order to manage library operations more effectively."

Silent Generation	Baby Boomer
1925-1945	1946-1964
Patriotic	Traditional
Ambitious	Professionally loyal
Use technology of the time	Jump started new technology
Generation X	Millennials
1965-1976	1977-1998
Self-reliant	Self-inventive
Reject rules	Re-write the rules
Use technology	Assume technology

As we can tell from the table, the change in the generations does affect how Technical Services functions, what services and support are offered, and how the staff interacts within Technical Services and with other sections of the library – even patrons themselves.

As for our Technical Services department, we number 16: one administrator/faculty librarian, four faculty librarians, and 11 support staff. Three individuals are in the Silent Generation, ten are Baby Boomers, and three are in Generation X. Of the ten Baby Boomers, two individuals at times identify with Generation X. It is interesting to note that we do not have any Millenials at this time. While there are a few Millennials in our Libraries, none are in Technical Services.

And one last item to mention that is appearing in the literature: our numbers. Based on the 2000 census, data reveals that retirements should be peaking between 2015 and 2019 —there may be a shortfall in the profession. The number of new, MLS-degreed librarians entering the field has been declining since the early 1990s—and the number of men in the profession is declining.

A closer look at where we are now, what challenges all of us are experiencing, and what possible solutions are available may reflect what many of you are doing now.

THE PRESENT

Jenny McCarthy, writing "Planning a Future Workforce: An Australian Perspective," says "Libraries throughout the world are facing the dual challenge of an aging workforce and a workplace which is requiring significant reassessment of the skills base of its staff as a result of the impact of technology on the delivery of information services…" (p. 41).

Kathleen Wells says, "Technical Services administrators are making the best of hard times by reallocating staff and resources to meet the needs of their users, they still feel the losses caused by shrinking budgets; many of those who have lost positions would like to have them reinstated, and even those with stable staff levels may prefer to add positions" (p. 29).

Over the last thirty years we have seen a shift from Baby Boomers entering the prime years of their professional library career to the beginning of their exit from the workplace. In this time also two new generations have made an appearance. Between 1990 and 2000, the average number of male librarians dropped from 20 percent to 18 percent of the workforce. Between 1990 and 2000, the number of female librarians (who most heavily populate professional technical services positions) entering the mid-years of their professional career swelled by thirty percent (Lynch, Tordella and Godfrey, *Retirement & Recruitment: A Deeper Look*, updating a report by *American Libraries* published in March 2002). This same demographic wave will begin retiring in droves in about a decade. In the meantime, the number of young people entering the profession, although a healthy number, cannot possibly reach the numbers of the previous generations. To compound this shortage, those choosing technical services careers lag more than ever behind those opting for the more glamorous public services careers.

In the last thirty years, a number of changes have impacted the workplace, and libraries have been no exception. These changes have been in part societal, technological and economical, technology being the central theme around which the other two revolve. During this time, society in the United States has become more mobile, more educated, and more global. Librarians who once conducted proprietary Dialog searches for their patrons now struggle to keep up with the latest modes of information retrieval popularly used by Millennials (whether or not they retrieve any information of value!). Individual knowledge consumers now "catalog" their own personal libraries and publish and tag their own blogs. Self-service delivery of information content is everywhere, but do users read what they retrieve? Meanwhile our economy can no longer easily support both the explosion of content and the rapid technological changes of format required for libraries to deliver that content. Thus it has never been harder to keep collections current and relevant. Collections must be in-demand or they won't be used. And librarians must be willing to keep their content fluid to avoid obsolescence by format.

Technology's central revolution has been one of communication. As society has moved toward a democratization of education, learning has become less obstructed. Where once night school was the only option for those who couldn't attend classes on a traditional schedule, distance and e-learning without walls or schedule constraints are now nearing the norm. How can technical services librarians not only address these needs, but stay ahead of the wave? We must become smart about new technology and methods of learning and communication. In Technical Services this may mean encouraging librarians and staff to experiment with new technology (such as widgets, blogs and wikis and other social networking tools). It may mean coming out of the back room to bring expertise to the reference desk. If technical services librarians don't learn how to operate within these modes of communication, how can they transmit content or information to their users in any meaningful manner?

As a tangible example of the technological revolution, remember how in the old days, you could expect to receive a print overdue slip in the mail *after* the fact? Now you can get an email message (or perhaps even a text message) from your library stating that your materials are coming due in three days. The central economic challenges for libraries have been funding for education, inflation, and the need for technological currency. Various libraries have handled these challenges by educating their parent institutions or states, advocating for the library, or participating in helping to develop the technological revolution, rather than just reacting to it. As budgets have shrunk and technology has streamlined information, technical services staffs have been forced to contract. When budget cuts strike operations lines, technical services positions are most likely to be cut or transferred.

In technical services departments, lack of funding for positions and lack of funding for collections means staff end up being moved, collections are forced to be weeded or de-duplicated, resources are ever more shared, document delivery becomes the prime option and libraries decide to collect and maintain only a core of traditional materials. As an example (we mentioned earlier that this had happened to us), the loss of a binding budget means that staff who formerly had a steady stream of work are now suddenly displaced. In order for Technical Services departments to thrive, they must listen to and engage the younger generations. This means both by directly involving their staff, and indirectly by understanding how patrons use library resources and communicate with the library. We must also trust the wisdom of those who have "been there". Without institutional memory we run the risk of repeating costly and senseless mistakes—for instance, ordering useless supplies or equipment that ends up sitting idle just because we've not bothered to check with those who know from experience what works and what doesn't.

Technical Services departments must be indispensible, visible and proud. In addition to organizing library content, we must focus on creating innovative avenues for the delivery of that content. This means we cannot just do things as we have always done them. It may mean going with the flow and doing what our patrons and students are doing, but it also means being out front, letting patrons meet us, and letting them understand what we do and why it matters.

THE FUTURE

What does all of this mean for Technical Services of the future? First, it means that Technical Services will have to do more long range planning. This is necessary to meet the demands of budgets, intergenerational staffing and evolving technologies and will continue to be so in the future.

When working with planning especially with intergenerational staffing, McCaffery and Garner in their 2006 article "Long-range planning across generational lines," discuss eight tips that you should consider when planning with the various generations in a library:

Foster respect between generations,

Represent every constituency

Create a timeline, (with a beginning, middle and end)

Provide opportunities for all voices to be heard,

Apply professional standards (ACRL)

Incorporate succession planning, (feed into next planning stage-continuity)

Gather data (numbers and statistics are good!)

Get outside opinions.

Give yourself a break and identify those issues that are easy to solve. Remember we are building a bridge between the staffing groups and staff themselves.

Second, we must become more creative with our budgets. By that I mean, know your collections, do an inventory, develop a collection evaluation policy along with your collection development policy, and collaborate with other libraries of the same type in purchasing materials or sharing resources (which is library strength). Eliminating duplication as much as possible and spreading those dollars around.

Future collections will be local or core collections of books and media. There will be more consortial purchases being made, but the local library should not lose sight of their individuality. They should continue to purchase books and media for their local collections and constituents.

As we all know, serials management did not go away with the advent of electronic resources. We have learned that electronic resources need another type of management, which can be as labor intensive as the management of print resources. Print serials will continue to remain a prime target of cutting, but this should slow down. Consortial and collaborative purchasing for both print (serials and books) and electronic resources will be necessary to stretch our dollars. It is important to establish good consortial relationships and to maintain them.

Third, with all of the activity of the budgets, the staff begins to become confused about their jobs, their duties and their responsibilities in the organization. Staff demographics: Baby Boomers, GenXers, Millennials and the next generation require different techniques to alleviate this confusion. Leslie Burke and Stephanie McConnell in their 2007 article, "The Four R's," provide a good guide to follow in alleviating staff confusion:

Re-assess—Job descriptions keep updated and current

Re-assign—New tasks and procedures (workflow)

Re-train—New skills

Re-energize—Communicate and motivate

Catherine Essinger's article, "X/Y Managing the Millennial Generation," describes these difference skills sets between Millennials, GenXers and Boomers and how to manage these different groups. For example, Millennials: don't work well alone, but work well with partners, should be offered projects to develop leadership skills, need to understand the chain of command, like to have more education and training workshops, don't respond well to subtlety, have zero tolerance, like written instructions to be exhaustive, and know how to organize their time. In addition, subtlety is lost on Millennials; you will have to communicate more directly with them, but then subtlety is sometimes lost on all of us. A quote from the 2007 article by Burke and McConnell. "The manager's objective is for each individual to achieve excellence within the limits of his or her talents and abilities" (*Against the Grain* [Nov. 2007], p.62).

Lastly there are evolving technologies that Technical Services staffs have to learn and deal with so that the following is not heard: "I am not a techno guru." Most Technical Services supervisors find experts in the field that they understand, such as:

- Marshall Breeding who is the trendspotter to read for technology changes especially in the area of the ILS vendors.

- Rachel Gordon's columns in LJ spots trends in social networking tools and other millennial thoughts on librarianship.

We recommend that you find your techno guru or become one yourself.

We think we are safe to say that Technical Services will continue to be a part of libraries for the future. If we keep these transformational challenges, changes and visions in perspective, technical services will be a far, far better place.

BIBLIOGRAPHY

Brisson, Roger (1999). "Online Documentation in Library Technical Services." *Technical Services Quarterly* 16, no.3: 1-19.

Burke, Leslie, and Stephanie McConnell (2007). "Technical Services Departments in the Digital Age: The Four R's of Adapting to New Technology." *Against the Grain* 19, no.5: 58-64.

Carpenter, Kenneth (1996). "A Library Historian looks at Librarianship." *Daedalus* 125, no.4: 77-96.

Cooper, Julie F. Cooper, and Eric A. Cooper (1998). Generation Dynamics and Librarianship: Managing Generation X. Illinois Periodicals Online (IPO). www.lib.niu.edu/1998/il980118.html.

Essinger, Catherine (2006). "X/Y Managing the Millennial Generation." *Texas Library Journal* 82, no.3: 104-107.

Lynch, Mary Jo, Stephen Tordella, and Thomas Godfrey. *Retirement & Recruitment: A Deeper Look* (Chicago: ALA Office for Research and Statistics, 2004). www.ala.org/ala/aboutala/offices/ors/reports/recruitretire-adeeperlook.pdf

McCarthy, Jenny (2005). "Planning a Future Workforce: An Australian Perspective." *New Review of Academic Librarianship* 11, no.1: 41-56.

McCaffrey, Erin, and Martin Garner (2006). "Long-range Planning Across Generational Lines." *College & Research Libraries News* 67, no.3: 144-164.

Wells, Kathleen (2004). "Hard Times in Technical Services: How Do Academic Libraries Manage? A Survey." *Technical Services Quarterly* 21, no.4: 17-30.

CHANGING CHANGE TO MAKE A CHANGE

Tinker Massey, Serials Librarian, Embry-Riddle Aeronautical University Libraries, Daytona Beach, Florida

Change is a constant everyday at work and in our regular lives. As we prepare ourselves to adapt to the changes and use them to institute more change, we have to recognize a basic fact. Characteristics that we display upon trying to cope with change are those of the grieving process. As a supervisor, we should look for problems within the organization that stem from those in various aspects of grief. Sometimes it isn't possible for people to make rapid adaptations to change until they have had a chance to deal with the anger and release of their grief. It is wise to let the employee help design the coping structure and relate the stresses he/she feels. You can work with the employee suggesting many different stress releasers, for instance, exercise (many walk on breaks or at lunch), meditation (also available on breaks or lunch periods), and perhaps even massage (available off-times).

It is essential that we respect each other's feelings and coping skills, helping when needed, supporting when necessary. As the changes and coping progress, we will see a change in the ability and skills that are shown personally and in the work processes. This leads to personal development in the workplace, which will continue to grow as we nurture it. You will gain an improved employee during this time.

When we change work processes/procedures, we need to be sure we have ample communication that is simple and direct. Allow employees to ask questions and feel comfortable with the directions involved. Evaluate how things are changing as they do so. Restructure when necessary and re-evaluate again. Try to be proactive rather than reactive and allow the employees to feed back information that helps the process. I like to get my employees to work in teams. We divide the work by their skills and abilities and help each other dependent upon the needs of the specific crises. We all work together when it is necessary, and we all lend ideas for new situations that need to be solved. Many times we are able to use older changes and build new changes into the present system. As long as communication is strong and respect is shown for everyone, there is an easier time to establish and cope with changes. Don't take things personally. Life continues!

We discussed many aspects of communication, personnel management and cooperative productivity. The packets distributed contained hints for good management, outlines and bibliographies. This session was a very interactive program allowing people to give ideas, ask situational questions and promoted solutions that were "out of the box."

TALK BY PAT SCHROEDER AT THE CHARLESTON CONFERENCE

Pat Schroeder, President and CEO, Association of American Publishers, Washington, District of Columbia, is a Plenary Speaker at the Charleston Conference

Summarized by John Tagler, Executive Director, Association of American Publishers, Washington, District of Columbia

AAP President and CEO Pat Schroeder was one of the opening plenary speakers at the 28th Annual Charleston Conference on book and serial acquisition Issues on November 6. The theme of the conference was "The Best of Times . . . The Worst of Times."

Addressing some 1,200 librarians and publishers, Mrs. Schroeder took her cue from the Dickens' theme, setting the stage with observations about the current environment for scholarly communication in which the Internet has fostered a multitude of new possibilities in the delivery of information, while at the same time blurring distinctions about the origins, integrity, and quality of much of that information.

Invited to speak about "News from the Publishing World," Mrs. Schroeder underlined the common goals shared by librarians and publishers, stressing that "we need to work together to create a structure for information that is reliable and makes sense." To illustrate her point, she shared an anecdote about an elementary school student who was asked to prepare a report on Magellan and turned in a paper on the fund management group, not the explorer. "In a world where change is coming so fast," she commented, "we need to assess what are reliable, durable tools to get to content, determine what is and is not essential material to retain, and then develop a strategy for preserving it going forward."

Mrs. Schroeder discussed the publishing issue most on the minds of her audience: the landmark settlement reached by AAP, the Authors Guild, and Google that had been announced just a week prior to the conference. Reviewing key provisions of the agreement, she focused particular attention on those applicable to libraries, including wider access to out-of-print books, additional ways to purchase copyrighted books, and a provision for institutional subscriptions to millions of books online, underscoring the fact that the smallest U.S. public library can now have access to great library collections.

Mrs. Schroeder conveyed the significance of the new Book Rights Registry as a component of the rights management infrastructure, but it was evident as she began to answer detailed questions from the audience that many complexities and issues remain to be resolved. Most importantly, as she communicated in wrapping up her 45-minute session, after three years of discussion and negotiation, the Google settlement provides "a model for going forward, but there's still a lot of work to be done."

WHEN COLLECTIONS MERGE: IMPACT OF SPACE & FUNDING ON BRANCH LIBRARY COLLECTIONS, SERVICES, AND SPACE

Mary Beth Thomson, Associate Dean for Collections and Technical Services, University of Kentucky Libraries, Lexington, Kentucky

Introduction: Who Doesn't Need Space

The lack of available space on college and university campuses is legendary. For the last several years, librarians have discussed remote storage facilities, re-purposing of space, building renovation projects, weeding, purchasing electronic books and journals, and the consolidation or closing of branch libraries, all in an attempt to deal with ever present space concerns. The University of Kentucky Libraries has a history of consolidating collections and branch libraries that dates back several decades. In the *Science and Engineering Library – A Vision for the King Library Addition*, Diedrichs and Greider noted the "consolidation of collections and service points has been ongoing since the 1960s. As a result of changing user needs, multiple individual departmental collections in Agriculture and Engineering were consolidated under library administration in two libraries. Independent Chemistry and Physics departmental libraries were consolidated into one library. With the construction of the Young Library in the late 1990s, the life sciences collections from biological sciences, agriculture and medicine were consolidated in Young. In 2001, the Art and Music libraries were consolidated in the Lucille Little Fine Arts Library. In 2002, the Geological Sciences Library and Maps Collections were consolidated in the King Library Addition."

Many libraries face funding pressures on an annual basis. The cost to purchase and provide access to new information resources coupled with the need to preserve and manage legacy print collections continues to increase. If university administrators are able to provide the funds to cover the increased cost of collections, they often do not have additional funds for other needs such as remote storage facilities or building renovations.

Universities plan capital projects a decade or more in advance. It's not unusual to begin discussing a new building or major renovation project 10 to 15 years before funding is secured and there is always much competition for that capitol project funding. UK's current construction projects include a new $450 million UK Chandler Hospital to be completed in 2011 and a $120 million pharmacy building which had to be funded over 2 biennial state budget (4 years).

UK's main and branch libraries are either out of available collections space or very close to it. We have over the years moved both books and journals to both on-campus and off-campus storage areas. Investigating a variety of storage facility options was the beginning point of our recent planning process for a merged science library. We continue statewide, consortia, and university-based discussions of building a remote storage facility but for now the funding is just not available. We are however moving forward with the merger of 3 independent branch libraries into a new science library.

The UK Libraries is in the final stages of completing the merger of a Chemistry/Physics Library, Mathematical Sciences Library and Geological Sciences Library and Map Collections into a Science Library. Ours is an example of the needs of the university administration, departmental faculty, and the needs of the library colliding. In 2002, architectural plans and renderings were contracted for and costs were determined for a complete renovation of the

Margaret I. King Library Addition. The 2002 plan proposed a combined Science and Engineering Library including the merger of materials from four branches: Engineering, Chemistry/Physics, Mathematics, and Geological Sciences/Maps. The costs of a comprehensive building renovation were too high at that time.

Years later other university and library projects had moved forward but not the renovation and creation of a Science and Engineering Library. Then in 2007 the University began addressing the need for new faculty labs and offices as a result of ambitious business and strategic plans aimed at moving UK into a top 20 public research institution ranking.

The Chemistry/Physics Library is located on the main floor of the Chemistry/Physics building and thus located in prime real estate, real estate the administration desperately needed for additional labs and faculty offices. This branch collection includes over 87,000 book and journal volumes on Chemistry, Physics and Astronomy and subscribes to approximately 300 journals. The library is staffed by one librarian, one senior level technician and student assistants.

The Mathematics Library, while not in a prime real estate location, was in desperate need of additional space for both the collection and user seating. It is located in the basement of a main office tower that houses offices for several major departments within the College of Arts and Sciences as well as Research and Graduate Studies. Overall the Mathematics Library is not in a good place for students and the environment is not conducive for print collections. It has over the years had water leaks and, by being in the basement, is in a somewhat isolated location. Nonetheless, UK's campus planning department has plans for the use of that space as soon as we move the library out. The Mathematical Sciences Library serves the mathematics and statistics departments with materials in pure and applied mathematics, statistics and related fields. This branch provides access to approximately 47,000 book and journal volumes and subscribes to 235 print and electronic current journals. It is staffed by a librarian, a technician and student assistants.

The Geological Sciences Library and Map Collections are already located on the 4th floor of the King Library Addition and, therefore, would not have to be moved out completely. Although the university would not gain any additional space, the merger and renovation would provide the library with the opportunity to adjust and improve how the space was being used. This branch collection includes approximately 62,000 book and journal volumes and subscribes to around 325 journals relating to all aspects of the geological sciences. The map collection is international in coverage and includes maps, aerial photos, atlases, and gazetteers. The Geological Sciences Library and Map Collections are staffed by a library manager, 2 senior level technicians and student assistants.

As a result of various discussions, particularly the issues concerning the Chemistry Department's space needs, the library administration proposed and the university administration provided funding for a $2,225,000 capital building project. Part of the overall project was the partial renovation and creation of a merged Science Library based primarily on the libraries' earlier planning documents. The Libraries would finally have the funding to move forward with a science library.

Project Motivation

The university's primary interest in moving forward with this capital project was in creating more office and lab space for faculty being hired as a result of the university's push towards a top 20 status. The university, in general, is also in need of classroom and storage space. What was providing the motivation for the libraries to continue to consolidate branches? First was the consolidation of service points to help relieve pressure on a very tight operating budget. The consolidation of three branch libraries into a single facility would improve the utilization of staff and support increasing the library hours. Additionally, we were interested in increased student seating, updated group study space, additional computing capabilities, quiet study areas, a safer environment, and an interdisciplinary collection. In addition to moving the Chemistry/Physics Library, the departmental computer lab was also going into the newly renovated building. This afforded us with the opportunity to create a second information commons on campus in cooperation with the Information Technology Division. The Libraries opened the first information commons area in the William T. Young Library, the main campus library, in 2007.

Although the first phase of the revised science library plans outlined the merger of the Mathematics, Statistics, Chemistry, Physics, Geology, and Map collections into one renovated space, the second phase detailed the incorporation of the Shaver Engineering Library. The current capital project only covers phase one of what was originally termed the merged Science and Engineering Library. As a result the College of Engineering decided to move forward with the renovation of the Shaver Engineering Library in order to provide much needed user space, small group study rooms, improved lighting and furniture and to address concerns in an accreditation review. In 2006/07 funds for renovating the Shaver Engineering Library were provided by the Dean of Engineering and Provost. It is still a future goal to consolidate the Shaver Engineering Library into the Science Library but is considered as phase two and would be funded by a future capital project plan.

There were, of course, some obstacles or disadvantages to the moving and consolidation of facilities. Both the Mathematics Library and the Chemistry/Physics Library were in the same building as the departments' faculty and students. This provided the branch librarians with the ability to concentrate on specific subject areas and to be in regular, if not daily, communication due to their close proximity to the faculty and students. Additionally, faculty in Chemistry, Physics, Mathematics, and Statistics had key or key card access to the library branch and, therefore, had 24-hour access. Each of these factors was a key point of discussion with the departmental faculty as the project continued moving forward.

Project Management Process

The project management process included the creation of two library working groups, several planning documents, a construction project group, a RFP for a commercial mover sub-committee, and the identification of the various stakeholders that would need to be a part of the on-going discussions. In addition to the stakeholders already discussed, the library and university administrators, plant facility administrators, faculty, students, and branch librarians and staff, there are two others. The University's Information Technology Division has a stake in this renovation project as well. They will be maintaining a computer lab on the main entrance floor as well as computers on each of the other floors. Information Technology staff will also use a portion of the reference desk and work closely with library staff members.

There is also an outside community group, Central Kentucky Radio Eye (CKRE) whose studios and offices have been housed in the King Addition for many years. CKRE is a volunteer based group that provides a radio reading service for the blind and visually impaired. CKRE had plans to relocate to a new public library branch being built but not until well after the renovation project began.

Two working groups were formed in January 2006: the Science & Engineering Library Storage and Staging Working Group and the Science & Engineering Library Service Design Working Group. The storage and staging working group's main focus was to plan for the transfer and storing of the materials currently housed within the King Addition and the development of a detailed plan for moving and merging the science collections into the renovated space. The working group consisted of staff and librarians from several departments and a representative from the university's capital projects management office. The head of the library's facilities and storage department chaired the working group.

The service design working group was specifically tasked with the development of the service concept. This working group consisted of the branch librarians, faculty and student representatives from each of the college departments, representatives from the University's Information Technology Division, Capitol Projects, and the Provost's office. The library's associate dean for Research and Education chaired the working group until the fall of 2007. At that point the meetings began to include more discussions dealing with the collections and the author joined the group as co-chair.

There were areas of overlap between the groups as several individuals served on both groups and the charges were broadly stated. Much of the information gathered by each group was important to both groups and the path to final decisions was not always clear. Delineating responsibilities between the development of the service and design concept and the implementation of the actual move was difficult at times. Numerous library departments and units were either directly or indirectly involved in the various stages of the collection moves and building renovation. The library departments and units most heavily involved were the Facilities and Storage, Special Projects and Database Integrity, Collection Development and the Branch Libraries. The timeline for the first eighteen months of the project included activities which had to occur before the Science Library activities could commence: the move of a collection of older medical monographs to storage and the relocation of the International Documents & Research Collections (IDRC).

International Documents & Research Collections

The International Documents & Research Collections were the first to be reviewed for relocation and retention decisions. Before any renovation work could begin in the MI King Addition, IDRC materials currently housed on the 3rd floor had to be moved and the service center closed. The decision was made to close the IDRC service point before the fall semester began in 2006 and to then disperse the collections. Subject librarians were asked to forward the branch closure announcement to their faculty members. The announcement was also posted to the library's website and faculty known to be regular IDRC users were contacted directly by their subject liaison well before the actual closure.

Large portions of IDRC were to be identified for relocation to the Young Library including the United Nations and European Union documents. In order to make room in the Young Library stacks, approximately 44,000 older medical monographs were reviewed as a group, not title-by-title, and selected for transfer to storage beginning in the summer of 2006.

The author worked with the collection managers responsible for the materials that comprised the international documents collections. The IDRC included a reference and statistical yearbook collection, journals, United Nations, European Union Depository, League of Nations, Scott/Greenslade Russian military and history collection, and the Great Britain bound collections (Parliamentary Debates, Irish University Press reprints, and House of Lords Papers). Almost all of our work was completed through e-mail exchanges and the use of inventory spreadsheets. Numerous management reports were pulled from our Voyager ILS system by the Libraries' Special Projects Coordinator, and a member of the Storage and Staging Working Group. We would return to these reports numerous times during the various stages of the collections relocations. The first reports run were those listing the various books, journals, documents, microfilm, and technical reports housed in IDRC. The inventory spreadsheets were posted to a SharePoint site created for the working group. The inventory spreadsheets included call number, item counts, organization, such as UN or EU, format, author, title, and notes. We added columns to indicate our collection retention decisions – withdraw, transfer to storage, or transfer to Young. To aid our collection decisions we also had spreadsheets of items circulated within the last two years and one indicating the number of circulations within the last seven years. By the end of the IDRC moves we had used a half dozen or more inventory spreadsheets. Items marked for withdrawal or for transfer to storage were processed before the rest of the collections were moved to the Young Library. These efforts were coordinated and completed mainly by the Facilities and Storage Department and the Special Projects Unit, a unit of the Collections and Technical Services Division.

The House of Commons Parliamentary Session Papers presented the first opportunity to purchase an electronic version of a print resource as a part of the consolidation project. We purchased the House of Commons Parliamentary Papers online. ProQuest describes this collection as "200,000 House of Commons sessional papers from 1715 to the present, with supplementary material back to 1688." Our print collection was used on a fairly regular basis by a small number of faculty members but was in extremely poor condition. We were concerned with the idea of having to move the collection and, so far, are pleased with the electronic resource. During this first year there have been close to 4,000 full-text downloads. Staff members stabilized the fragile parliamentary paper items in preservation quality bags before placing them into approximately 207 boxes for transfer to storage. Cataloged on collection level serial records, the individual items were not bar coded but instead records were created for each storage box identified by session year and number range.

Commercial movers were hired to transfer the United Nations and European Union depository materials, the League of Nations and the Great Britain Collections to the William T. Young Library. As often happens with this type of collection intensive project, smaller projects were created for various units. In this case, a year later the cataloging and database integrity units continued to catalog, process and resolve problems for a variety of materials. One of these projects is an uncataloged collection consisting of approximately 1,500 Russian monographs and our government documents unit student workers spent several months shelf-reading the United Nations collection.

Service Design Working Group

While the storage and staging working group began its investigation into the cost and options for a remote storage facility, the transfer of the medical monographs, the IDRC move, and the RFP for a commercial mover, the service design working group began the development of their concept paper. As a result of their discussions "Science and Engineering Library for the University of Kentucky: A Concept Paper" dated June 2006 was distributed. The paper's first paragraph described the overall concept as "The Science and Engineering Library will bring together the current departmental libraries in Chemistry, Physics, Engineering, Geological/Earth Sciences, Mathematics and Statistics, to provide well-staffed, 24-hour access to these collections for faculty researchers and establish an attractive working space for students. While the integrity of departmental collections will be preserved, housing the departmental collections in a single facility will facilitate interdisciplinary research, support collaborative learning, and better serve the information needs of faculty and students in the Science, Technology, Engineering, and Mathematical Sciences disciplines. The Science and Engineering Library will house the traditional print collections of these departmental libraries and provide additional space for group work and quiet, individual study."

Then in August 2007 Carol Diedrichs, Dean of Libraries, completed "Comparative Analysis of Proposed Science & Engineering Library," an analysis required by the university before an existing branch is closed. In responding to the space and equipment requirements portion of the needs analysis, Diedrichs wrote "Most academic research libraries continue to need additional space for collections. To meet this challenge, major research libraries continue to build their digital collections and store their lesser used, but important, print resources in an off-site state-of-the-art storage facility. Currently our stored materials reside in a storage facility off the central campus with regular delivery of requested materials to campus. The space in the Science and Engineering Library will be devoted to attractive, comfortable and safe people space, the core print collections which require immediate access, and state-of-the-art equipment to support the teaching and research needs of the sciences. The collection space will be static with space for new materials achieved by the removal of lesser used materials to storage."

As the project continued to move forward discussions were held to further define the design and service aspects of the first phase of renovation. In September 2007 a draft program document, "Science and Engineering Library for the University of Kentucky Phase 1: Combined Geology, Chemistry/Physics, and Mathematical Sciences Library" was distributed. This document identified floor by floor function, space and service requirements. The document indicated the majority of the collections would be housed on the 3rd and 4th floor. The books and journals would start on the 3rd floor by LC classification and continue on the 4th floor but be shelved in separate groups. At least a portion of the shelving on the 3rd floor was to be compact shelving if possible and subsequently the compact shelving was purchased as a part of the overall project expenditures.

Around the same time that we were moving the IDRC, writing concept papers, analyzing the size of the current branch collections and working with the faculty, the university's capital projects department was moving forward with the process of hiring an architect and contractor for the renovation project. The review and evaluation process included representation from the library. Once the architect was awarded the project, she began to work with us and met on several occasions with the service design group and faculty representatives. As we moved through the various renovation designs, opportunities were provided for input from the departmental faculty members, working group members and library administration. These discussions were important not only to the branch librarians but also to the departmental faculty and students. Faculty and students were very accustomed to "their" library and "its" arrangement. We needed to provide opportunities for faculty input, to stay within the construction projects timeline, and to not complicate the process any further. The architectural planning review process was completed during the fall of 2007. Construction bids were then received and a contractor hired. The actual construction work began in the spring of 2008 and was completed in fall 2008.

Science Collections

There were numerous collection issues that had to be discussed in order to determine the materials to be included in the merged collection and the physical arrangement of the collections. One of our main tasks was to review the various collections within the three branch libraries and decide on those volumes that would be included in the science library. The four collection managers involved met to begin discussion of the various collection issues and to make some initial decisions. The end result of the initial review process was an overall shared collections concept. Although the service design working group had discussed the collections at a conceptual level, the collection manager meetings began the actual process of identifying specific materials to include in the merged collection. Based upon an earlier collection analysis process, we knew that a sizable portion of the existing print collection would have to be transferred to storage. The renovated space, even with the inclusion of compact shelving, would not hold all the print volumes from the three branch collections.

Each disciplinary group had a different response to sending print collections to storage. The Geological Sciences Library, up until that point, had not transferred any material to storage. Math had transferred some journal back files and books into on-campus storage due to water leaks with the hope that the volumes would be transferred back into the library's collection at some point. The Math and Statistics faculty were very concerned with the prospect of sending material to storage and had stated that they wanted all of their books in the merged science collection. The Chemistry/Physics faculty members were very open and supportive of electronic access to journals and of transferring the print journal volumes to storage.

One key question was how to decide on the size of the print collection to be included from each branch. One of the questions asked was would each branch have to identify a set percentage of their collection for storage? The collection managers also wanted to address the issue of the books and journals already in storage, especially the math materials. Would those volumes be a part of the merged science collection? These discussions helped us move beyond thinking about each branch's collection as an individual collection being moved to a new location and more towards what the combined collection needed to look like in terms of the printed books and journals as well as the electronic resources. The decision was made that we would not target specific branch collection percentages for inclusion but would proceed with making collection decisions based upon the actual materials and their appropriateness to the research and instruction needs of the faculty and students.

To begin the collection review process, we once again called upon the special projects coordinator to query our Voyager system and provide a comprehensive spreadsheet listing of materials within each of the branches based upon location codes and material type. Each collection manager was also provided with a listing of their books and journals in call number order. In addition to the branch materials spreadsheets, the special projects coordinator provided the collection managers with a list of the merged collections in call number order and separated by material type. The various spreadsheets were posted on the SharePoint site for ease of use. A revised merged listing of the books and journals was also included as an important part of the RFP issued to select and hire a commercial moving company. As journals were identified for transfer to storage their records were removed from the comprehensive list. The special projects coordinator also completed a good deal of basic database maintenance work within the Voyager system as the project moved along.

Additionally, the collection management department provided the science librarians with a list of their current journals subscriptions. This listing indicated the format of each journal: electronic only, print only or print plus electronic. As a part of the earlier collection analysis process, each collection manager counted the number of shelves currently in use for books, journals, theses, reserves materials, reference, special collections, and oversized materials. Shelves and collections were counted and measured in a variety of ways and multiple times as the project progressed.

Our initial decisions included the need to identify the journals currently purchased as e-only. The back files for the journals no longer purchased in print would be transferred to storage. We made the decision early on that we did not want to move print journal volumes to the new Science Library if electronic access was available. The Libraries made an aggressive move towards e-only journals during the last few years both for increased remote access and as a way to reduce serials expenditures. One of the first strategic decisions made was to work with the Libraries' Collections Advisory Committee to focus most of the budget's general endowment funds towards the purchase of additional electronic journal back files and other appropriate electronic resources. The purchase of additional journal back file volumes allowed us to transfer complete print journal runs to storage. The increased access added more coverage in chemistry and physics than in the other subject areas. As the additional back file collections were identified and purchased, the print versions were boxed and transferred to storage. In the end, we transferred approximately 41,000 volumes to storage from the branch collections. This work was completed before the commercial movers arrived and the move and merging of collections began. This allowed the movers to tour each of the branches and see only the materials that were to be moved.

As the project progressed other collection decisions were made including the migration of additional journals to e-only as a result of a serials review project conducted during the spring of 2008. The collection managers also decided that the journal back files and books that were already in storage, including the Math journals in temporary storage, would remain in on-site storage. The exception to that decision was that the Math and Statistics books previously sent to storage would be included in the merged collection. The combined collection would therefore include all Math and Statistics books but not all print journal back files. Due to the increase in electronic access, Math and Statistics faculty agreed and were supportive of the decision to not include the print journal back files.

Another collection issue discussed by the collection managers was the arrangement of merged current journals collection. The Chemistry/Physics current journals were alphabetized by title, whereas, Math, Statistics and Geology journals were arranged by LC call number. It was decided that the current journals area would be on the 3rd floor and that the journal issues would be arranged alphabetically by title on short shelving units. The concept for the area was one that included comfortable seating and more of a reading room arrangement.

The collection managers also discussed the floor by floor collection arrangements. In working with the architect, the group specified that the reference collection would be merged and located on the 2nd floor along with the information services desk and information commons area. The 2nd floor is the entry level floor. Map and atlas reference materials however would remain on the fourth floor with the various map collections. Books would be shelved on the 3rd floor beginning in the free standing shelves and continuing into the compact shelves. The journals would then begin at the end of the books in the compact shelving and continue on the 4th floor. The 4th floor would also house the map collections, theses, several small geological sciences special collections, and some government documents.

The floor by floor collection arrangement was discussed with the service design working group in order to obtain comments from the college departments. Each faculty representative was asked to communicate to their departments the recommended overall collection arrangement and floor plan. Each department had copies of the architectural plans that were available for review in their branch library. Faculty members were extremely concerned, and still are, about the split in the journal collection between the 3rd and 4th floor. Our target was that the journal collection would split after QD. Everyone was very pleased with the concept of the books being available on one floor. The collection managers were also in favor of having the books and journals shelved separately and not interfiled. There were considerable ongoing conversations about having separate book and journal collections or one interfiled collection. We are anticipating that the print journal collection will continue to grow but at a much slower rate than in previous years. As more journals become available online, we will continue moving the print volumes to storage. We've allowed slightly more growth space for the journals still received in print within the compact shelving plus general collection management spacing.

Conclusion

As the almost three year saga comes to a close, everyone is excited about the opportunities the new Science Library provides as we strive to enhance our service to the UK community. The merged science collection provides support for the interdisciplinary nature of research, as well as, increased electronic access to the literature. The renovated building provides both quiet and interactive study areas for students, an information commons area, computers on each floor, and extended hours of operation overall. UK librarians and staff have a wealth of knowledge and experience about how to make a move of this nature happen. Experience that will be useful in the near future, after all, there are other branches to consider.

Sources

"Comparative Analysis of Proposed Science and Engineering Library," prepared by Carol Pitts Diedrichs, Dean of Libraries, dated August 17, 2007.

"Science and Engineering Library – A Vision for the King Library Addition," prepared by Carol Pitts Diedrichs, Dean of Libraries and Antoinette Greider, Associate Dean for Research and Education. Revised January 31, 2006.

"Science and Engineering Library for the University of Kentucky: A Concept Paper," dated June 2006.

T his topic, out-of-the-box thinking, was new to the Charleston Conference this year. The demand for librarians to provide more and more services to their patrons with fewer resources continues. The contributors to this section discussed innovation with a purpose and also the Charleston Observatory concept.

Out-of-the-Box Thinking

RESEARCHER: THE OPEN SOURCE SOLUTION FOR MANAGING ELECTRONIC RESOURCES

Rachel A. Erb, Systems Librarian, University of Nebraska, Omaha, Nebraska

Abstract

The onerous cost of traditional vendor electronic resource management products have often excluded smaller academic libraries from providing basic services such as OpenURL link resolving, federated searching, etc. At very best, libraries often forsake one service for another, and therefore, are unable to provide the same level of comprehensive research capabilities as larger, well-funded academic libraries. Fortunately for small academic libraries, the zeitgeist of open source software has inspired the Simon Fraser University Library to provide an open source integrated suite of electronic resource management products called reSearcher which has been adopted by a broad spectrum of academic libraries—from research to community college libraries.

This session will focus on demonstrating several components of reSearcher as well as describing its implementation. *reSearcher's* efficacy will also be compared to some commercial offerings

Introduction

As many community and two-year colleges experience unbridled enrollment growth, library budgets at many of these institutions either remain stagnant, or even worse, are reduced. Located in the Upstate region of South Carolina, Greenville Technical College (GTC) enrollment has grown from 7,000 to 10,000 full-time students in the past several years and boasts the largest number of matriculated students of all technical colleges in the state. Despite the College's recent overall success in attracting students and gaining a statewide reputation for some of its academic programs funding consistently remains earmarked toward developing academic programs and the construction of several branch campuses. Unfortunately, the Greenville Technical College Library's budget has not been increased in four years. Concomitant to physical campus growth is the expansion of distance education within several academic disciplines. In addition to several existing programs in computer technology, health sciences, business, and liberal arts, GTC began offering an Associate of Science degree via distance education in 2007. This climate could be very challenging for a library with a modest and vulnerable budget to provide effective services that meet the needs of a growing, diverse student body and faculty.

In terms of electronic resources, the Library's online presence needed to move beyond remaining a static portal for database access and become a more proactive environment for resource discovery. It was imperative for our services to fully address the fact that our students and faculty heavily rely on electronic resources, the former primarily concerned with retrieving full-text articles whenever possible. Other two-year institutions, moreover, were providing resource discovery technologies such as an interactive journal database, an Open URL link resolver, federating searching, etc. Out of the sixteen technical colleges in South Carolina, three have an A-Z journal title list service and federated searching. It is not surprising that the second and third largest technical colleges are in that group. None of the technical colleges have

Please note this article was left out of the 2007 Charleston Conference Proceedings.

an Open URL link resolver, or an Electronic Resource Management System (ERMS). This is in stark contrast to most four-year colleges in the state that have most of the aforementioned electronic resource access and management technologies. Even though this digital divide is not surprising, there is now a way for indigent institutions to narrow this gap. This paper illustrates how the Greenville Technical College Library effectively narrowed the digital divide between themselves and four-year institutions in South Carolina by opting for a comprehensive open source solution for managing electronic resources.

Discovery and Implementation

The path leading to open source solution began with many attempts to secure a vendor-based A-Z journal listing service and Open URL link resolver package that was affordable. Initially, in 2004, the Library purchased EBSCO A-Z and included print titles in this database. Over time, numerous open access titles were added to EBSCO A-Z, but these resources were not "free" as the overall cost of EBSCO A-Z sharply increased, rendering this product unaffordable. How can a library of modest means continue to provide open access journals when the vendor of the electronic journal listing service increases the subscription rate based on the number of titles added? Instead of tacitly accepting these circumstances, the Library sought alternate solutions such as partnering with other institutions. The Library approached members of their consortium, the South Carolina Information and Library Services Consortium (SCILS), for a possible group purchase of a vendor-based product. Two member institutions already subscribed to packages from Serials Solutions and had no desire to expand beyond A-Z listing and federated searching. The other nine member institutions were not interested and determined it would be best to wait until the Partnership Among South Carolina Academic Libraries (PASCAL) purchased these products. (As this is written, there has been discussion of PASCAL's possible statewide purchase of EBSCO's WebFeat to provide federated searching, but nothing has been finalized.)

Due to lack of interest from SCILS members, the Library had to seek other alternatives. The Library investigated other vendor-based products with little success; in some cases, the subscription costs were cheaper than EBSCO, but the Library would have to choose both journal listing software and federated searching, in favor of journal listing software and link resolving package. Because an Open URL link resolver was a priority over federated searching, this was not tenable. Even when an Open URL link resolver was bundled with a journal listing service, the subscription rates were still prohibitively expensive for the Library. At this point, finding a vendor-based ERM was not a consideration. The Library, however, entertained the notion of creating an in-house ERM system with *Microsoft Access*, but there were not enough personnel to devote time to develop and manage this project. Consequently, the Library continued to rely on spreadsheets and emails stored in disparate workstations. Cognizant of open source ILSs such as *Evergreen* and *Koha*, the Head of Technical Services, Rachel Erb, searched for open source software that was analogous to commercial products. She stumbled upon *reSearcher*, e-mailed a technical contact, Kevin Stranack, and received a response within several hours. Due to the lack of technical support at GTC, it was not possible for the library to become a "software only" site. The Library negotiated for hosting and technical support, paying Simon Fraser University $6000.00 for the first year of implementation, and $5000.00 for the second year. Despite these costs, the Library still saved several thousand dollars.

reSearcher Modules

CUFTS A-Z

Developed in Canada at the Simon Fraser University for the Council of Prairie and Pacific University Libraries (COPPUL), *reSeacher* is an open source suite of electronic resource management products. *reSearcher* comprises several modules: CUFTS A-Z for serials and ERMS; GODOT for Open URL link resolving; dbWiz for federated searching, and Citation Manager for personal bibliographic management. Currently, CUFTS A-Z only allows databases that provide full-text e-journals in its database. This is a bit more restrictive than EBSCO A-Z which permits the inclusion of citation databases in its A-Z serial management tool, but the Library's patrons are more concerned with full-text articles. It was serendipitous that CUFTS A-Z met the needs of the Library's patrons more than EBSCO A-Z. Furthermore, the fact that the GTC Library could now have an Open URL link resolving feature in its databases overshadows this concern regarding the exclusion of citation databases in the knowledgebase.

The knowledgebase contains information for more than 375 collections from a wide-variety of providers such as Gale, EBSCO, Blackwell, and open access collections such as the Directory of Open Access Journals, PubMedCentral, etc. (Stranack, 2008) (see Figure 1). CUFTS A-Z is frequently updated by the project managers at Simon Fraser University and simultaneously benefits from participants adding titles to the knowledgebase. The Library was able to include aggregator, print and electronic publisher titles in the knowledgebase. The Library was primarily responsible for maintaining the collection, but occasionally sought the assistance of the SFU Library. Being the first library in the United States to become a part of the *reSeacher* community, GTC had several unique resources that needed to be added to the knowledgebase by the project managers at the SFU Library.

	name	provider	type	titles	active	rank	title list scanned
view | edit | delete	AAAS Journals	American Association for the Advancement of Science	fulltext journals	3 of 3 (bulk)	yes	100	2007-01-17
view | edit | delete	Academic OneFile	Gale	fulltext journals	10571 of 10571 (bulk)	yes	100	2007-07-23
view | edit | delete	Academic Search Premier	EBSCO	fulltext journals	8454 of 8454 (bulk)	yes	100	2007-11-02
view | edit | delete	AMA Journals	American Medical Association	fulltext journals	1 of 1 (bulk)	yes	0	2006-03-24
view | edit | delete	Biography Resource Center	Gale	fulltext journals	270 of 270 (bulk)	yes	95	2006-12-08
view | edit | delete	BioMed Central	BioMed Central	fulltext journals	176 of 176 (bulk)	yes	100	2007-04-25
view | edit | delete	Blackwell Synergy	Blackwell	fulltext journals	3 of 941 (bulk)	yes	90	2007-05-31
view | edit | delete	Business & Company Resource Center	Gale	fulltext journals	5268 of 5268 (bulk)	yes	100	2007-07-25
view | edit | delete	Business Source Premier	EBSCO	fulltext journals	12947 of 12947 (bulk)	yes	100	2007-11-02
view | edit | delete	CIAO: Columbia International Affairs Online	Columbia University Press	fulltext journals	36 of 36 (bulk)	yes	95	2006-03-24
view | edit | delete	Computer Source	EBSCO	fulltext journals	464 of 464 (bulk)	yes	95	2007-11-02
view | edit | delete	Directory of Open Access Journals	DOAJ	fulltext journals	2733 of 2733 (bulk)	yes	99	2007-07-03
view | edit | delete	Expanded Academic ASAP	Gale	fulltext journals	4245 of 4245 (bulk)	yes	100	2007-07-23
view | edit | delete	General Business File ASAP	Gale	fulltext journals	4567 of 4567 (bulk)	yes	100	2007-07-24
view | edit | delete	General Reference Center	Gale	fulltext journals	1381 of 1381 (bulk)	yes	100	2007-07-23
view | edit | delete	Greenville Tech Journals	Greenville Tech	fulltext journals	9 (bulk)	yes	0	2006-12-20
view | edit | delete	Health & Wellness Resource Center	Gale	fulltext journals	1107 of 1107 (bulk)	yes	100	2007-07-25
view | edit | delete	Health Reference Center Academic	Gale	fulltext journals	1081 of 1081 (bulk)	yes	100	2007-07-24
view | edit | delete	Health Source: Nursing/Academic Edition	EBSCO	fulltext journals	845 of 845 (bulk)	yes	100	2007-08-29
view | edit | delete	Highwire - Free	Highwire	fulltext journals	269 of 269 (bulk)	yes	100	2007-10-22
view | edit | delete	InfoTrac™ Junior Edition	Gale	fulltext journals	325 of 325 (bulk)	yes	90	2007-07-24
view | edit | delete	InfoTrac™ Kids Edition	Gale	fulltext journals	114 of 114 (bulk)	yes	90	2007-07-24
view | edit | delete	InfoTrac™ OneFile	Gale	fulltext journals	11135 of 11135 (bulk)	yes	100	2007-07-23

Figure 1. CUFTS Knowledgebase

Statistics may also be generated from CUFTS A-Z to assess usage and compare up to four resource title lists. The latter is useful in discovering overlap between two or more databases.

The user interface also engages users in an interactive, intuitive research experience. The tabbed search feature clearly presents search indexes such as keyword, subject, association, or social tag (see Figure 2). Browsing by alphabetical title is a standard feature identical to analogous commercial products. One of the more interactive features of CUFTS A-Z is the option for users to assign tags to their favorite journals for the purpose of creating custom lists based on subject, course name, etc. The spirit of social book-marking sites such as del.icio.us, LibraryThing, etc., is fully realized in CUFTS A-Z. The Library also has the option to restrict the social tagging feature to library staff, but the public can still browse the tags to access journal titles.

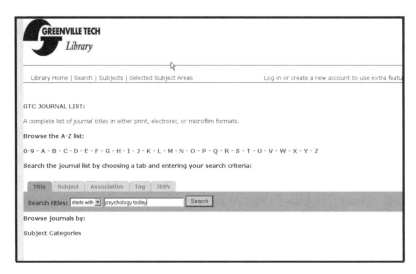

Figure 2. CUFTS Search Interface

The journal record displays all print and electronic holdings as stored in the knowledge base (see Figure 3).

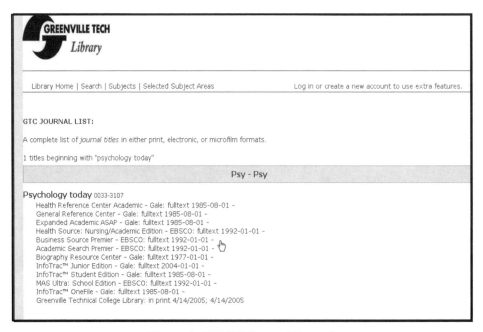

Figure 3. CUFTS Journal Record

The inclusion of social tagging is one of several key differences that set CUFTS A-Z apart from other commercial journal listing products. Social tagging is currently not a feature of either EBSCO A-Z or Serials Solutions A-Z journal listing products. Live updating of the knowledgebase is feature of CUFTS A-Z and is consistently reliable. Even though EBSCO A-Z permits live updating, the Library has found there were frequent extended time intervals (sometimes up to 24 hours) between updating and when these changes were realized in the public A-Z journal interface. Live updating is not a feature of Serials Solutions A-Z and the knowledgebase is consistently updated within 24 hours.

Also, both EBSCO and Serials Solutions offer more database choices. Unique databases, however, can be added to CUFTS A-Z by simply contacting technical support. Despite this, the process is often expedient—updates are made within a few business days.

The A-Z journal listing databases often vary to what extent the public display is customizable. CUFTS A-Z and Serials Solutions A-Z offer more extensive options to brand and customize. For example, headers and footers are customizable to the extent that they can match the headers and footers of the library's website. On the other hand, EBSCO A-Z is rather restrictive, allowing the insertion of a logo and a few color changes.

CUFTS2MARC

The CUFTS knowledgebase also facilitates the access of electronic journal titles through the online catalog because it has the capability to generate MARC records which can be uploaded to an integrated library system (ILS) (see Figure 4).

```
LDR 01083nas  2200229za 4500
005     20071105100345.0
006     m         d
007     cr u|||||||||
008     071105|||||||||||||||||||||d|||||||||||||
022 1   _a0098-3500
024 8   _aCUFTSResourceID93
050 00  _aQA76.6
        _b.A8a
082     _a510/.28/542505
245 10  _aACM transactions on mathematical software.
        _h[electronic resource]
246 3   _aAssociation for Computing Machinery transactions on mathematical software
500     _aFull text is available from 1997-03-01 to 2001-03-01.
540     _aILL allowed
590     _aRecord derived on 2007-11-05 from the CUFTS (http://cufts.lib.sfu.ca/) title list for Academic ASAP (CUFTS Resource ID 93, last updated
650  0  _aComputer programming
        _vPeriodicals.
650  0  _aMathematics
        _xData processing
        _vPeriodicals.
650  0  _aMathematics
        _xComputer programs
        _vPeriodicals.
856 4   _uhttp://infotrac.galegroup.com/itw/infomark/1/1/1/purl=rc18%5fAIM%5F0%5F%5Fjn+%22ACM+Transactions+on+Mathematical+Software%22
        _zClick here to connect
```

Figure 4. CUFTS2MARC Record

The CUFTS2MARC module is essentially an online form that allows the cataloger to customize MARC records. Essentially, libraries are able to generate locally enhanced records either by the addition of MARC tags or by customizing existing fields. For example, many fields, such as the one pertaining to the URL (MARC 856) can be enhanced to reflect access issues. Specifically, the URL in the 856 field may be prefixed to show an EZProxy login URL. Both commercial vendors, EBSCO and Serials Solutions, provide a subscription service for MARC records, but CUFTS A-Z provides free MARC records.

ERM

The ERM is accessed from the administrative module of CUFTS. At the time of implementation at Greenville Technical College, the ERM was fairly skeletal and did not provide an extensive range of data fields. In 2007, the ERM has been upgraded based on the *Functional Requirements of Electronic Resource Management: the Report of the DLF Initiative.* The ERM now provides enough data fields to manage cost and renewal details, administrative information such as usernames, password, and trials, and links to license information (see Figure 5). Because of these significant enhancements, the Library is finally able to manage their growing collection of electronic resources. Prior to implementing the ERM, the Library's cumbersome way of managing electronic resources consisted of storing usernames and passwords in a Word document.

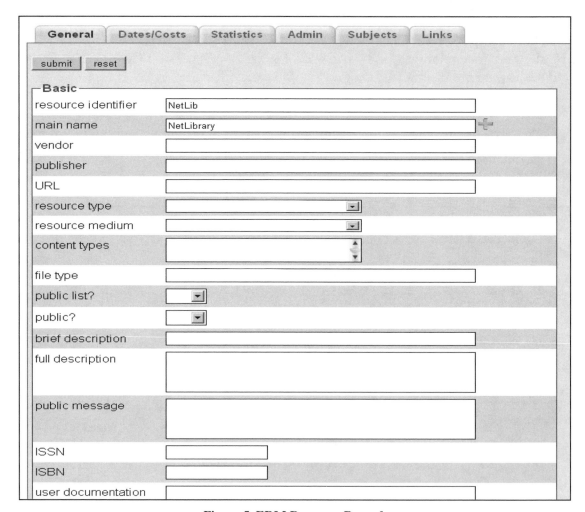

Figure 5. ERM Resource Record

The ability to manage database usage statistics provided by vendors is also a key feature of most commercial ERMs. In response, the CUFTS ERM can track statistics that are COUNTER compliant. At the time of writing this paper, the research team is investigating how to import Standard Usage Statistics Harvesting Initiative (SUSHI) compliant statistics in preparation for when most vendors will provide statistics that adhere to these standards. The ERM now allows the Library to harness the potentiality of administrative, technical, and statistical information from its electronic resources.

GODOT

One of the more significant modules to impact the research experience of the GTC community is the Open URL link resolving module of reSearcher, GODOT because they can finally access full-text articles from citation or citation-dominant databases. Depending on the database, GODOT will usually link the citation with a direct link; when a direct link is not available, the software will provide issue or journal level links to the resource (Stranack, 2008). In order to use the full power of GODOT, it was configured to search GTC's online catalog (SIRSI), Google, and Google Scholar. In the event an item is not found in any of the resources, a link to the Library's interlibrary loan form is included. This has been proven to be an effective way to promote interlibrary loan services. Since the implementation of GODOT at GTC, there has been a marked increase in interlibrary loan requests.

2. Don't Quit Your Day Job, Podcasters. By: Green, Heather. Business Week, 4/9/2007 Issue 4029, p72-74, 2p; (*AN 24560485*)
📄 **HTML Full Text**
📁 Add

3. Test Ride. By: Applebaum, Michael. MediaWeek, 4/9/2007, Vol. 17 Issue 14, p25-36, 6p; (*AN 24591533*)
[Where can I get this?]
📁 Add

4. Medical Librarian 2.0. By: Connor, Elizabeth. Medical Reference Services Quarterly, Spring2007, Vol. 26 Issue 1, p1-15, 15p, 6bw; (*AN 23540457*)
Cited References (7)
[Where can I get this?]
📁 Add

5. *Podcasting* at the University of Virginia Claude Moore Health Sciences Library. By: Ragon, Bart; Looney, Ryan P.. Medical Reference Services Quarterly, Spring2007, Vol. 26 Issue 1, p17-26, 10p, 6 charts; (*AN 23540458*)
Cited References (1)
[Where can I get this?]
📁 Add

Figure 6. Search in Academic Search Premier. Note: Greenville Technical College, like most *reSearcher* partners, opted for the phrase "Where can I get this?"

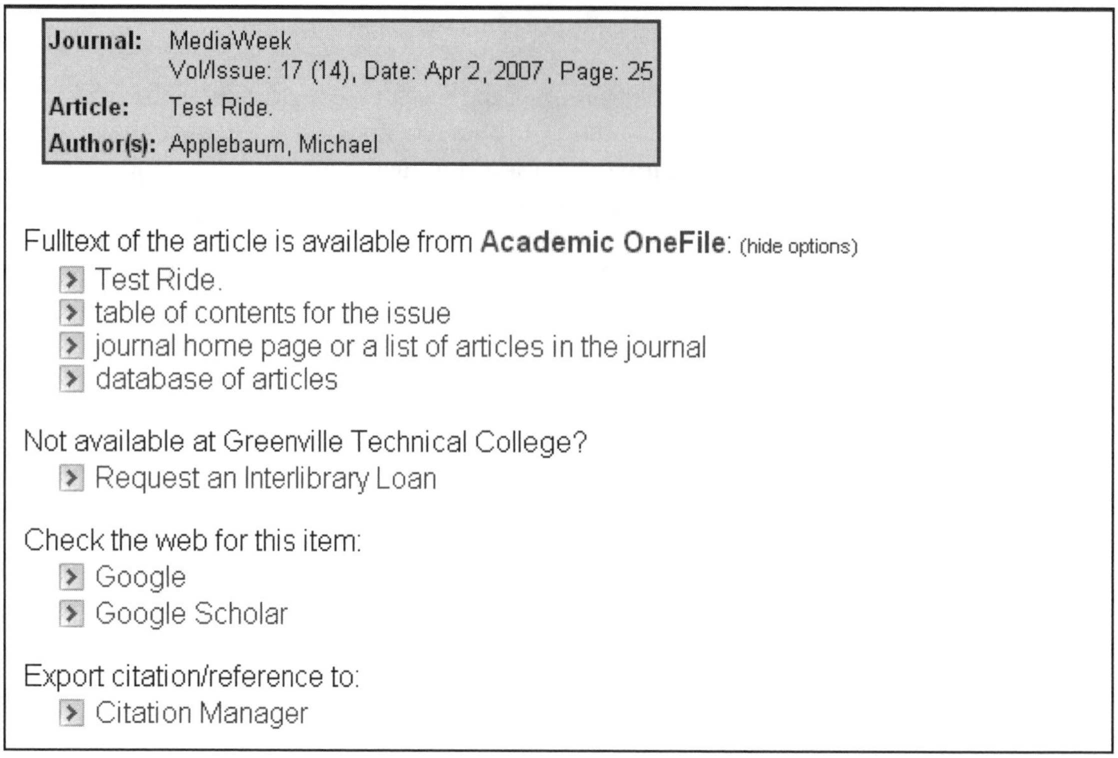

Figure 7. User Interface of GODOT after citation #3 is selected.

A feature that works in tandem with GODOT is Citation Manager. This product is analogous to other citation management products such as RefWorks, EndNote, etc. Citations can be either culled from GODOT or added manually and can also be organized in folders. Citation lists can be exported in XML, tab delimited format, etc., and are also compatible with Citation Manager's major commercial reference management analogues.

An advantage that Citation Manager has over commercial citation management products is that access can be maintained after graduation (Stranack, 2008). The library can determine if access is to either cease upon graduation or continue indefinitely for alumni. At the time of implementing *reSearcher*, the GTC Library did not actively promote Citation Manager and whether or not it will be incorporated into its bibliographic instruction program remains uncertain.

dbWiz

One of the modules currently not implemented at the Library was the federated search engine, dbWiz. Implementation was forestalled due to personnel changes. The person primarily responsible for configuring dbWiz resigned to take another position in another state. Because dbWiz employs the CUFTS knowledgebase, configuration of this utility is quite simple. Like most federated search engines, dbWiz searches traditional library resources such as library catalogs, Z39.50 databases, and full-text/citation article databases. Web resources such as Google (even EBay!) may be included. dbWiz also permits the clustering of databases by subject and course title or number. The ability to rank databases for each federated search cluster makes it possible to manipulate the order of preference in which databases are searched. To circumvent overwhelming students, the retrieval limit can be set to a certain number of hits. The end-user is able to sort the search results by date or by database alphabetically. dbWiz is not as robust as other commercial federated search products. Serials Solutions' Central Search, for example, allows more sorting options and has an export feature which dbWiz currently lacks. In essence, dbWiz is an inexpensive way for institutions to delve into federated searching.

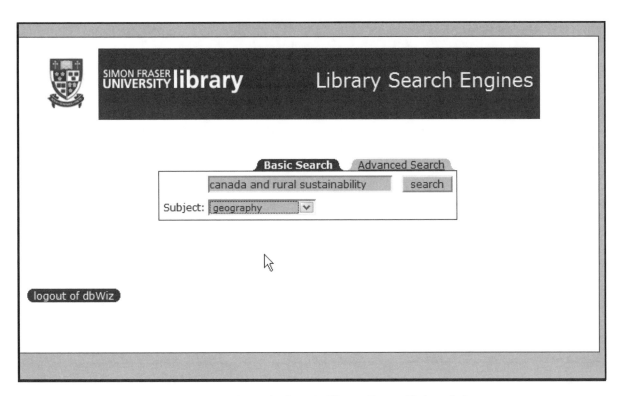

Figure 8. dbWiz Basic Search (Simon Fraser University)

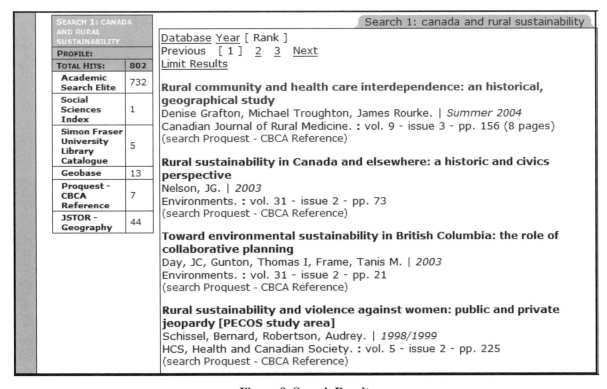

Figure 9. Search Results

Future Developments

One of the potential pitfalls of taking the open source route is that there is a risk the software development will be either indefinitely stymied or permanently discontinued. There is clear evidence that this is not the case with reSearcher. In the near future the Greenville Technical College Library will benefit from several initiatives driving the evolution of this product. Specifically, there are concrete plans to enhance the ERM module. ERM fields will be fully customizable. The ERM will also permit variable staff permissions, allowing some full administrative rights (Stranack, 2008). Most significantly, ERM data will be able to be imported from an institution's ILS. Also, dbWiz will not remain rudimentary for long—there are plans for an improved iteration.

In addition to future enhancements of existing modules, a new module is under development—CUFTS Resource Database (CRDB) (see Figure 10). Essentially, this is a database of databases for libraries and it eliminates the need to maintain a separate list of resources outside the CUFTS system (Stranack, 2008). CRDB will have standard browsing and searching features and faceted browsing. Each CUFTS library will also have the ability to include additional Subject, Resource Type, and Content Type terms.

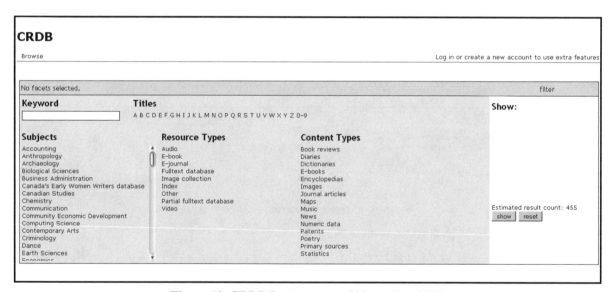

Figure 10. CRDB Prototype as of November 2007

Conclusions

Implementation at GTC was very successful and the Library is very proud to be the first participant from the United States in the *reSearcher* community. As one who was directly involved in all phases of its implementation, I can attest to not only the quality of this product, but to also the high level of professional service and assistance from the developers at Simon Fraser University. *reSearcher* is slowly starting to garner attention from the open source library software community and some academic libraries in the United States are deciding to implement this product. For example, the Baker University Library, in Baldwin City, Kansas is using GODOT and CUFTS A-Z. Lee College in Baytown, Texas is in the process of implementing *reSearcher*. In late 2007, I presented *reSearcher* to librarians at the College of St. Mary in Omaha, Nebraska and there are plans for implementation in late 2008. As *reSearcher* emerges as part of the discussion regarding electronic resource management software, it will be interesting to see its overall impact on the development of subsequent open source library applications and commercial products.

References

Copeland, L. (2006). There be dragons: Learning management and library systems in Canada. *IFLA Journal, 32*(3), 200-208.

Copeland, L., Long, K., & Mundle, T. (1999). The COPPUL virtual library resource sharing software. *Library Hi Tech Journal, 17*(2), 165-171.

Digital Library Federation. (2004). *Functional Requirements of Electronic Resource Management: The Report of the DLF initiative*. Retrieved November 6, 2007, from http://www.diglib.org/pubs/dlfermi0408/.

Mah, C., & Stranack, K. (2005). Db wiz: Open source federated searching for academic libraries. *Library Hi Tech, 23*(4), 490-503.

Renaud, J. P. (2006). CUFTS: Open source serials management. *Choice: Current Reviews for Academic Libraries, 43*(9), 1789-1790.

Simon Fraser University. (2007). *reSearcher: Open source software for libraries*. Retrieved November 6, 2007, from http://researcher.sfu.ca/.

Stranack, K. (2006). CUFTS: An open source alternative for serials management. *Serials Librarian, 51*(2), 29-39.

Stranack, K. (2008). The reSearcher Software Suite: A Case Study of Library Collaboration and Open Source Software Development. *Serials Librarian, 55 (1/2)*.

INNOVATING WITH PURPOSE: THINK GLOBAL, ACT LOCAL, AND THEN GIVE BACK

Rachel L. Frick, Senior Program Officer, National Leadership Grants, Library Services, Institute of Museum and Library Services, Washington, DC

Elisabeth Leonard, Doctoral Student, University of North Carolina Chapel Hill, Chapel Hill, North Carolina

Abstract

How can we thoughtfully alter traditional modes of research, development and communication in libraries and leverage creative problem solving activities from a model of local, incremental change and continuous improvement to a more dynamic, radical, risky, course of innovation that yields far reaching solutions? This paper provides suggestions on how innovation can help libraries address the issues that face them, through both theoretical and practical perspectives, with information on resources available to assist libraries in their efforts.

Introduction

In 2007, the authors presented papers at the Charleston Conference that discussed innovation (McDonald & Leonard, 2007)[1] and the re-evaluation and restructuring of entrenched organizational structures (Frick & McDonald, 2007).[2] Feedback and discussions from these presentations established that there was more to be explored. Why are libraries not innovating to adequately meet the challenges of the 21st century scholar and research community? What is holding us back? How can we effectively create strategies to best leverage the expertise, talent, knowledge and creative ideas we know exist in libraries for the greatest impact that will drive the profession forward, now? What are the challenges for the academic research library? What are the management and leadership issues? Where do libraries fit in the new information universe? How do we know we are traveling in the right direction? How do we measure our success? These questions keep resurfacing and need to be explored strategically.

Before we can begin to solve these issues, the first step is to acknowledge them, then establish their context in order to define them and move towards resolution. We must remember why we came to this profession and why we are still here. This is a period of great change and potential; a time to be viewed as rich with possibilities.

We are not attempting in this paper to identify specific operational problems and prescribe detailed solutions, but instead we want to share ways to think strategically and to develop local solutions for problems that could possibly have national impact, if shared effectively. In order to provide a rich set of recommendations, the authors interviewed four innovators, Susan Perry (Senior Advisor for the Liberal Arts Colleges program at The Andrew W. Mellon Foundation), Jeremy Frumkin (Assistant Dean for Technology Strategy, University of Arizona), Andrew Pace (Executive Director for Networked Library Services at OCLC), and Scott Walter (Associate University Librarian for Services and Associate Dean of Libraries, University of Illinois at Urbana-Champaign).

Environmental Scan

When thinking strategically, it is critical to first examine what is going on in the current environment and then to establish a context for the future. How you frame your definition or roster of stakeholders greatly influences the results of an environmental scan and, ultimately, the direction of organization. Furthermore, the perspectives, the lenses, used to view the present and future determine your vision of the environment.

For academic libraries, in addition to the traditional stakeholders of students, faculty and staff, you may want to include stakeholders, such as other campus information technology entities. Pace[3] recommends considering PeopleSoft and Blackboard when envisioning the library's webspace. In terms of stakeholders, that could include the university's registrar, finance office, and IT department. Also consider adding to your stakeholder roster peer and aspirant libraries, which may include K-12 libraries, public libraries, consortia, information providers such as publishers, book vendors, and library systems vendors, and, yes, even your own librarians. For example, when considering changes in public services, adding members from campus academic technology groups and cataloging librarians can contribute a valuable dynamic to the conversations.

What makes an environmental scan different than strategic planning is that it should not only scan and observe stakeholders, but also actively engage them in a true two-way conversation. For example, if middleware providers from the mobile devices community were engaged in our discussion of libraries in the 21st century, would it be possible to create new products and services beneficial to a broader community?

Traditionally, the questions we pose are the following: What are the faculty pursuing? How are they being challenged? We need to bring these questions into a larger context of national and international information infrastructure initiatives. How do tectonic movements like the National Science Foundation's Datanet program[4] and the Mellon funded Project Bamboo[5] affect local faculty research and teaching behaviors and needs? How will it affect their working relationship with the library? We must gather what our new context is[6] so that we can bootstrap ourselves to what the best of us are doing, what we could be doing, and how we can be doing it collaboratively.[7]

When we are engage our peers, partners and other players in conversation – what is the framework? What are the foundational concepts that are driving the conversation?

The library will need to focus clearly on two specific roles: one that is local and the other that is networked and part of a national and transnational research cyber-infrastructure. In its local role - the library will be optimized to meet the needs of its campus community in its networked role the library will be able to support research and dissemination to the extent that it is tightly networked into the increasing cluster of inter institutional collaborations that enable the creation and use of scholarly content.[8]

The basic question shifts from how to draw users into library systems to how to make certain that the content and services provided by the library can be found within the broader systems that users take part in while conducting their work.[9] There is a need to have and utilize a platform to share so that we are not recreating the wheel or redundantly providing the same services, but instead, using our resources to build on top of that to provide local more unique services specific to our communities of users.[10]

Changes in Attitude

It is paramount to begin viewing our local activity with a global context. Ten years ago, new librarians may have felt bombarded with a message of doom and gloom, resulting from the rapid changes in the information environment and the libraries' inability or inertia to react. The defeatist tone has lingered far too long. We are now talking proactively about creating our future. These following factors have contributed to the positive change in outlook:

- Thinking as entrepreneurs; deliberately creating new products and services, some of which may involve a higher level of risk than libraries' are used to dealing with.

- Assessment is becoming business intelligence.[11] It is more than statistics, more than learning outcomes; it's a performance dashboard melded with a look at the outside world and toward the future. "Traditional measures are not as relevant or stable as they were in the past. As a whole, the library community realizes this and is finding ways to better measure our success, impact and contributions. The task at hand is creating those new measures, combining them with our more traditional metrics, and finally understanding what the information means so that we can apply the knowledge in a proactive and meaningful way."[12]

- A growing demand to build on our core services of provision access to information into new areas and service models. While reports may decry researchers' interest in using the library, at the same time, our communities are calling out for assistance navigating through what is a complex and cluttered info-scape.

- Grants and national initiatives that call for the sharing and actively curating research data.

- Influx of new librarians who received their degrees from iSchools with a more progressive vision of information and library services.

Resources

Collaboration often brings a larger impact and more opportunities for knowledge sharing and skill enrichment. So why aren't libraries collaborating on shared service needs? Often money keeps us from scaling our local efforts into larger, broader more resounding regional or national ones. But this should not be the case. There are ways to fund innovation – especially if it solves a shared problem in a replicable way that can be utilized across libraries:

- Seek grants from federal, state, local, and private funding agencies. The Institute Museum and Library Services has a program that funds just this type of activity, the National Leadership Grants.[13] For example when Virginia Tech wanted to explore solving the problem on how to better integrate electronic resources into their catalog, they successfully applied to the IMLS for a National Leadership: Advancing Digital Resources Grant to fund the development of LibX.[14]

- Individuals and organizations will give support if you are providing good and important services. It is good to find a champion to support your cause; your champion could be a faculty member, a neighboring library, library consortia, or service provider that would like to use the libraries' unique skills and resources to solve the problem.

- Pool your resources - across campus - in your neighborhood - among interest groups. Working with others in a local or regional capacity, it is possible pool your dollars and your staff toward a specific project that would benefit all those involved. Explore the possibility of bartering services and expertise. Do you know someone who did a great job with fine-tuning his or her acquisitions unit? Invite them to come to your library; maybe there is something they can learn from you in exchange.

- Turn your projects into products. When you develop a tool or service think of ways to commoditize it in order to support continued development. Develop a revenue stream that will fund the marketing and sustainability of the effort.

- Quit doing something - we have heard it many times before, including many times at the 2008 Charleston Conference, but it bears repeating - the only way we are going to be able to meet the information services needs of the 21st century is to let go of some of those 20th century services that are no longer relevant.

Prepare the Soil

Once you set your sights on a challenge, how do you foster creative solutions and fresh perspectives? How are you going to bring that good idea you thought about here at the Charleston Conference home to your library? What does your library do to facilitate good ideas? How do you sell a new idea to your staff and your boss? How to you get to the "yes" that moves your idea forward? How do you cull the best solutions for your problem?

There is a danger in coming home from a conference all excited and wanting to instantly create change. If you don't already have a culture of innovation in your organization, you need to begin a transition to one in order to ensure that you will not only hear *new* ideas, but that those some of those ideas will come to life. As a manager, you must foster an environment that encourages and rewards contributions. Not only must *you* be comfortable with the process of exploration, development and risk taking, but you must create an environment that makes those activities safe for everyone else. You must also make sure that in that time when you are all brainstorming, that every idea is initially seen as a potential flower, even if it may seem like a weed. Take the time to hear every idea with an open mind. Thus you have a fertile environment, seeded with multiple ideas from multiple perspectives, all of which have the potential of furthering your institution's strategic goals.

Some ideas will take hold and root, while others fail to germinate at all – that is okay. If a thousand ideas are allowed to bloom, you have a greater chance of growing a winner.

It is inevitable in the course of change staff will be scared, angry, uncertain, excited, and enthusiastic. Meet them at the point of need and love them through the process![15] By this we mean reminding staff of their strengths and experience and providing the staff development opportunities that continually refresh their abilities. As a manager, you must ensure that the staff has a firm foundation of the skills and knowledge necessary to be successful; you should not set them up to fail.

It is important to keep the focus on the end goal, even while acknowledging that the process is difficult, challenging, and can take an emotional and mental toll. Managers must create a safe space for staff to feel their emotions and managers must support staff through troubled times. Developing a new idea can easily be the best of times and the worst of times, all in the same day.

Additionally, there should be a champion for the ideas that you are working toward. A champion acts a coach and as a steward, rather than an owner. Having sole ownership of a new idea with a stifling strangle hold on the natural growth process without allowing others to have meaningful influence or contribution is a sure way is kill it before it can flourish. "Don't squeeze too tight – or it will slip through your fingers."[16]

Strategic Thinking

As your ideas grow, as you work through your solutions, a planned part of the activity should be some designated chin up time. The environmental scan we mentioned about earlier is one instance of chin up time. Take the time to check to in on the national, regional, or other community based conversations to see if your idea was tried before, has been developed and abandoned, or had preliminary success. Does your idea still have meaning in today's environment as it did 3 weeks or 3 months ago? Pausing to weigh in with your communities and share your goals as you progress can also uncover a partner to help enrich your process.

In order for the environmental scan to yield true and meaningful results, we need to re-think how and what we share, the ways we "publish" or announce our activities. We have grown comfortable with our usual means of dissemination. The journal article and the conference presentation are the usual comfortable modes to communicate the end product of the activities. But is this the most useful to our community? These traditional modes are the accepted ways to share our success, but often are to slow and too staid to influence and enact true innovation and change on a large, fast enough scale. The reach of these activities seems to limit the audience to those in the first tier of influence. Rarely do they ripple out to second or third tier communities that might find the information valuable.

When publishing findings in our journals, the time lag from submission to formal publication is too long, and the ideas do not get to the community when they are fresh and needed. Is there a better way to get our message out sooner? Possibly using social networking tools, like wikis and blogs on a project website to communicate ongoing activities, along with publishing regular interim reports could facilitate real time communication of efforts when they are the most meaningful.

We also need to re-evaluate our Conferences activities: where we attend, how we attend and why we attend. Have you gone to the same conferences for the past 3, 5, 8, 10 years?

How many from you library go to the same conference at the same time? Have you ever invited a faculty member - or IT person to a library conference? Have you thought about going to a conference outside the library profession? It was noted often in by our panel that one of the challenges in effectively communicating about changes in libraries, was that we tend to only talk to ourselves.[17] And in talking to ourselves - we tend to only talk about our successes - we need to talk about the whole learning experience.

The failures, or "learnings,"[18] are just as important as the times we succeed and need to be evaluated and discussed in order to gain an understanding and leverage that knowledge for future success. The times we fail and share why we failed, adds to the validity of our successes. It helps the community as a whole from repeating the same mistakes. Often in presentations, the focus is on the end product, or the details focus on the positives of the process - we need to tell the complete story. This is what makes a presentation a real dissemination and sharing of knowledge, versus a sales pitch. As you are disseminating information about new products, services or other ideas developed at your library, keep these questions in mind:

- Do you provide actionable results?

- What is the takeaway experience?

- When you have developed a product or service - do you present it and make it available in a way for someone to easily grasp the concepts and be able to apply them at their home institution?

- Can someone grab your idea and go, run with it, build on it, and possibly make it better? Are your outputs, services and products "open"?

- Are you leaving out key information that will hinder someone from following in your footsteps?

- How can you improve the share-ability of your work and ideas?

Some suggestions are to network your idea like you network at a conference. Talk to people and ask for feedback; shop it around and get interested people involved in the process. Actively seek supporters, develop efforts to build a community, recruit field testers, contributors, believers outside of your immediate vicinity.

The act of positive sharing is tied in to transparency. Libraries often hide their inner workings behind the curtain. How do you share interests, research and professional activities within your organizations? How do you share those same activities with those outside, to your campus community and beyond? Consider posting on the library web page papers, conference reports, and updates on the library's activities and projects. Providing information about staff travel schedules, the conferences and workshops they attend and why they are attending could open up some spontaneous conversation, unexpected areas of collaboration, or a new partnership. By publishing your staff's off campus professional activities, you might find a serendipitous shared interest with others in your community. To establish a quick way to get feedback on your libraries products and services, explore the possibility of a Twitter account for your library.[19] The developers of Zotero[20] and Omeka[21] at George Mason University's Center for History and New Media[22] use Twitter to interact with their users and others interested in where they are presenting, product updates and upgrades, as well as innovative uses for their services.

By offering a greater level of transparency - we increase the probability of creating opportunities of collaboration and innovation.

Call to Action

One of the best pieces of advice I ever got was to never go to your manager with a problem – you will either be sent away or the manager will offer you a solution you don't like! So, you offer a solution, not a problem. In terms of thinking innovatively, we need to think strategically about approaching the problems that already exist in libraries *and* in the communities we serve, and provide new solutions to those problems. While developing a radical innovation is difficult, it creates a new future while solving existing problems. As Andrew Pace said to us, "Greatness is in our grasp…take the leap of faith and endure the year of hell."

We can make that development time easier on ourselves. We must be more transparent internally with our goals for innovation AND with our partners about those goals. We must be willing to partnering with people who can inspire us, or who can provide skills/resources that we don't have. Why? To create a brave new world, built not on the ashes of librarianship, but on its fundamentals.

Notes

1. McDonald R. and Leonard, E. (November 2007). *Innovation in Practice: Transforming Everyday Complexities with New Discoveries.* Plenary session, Charleston Conference, Charleston, SC.

2. Frick, R. L. and McDonald, R. (November 2007). *Electronic Resources Management: The Future of Library Technical Services and Other Ideas on How to Dismantle an Atomic Bomb.* Concurrent session, Charleston Conference, Charleston, SC.

3. Interview with Andrew Pace, conducted on September 16 2008.

4. http://www.nsf.gov/funding/pgm_summ.jsp?pims_id=503141&org=OCI

5. http://projectbamboo.org/

6. Interview with Jeremy Frumkin, conducted on September 23, 2008.

7. Interview with Susan Perry, conducted on September 9, 2008.

8. Smith, Abby. *The Research Library in the 21st Century: Collecting, Preserving, and Making Accessible Resources for Scholarship, No Brief Candle: Reconceiving Research Libraries for the 21st Century,* CLIR report 142, August 2008, pg. 18.

9. Interview with Scott Walter, conducted on September 23, 2008.

10. Frumkin interview.

11. Pace interview.

12. Frumkin interview.

13. http://www.imls.gov/applicants/grants/nationalLeadership.shtm

14. http://www.libx.org/

15. Perry interview.

16. Frumkin interview.

17. Pace interview, Frumkin interview, and Perry interview.

18. Frumkin interview.

19. http://www.twitter.com

20. http://www.zotero.org/

21. http://omeka.org/

22. http://chnm.gmu.edu/

THE CHARLESTON OBSERVATORY: A POSITION PAPER

David Nicolas, Professor, University College London, London, United Kingdom

The General Idea

The Charleston Conference is renowned for the quality and currency of its proceedings and debates, as well as for the eminence of its speakers and delegates. The Proceedings provide a partial legacy and testament to this but we can and must do more to take further the new/big ideas and great challenges raised; in other words to enhance the Conference's ability to assist the information and publishing professions in their development. Currently there is no mechanism by which the exciting ideas and challenges raised can be tested or researched further and the results reported back to Conference to ensure build, continuity and dialogue. This position paper puts forward a mechanism by which this can be done – the Charleston Observatory. The Observatory would be the research adjunct for the Conference, the medium by which the ideas generated are turned into robust research projects, which provide the evidence base for strategic planning. The Observatory would be a place where information experiments can be undertaken and witnessed, where evidence can be collected in a robust and validated manner and where diverse communities can come together and share their data to the benefit of all. The Observatory would promote international research collaboration, global problems require global solutions.

The Mechanics

To kick start the process (and proof the concept) we might start with topics which seem to obtain universal interest from the publishing, academic and library communities: a) the information seeking habits of the young (undergraduates) or future researchers (The Google Generation); b) the impact of e-books on the scholarly community. In following years we can ask conference to suggest or vote on topics. We would seek two types of partners (or sponsors) to take part in observatory experiments – library communities who would be willing to contribute data and take part in live research studies and research funders who would provide the necessary resources to enable the projects to be undertaken, these funders would probably come from the commercial sector - information service providers, aggregators, publishers etc. and would have some interest in the topic being funded.

The idea is that we would canvass the community to see what level of interest and co-operation the idea receives and depending on what we get back set up a group that would establish the Observatory and oversee its activities.

Technology is changing the way libraries do business. These changes are coming quickly and sometimes without time to research or analyze them. The 2008 Conference provided librarians with the opportunity to discuss technology issues such as how to deal with Google, use of access databases in acquisitions, and the use of blogs in libraries today.

Techie Issues

165

BRIDGING THE GOOGLE GAP

Darrell W. Gunter, EVP / CMO Collexis Holdings, Inc., Columbia, South Carolina, Moderator

Panel:

Dennis Brunning, Arizona State Univ., Library Reference Service, Academic Prof w/Admin Appt

Mark Hyer, Vice President of Science and Technology Publishing ProQuest

Sue Polanka, Head, Reference/Instruction, Paul Laurence Dunbar Library, Wright State University

Steve Leicht, COO Collexis Holdings, Inc.

Introduction: Bridging the Google Gap—Google Friend or Foe
Darrell W. Gunter, EVP / CMO Collexis Holdings, Inc.

Back in early 2001, the library community was very concerned about the student's adoption of Google as they felt the students would not develop their research skills due to their dependency on Google. With the launch of Google Scholar and the other tools developed by Google, the academic community has come to embrace Google and all have benefited from its success. Our panel today will explore these developments and discuss how their companies have augmented their services in conjunction with Google.

Understanding Research(ers)
Dennis Brunning, Arizona State Univ., Library Reference Service, Academic Prof w/ Admin Appt

As other panelists point out, the Google Gap (or why do our users prefer Google for library search over library search engines) is ease of use. We can build—and do build—better mousetrapsl; but if there are easier and cheaper tools, people will use them.

Still, there is nothing simple about research. The goal is knowledge. Google's mission is to organize the world's knowledge—online or offline. Scholarship begins and ends with the printed word. Researchers surround themselves with books and journals. Most consider themselves writers; all are readers. Online is one tool of many. To find out more about how our institutional repository was used by researchers at Arizona State University, a colleague and I interviewed several dozen professors and graduate students.

We found out the following:

• Research may or may not start with Google; it is one search tool among many

• Many, especially faculty, understand the library's role in licensing electronic databases and content

• Purpose drives research and search method

• Keen interest in publishing management—how to get research out to reader

From these and other observations we suggest:

- Enhance their Property—academic publishing is about exposure

- Go Beyond Search—Google defines general search (digital content open to its search engine on the Internet); develop search techniques, approaches, that

- Leverage meta-data—our professional legacy is the information collected, organized, and archived in card catalogs, indexing & abstracting services, local records, and bibliographies

- Service data—faculty data sets are not new; what's new is our opportunity to curate these online

Mark Hyer, Vice President of Science and Technology Publishing, ProQuest

Sometimes Google has proven to be a great place for serious research to start searching, but this is not always the case.

Google Scholar is a comprehensive search tool for finding a large amount of information. However, Google Scholar does not provide specific navigation tools for all disciplines. Abstract and indexing services still provide unique navigation tools for students performing discipline specific searches—most importantly, controlled vocabularies and targeted journal and non-journal coverage relevant to the discipline. Advanced search options also provide navigational support not found in Google Scholar.

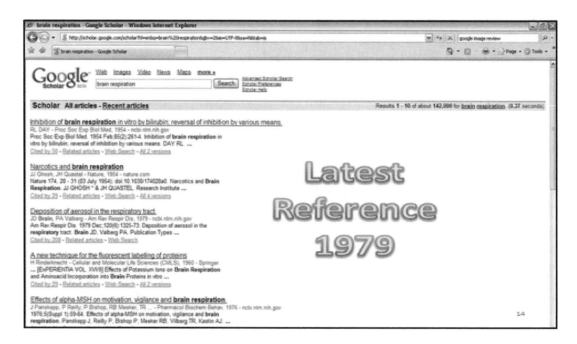

Google Images is not a serious search tool. With a lack of authoritative indexing around tables, figures, charts, and graphs, students would typically not find research related information.

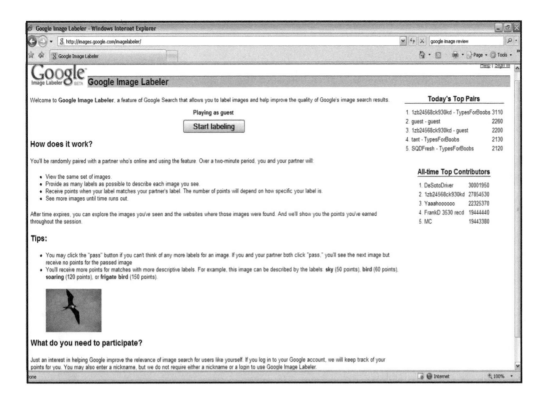

To increase the utility of Abstracting and Indexing services, ProQuest is currently investing in value added indexing of tables, figures, charts and graphs to Bridge the Google Gap.

Widgets have proven to be an effective tool for isolating and promoting search services. ProQuest recently released a series of widgets to support the ProQuest and Illumina platforms including a search widget to support Illustrata (deep index) searches of tables, figures, graphs, and charts.

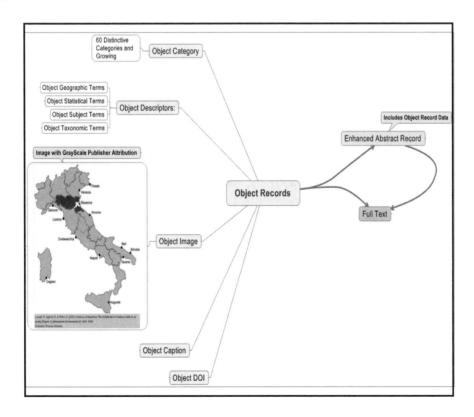

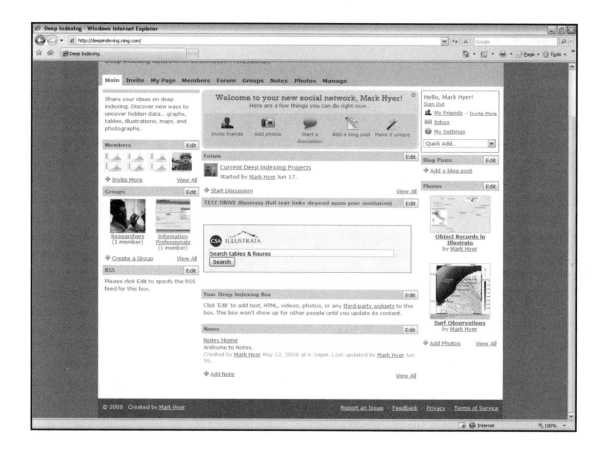

Bridging the Google Gap
Sue Polanka, Head, Reference/Instruction, Paul Laurence
Dunbar Library, Wright State University

As an academic librarian providing reference service, I was asked to comment on what is working for library patrons, what keeps the search, and results relevant to them. I'd like to discuss three things that are working for my school, Wright State University, and perhaps other libraries around the world—search widgets, library portals, and discovery layers.

What our students want is the "Easy Button." They want to search in one location to get quick, relevant results from authoritative sources, all in full text format. Since we cannot offer that—yet—we are doing what we can to make the web search experience relevant and successful.

First is through the use of search widgets, small search boxes embedded in websites. Plant them on any site or location (library or not) to direct students to good resources. Students will enter data into the first search box they find, so it needs to be effectively used on a website, not cluttered in/amongst other search boxes. Examples of successful widgets include the Credo Reference and Reference Universe search boxes, and Britannica's widgets, which provide colorful, factual information on a topic with links to more information.

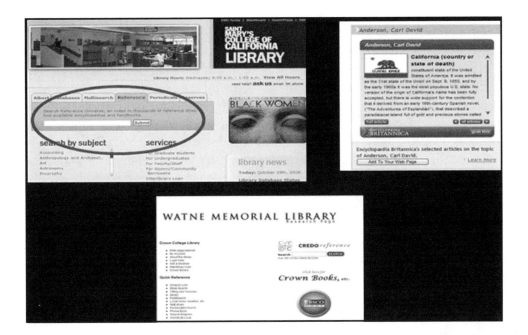

Second is the concept of library portals, otherwise known as "MyLibrary." This allows users to customize library and other web resources in one location, typically a site hosted by a library. Users have the flexibility to choose databases, journals, ebooks, and other links that are relevant at a particular time, and change these selections as often as necessary. Additionally, the Library can push information to users though news feeds, email, and other notification devices built into the software. This information can be customized by patron type—student, faculty, staff, and many times by major or course. Search widgets and chat/IM options can also be added. At Wright State University we use our campus portal to host a totally customizable library tab.

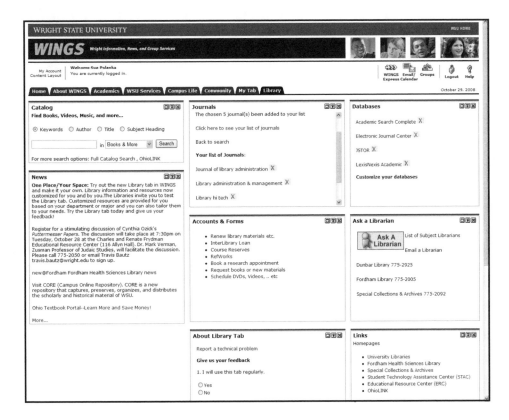

Third is the concept of a discovery layer. The discovery layer is a search engine that can retrieve results from hundreds of pre-indexed library databases at the blink of an eye, with facets, tags, and web 2.0 options. In other words, it becomes the Google of the invisible web, releasing the information locked behind the library firewalls. It is different from a metasearch tool in that data will be pre-indexed for faster searching and display of results, and the ability to make the best use of facets and limiters. OhioLINK, the academic library consortium in Ohio, is currently working with vendors to produce a discovery layer for the state. This tool will index the combined library catalog of all 90 members, and all databases subscribed to statewide and locally, including several OhioLINK hosted databases with full text of ebooks, journals, and thesis and dissertations. It's a concept, but will hopefully be reality.

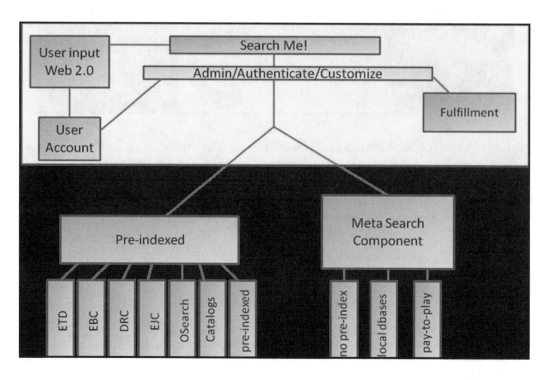

Since the Charleston Conference, EBSCO has announced the launch of EBSCO*host* Integrated Search, a discovery layer concept product.

Bridging the Google Gap - The Personalization of Information
Steve Leicht, COO Collexis Holdings, Inc.

The fundamental tenant of this talk is that the Library Community should rethink what we reference as the "Google Gap." Most of our talks will fundamentally approach this as a technical gap. If we consider it a technical gap, than the Google Gap has been technically addressable for over a decade. In fact, most information professionals could point to a wide variety of more efficient indexing and search platforms for manipulating and viewing information. Instead, we should think about the Google Gap as the gap of utilization of other tools. This is where there is an enormous gap, which is much more challenging to address. The common use by end-users of Google as the primary source of search is really the conundrum that continues to baffle information professionals. We can build a better mousetrap, but it appears that the mice have all left our house to be caught across the street by the Google Family. Their mousetrap might be slower, more basic, have less features, etc.—but everyone is using it.

Collexis has one unique approach in this utilization Gap. It is in personalizing and pushing information to the end user. By showing highly relevant, highly precise information to a user, without proactive input required from that user, there is an immediacy of attractiveness. Collexis has been able to achieve this goal in limited environments where a user or expert can be highly profiled without their input—by mapping authored papers or literature to its author. By accumulating literature-based "Expert Profiles" of an author (summarizations of their written ideas) - we have become a standard application at leading biomedical institutions like NIH, Johns Hopkins, Mayo Clinic, and 25+ other leading biomedical research institutions.

The advantage of this approach is that the profiles continue to update on an author, as long as they are generating documents—papers, grants, etc. These robust up-to-date profiles can act as a filter to mine through the enormous literature sources (of a library or other aggregated data source) to suggest highly relevant information on a daily, weekly, or monthly basis that is of interest to the scientist/user. Similarly, by mapping the social networks of these scientists through co-author relationships, we have been able to identify material which is highly relevant for conceptual profile and also highly relevant based on social connectivity. We have even turned a basic version of this into a standalone social network—www.biomedexperts.com— which is freely available for the health sciences research community. The site is gaining in usage, with over 10,000 researchers joining each month and over 30,000 unique users visiting the site daily.

THE EVOLUTION OF SERVICE: A TECHNICAL SERVICES PERSPECTIVE

Helen Heinrich, Cataloging Coordinator, California State University, Northridge, California

Donna LaFollette, Accounting & Receiving Supervisor, California State University, Northridge, California

Abstract

The behind-the-scenes work of Technical Services (TS) often goes unnoticed by the library patrons. However, they stand to benefit the most from innovative approaches in TS that curtail the challenges of shrinking budgetary and personnel resources. Leveraging existing technology, departmental reorganization, outsourcing and cross-training can help a library weather hard times and improve service at the same time. Qualities that create a good customer service workforce in Public Services can help coordinators for acquisitions, cataloging and processing to function more effectively. Relationships between library technicians, campus staff and faculty, and external contacts evolve as the tools we use to perform our work change. This paper will explore what Technical Services departments can do to improve service, using an academic library as a model.

Background

The campus of California State University, Northridge (CSUN) sits nestled in a valley at the north end of Los Angeles. CSUN's Oviatt library is the centerpiece of the campus, serving a population of 36,000 undergraduate and graduate students and 4,000 faculty and staff. The library's collections currently consist of 1.4 million volumes, 150,000 electronic books, 35,000 electronic journals, and 120 abstract and index or full-text databases. The Technical Services staff is divided into three main units: seven full-time staff in Acquisitions; nine full-time staff, one full-time and one half-time librarian in Cataloging; and one full-time staff and one full-time librarian in E-Resources.

Services

Within the Technical Services department, our mission is to select, acquire, organize, and process resources for users to the best of our abilities. Traditional materials processed in TS for the collections are passed on to Public Services, who are often thought of as custodians of customer service. However, it should not be assumed that TS does not play a significant role in access and the delivery of customer service:

> While a reference librarian interfaces directly with patrons in person, in classrooms, and by telephone, email, and live chat, a technical services librarian interfaces with patrons through the online catalog, the online journal portal, and through many links provided on the library website. The main concern for customer service is the same — helping patrons find the materials they need. (Skekel, 2008, p. 22)

Typically, contacts between TS and patrons are limited to the occasional access problem, such as locating a periodical issue that is within the office, awaiting binding. However, as we purchase more electronic resources, TS staff plays a greater part in access to those resources, affording us closer contact with the user:

> How the library delivers the content of its collection... may have consequences for patrons. Some of these consequences can be a direct result of Technical Services decisions about purchases, cataloging, or even technology used in the provision of resources. (Skekel, 2008, p. 20)

As the library's focus shifts from providing physical materials and spaces to information access across formats (Diaz & Pintozzi, 1999), Technical Services must be diligent in maintaining access as expected and promised to the user. Whether that entails establishing new services (such as a link resolver or metasearching) or maintaining and improving existing routes of access (such as the library's catalog), these responsibilities fall to TS staff, thus placing us at the forefront of customer service. Our relationships and communication with others (staff, institutional departments, and users) must be persistent and open to effectively meet their needs.

The model of the traditional vendor and library relationship has also evolved from one of merchant and client to a collaborative, symbiotic relationship. The increased volume of data exchange between our vendors and the library puts us in contact with them much more frequently, emphasizing our role not only as receiver of service but a provider as well.

Here is another side of our multi-pronged customer service provision. Amongst our users, our faculty is especially concerned with electronic resources. In a 2008 Library Satisfaction Survey, faculty listed e-resources as the most important issue to them. This includes the ease and availability of e-Reserves to their students. And it is TS who is providing ready access to e-Reserve materials, usually in the form of e-books or full-text articles, which gives our faculty flexibility in choosing materials to place on Reserve.

Furthermore, our faculty members request a large percentage of the materials through Inter-library loan (ILL). As an experiment, the Acquisitions unit in TS is investigating purchasing items that are initially requested through ILL. If Technical Services can fulfill these ILL requests through acquisition, in some cases faster than ILL could have borrowed the materials, we help create a user-generated collection management policy and provide better service as well. The expectation is that our faculty will be pleased that the library is reactive to their requests, that they will not be restricted by ILL loan limits, and that they may get their materials even sooner. Here again, we are directly offering service to our patrons, with faster-paced purchasing procedures.

Value

This year, we expect to spend $1.3 million in electronic resources alone. Are we receiving that much bang for our buck? In an effort to determine how much the services and resources we provide are actually worth, the library's Assessment Coordinator, Katherine Dabbour, conducted a valuation study in July, 2008. Although we subscribe to 120 databases, just one of them was examined. K. Dabbour (personal communication, December 8, 2008) determined that just one database (Academic Search Elite) provided over $20 million in downloaded articles over the course of one fiscal year.

At the same time, we have to balance the expense of the services offered by TS with the constraints on our budget. For electronic resources, the percentage of our materials budget expended on electronic resources has risen from 25% in the 2004-05 fiscal year to 65% in the 2008-09 fiscal year. The difficulties we face are the result of shrinking or stagnating personnel and materials budgets, coupled with rising costs for resources. Consortial agreements generally increase the number of resources we can offer; however, the fixed and hidden costs of these electronic packages limit our flexibility to expend our budget on electronic resources. "As many department heads know, daily duties can change dramatically from year to year as we are asked to do more with less while embracing new technology and standards" (Deeken, Webb, & Taffurelli, 2008, p. 211). The hidden cost of the workload associated with extra resources has been exacerbated by a 25% reduction in TS personnel since 2004.

Although we do need to save money, we have to take into consideration the provision of service in how we cut back. For example, earlier this year we purchased a certain platform for an e-book because it was less expensive than other options. But the result was a product that was not user-friendly, rendering the e-book unreadable by many users. In economizing, we must ensure that we do not undermine the integrity of the access to materials we provide. Access includes terms of use as well. If a user is turned away because we do not purchase enough simultaneous user licenses, have we adequately provided the service? Where is that balance?

Our users expect a high level of service with our electronic resources as well as our traditional materials. In fact, whatever we currently offer by way of e-journals, e-books, and databases, they want more. We cannot choose between delivering electronic resources and offering customary (old school) library collections. We need both. But how do we balance the provision of traditional materials and services with the explosion of popular electronic resources we now make available to our users? It is not simply a matter of answering, "What can we afford?" but, rather, "How do we get the most out of what we can afford?"

Since hiring more people to meet the demands of a greater workload was not an option for the Oviatt library, we looked to adjusting the current workflows in TS. This included reorganizing, consolidating, and paring down our procedures to make them leaner and to accommodate new workflows for electronic resources and electronic procedures. An ongoing reorganization of the department would impact our ability to meet budgetary constraints to not only bring service to our patrons but in many ways, to improve upon that customer service. In 2005, an opportunity for the reorganization of TS presented itself when newly hired Helen Heinrich brought a fresh perspective and diverse experience as the Cataloging Coordinator of the department.

Change

When Helen Heinrich started at Oviatt Library at CSUN as Cataloging Coordinator in 2005, she had over 13 years of experience working in Technical Services at the Getty Research Library. Both libraries fall under the classification of "academic and/or research", but the similarities end there. The Getty is a private library focusing on the research needs of Ph.D's, art history scholars and curators. It prides itself in a unique collection with 65% of materials being in foreign languages. Things could not be more different at the Oviatt Library. CSUN is a public institution serving more than 30,000, mainly undergraduate, students with diverse backgrounds. The primary mission of the library is to support undergraduate curriculum; therefore, to acquire mostly mainstream materials. The contrast between the Getty and

CSUN ensured that Heinrich had a different perspective of the work of Cataloging unit when she started her new job. Therefore, Heinrich's first order of business was to survey and assess the workflow in the department. She sat down with every staff member to learn what they do every day and how he or she does it. Being new gave her the advantage of asking "stupid" questions with impunity and encourages catalogers to think and rationalize why they do what they do the way they do. There were two prevailing answers to those questions: "I don't know" and "We've always done it this way". On the other hand, some people had ideas for how to do things more efficiently and they were eager to try it. Encouraged by those opinions and having a fresh perspective on the workflow, prompted Helen to approach Chair of TS, Doris Helfer, with a proposal for the reorganization. Doris Helfer welcomed the initiative and thus Oviatt library's TS department embarked on the road for change. The Reorganization Committee (the Committee) was formed, consisting of key personnel from all functional areas of Technical Services and chaired by the Cataloging Coordinator.

The process of reorganization at the Oviatt Library could be characterized by three R's: Review, Revise and Reorganize. Perhaps sharing some of the lessons we learned along the way will help others create an effective roadmap for implementing change in their organization.

Obtaining the support of library administration prior to launching the change process was vital. Doing so gave the Committee the authority and mandate to talk to people across various departments and request their cooperation and assistance in implementing the changes.

As mentioned earlier, a few members of the Cataloging unit were open to re-assessing their workflow and introducing improvements. However, the majority of staff members felt threatened by and wary of anything that would disrupt the status quo. There was, naturally, uncertainty in knowing what to expect from the new Cataloging Coordinator. The impending budget crisis in California and, consequently, at CSUN did not facilitate the establishment of trust in a reorganization. Employees were essentially concerned about job security and therefore resisted change within the department. It was crucial to open the lines of communication and explain the goal of the reorganization process to the staff by painting a big picture and underscoring the importance of staff's role in carrying out the library mission. Obtaining staff buy-in and their cooperative and candid participation required that they first feel safe.

Having staff on board, we performed a detailed workflow study. To create a complete picture and identify potential areas for improvement, we conducted internal and external reviews of our operations. The Committee identified the priority processes (e.g., the *monograph workflow*) and interviewed every staff member involved in the cycle. Typical interview questions included:

Describe in detail what you do on a daily basis?

Is there anything in your workflow that does not make sense to you?

Have you ever wondered why can't we do this differently?

Do we need to keep every step in a multi step process, or can a shortcut be created?

The survey of the external landscape was particularly important because many of the internal processes are determined by outside circumstances. As a state institution, CSUN is held accountable to auditing requirements and state regulations which define many financial procedures. However, the state requirements and the work of TS have not been synchronized for many years. For example, it was discovered that we no longer needed to keep records on the ethnicity of business-owners for the book vendors we use, or send out and file forms certifying a "drug-free workplace."

Numerous hours were dedicated to comply with these outdated procedures; these were numerous hours not used elsewhere and translated into wasted dollars.

The other major factor affecting daily workflow is technology. In addition to software upgrades, how do we keep up with other technological advances? This question raises the issue of staff vs. librarians. At CSUN, librarian positions are tenure-track, so librarians are required to attend professional conferences and satisfy the tenure requirements. However, daily work in TS is performed by staff, who do not routinely have the exposure to the latest developments in the industry. There had been a disconnect, especially in the Acquisitions section, between professional-level knowledge and standard workflow.

In order to explore all options, including outsourcing, in optimizing TS operations, we performed a cost analysis of cataloging and materials processing. We considered implementing PromptCat (OCLC) cataloging and shelf-ready services from our approval vendors, Blackwell and Yankee Book Peddler (YBP). Once we had figures on the actual cost of doing business, we were able to determine if outsourcing was an efficient option. After detailed analysis of the cataloging-to-shelf cycle, we compared our in-house cost with the vendors' cost. In our case the costs were about equal, so there was no savings in outsourcing. By the same token, it would introduce substantial savings in turnaround time, thus improving service to our users at no additional cost to us.

Revise

When we began the process of reorganization, the Cataloging unit had about three month backlog of books received on approval, with most titles having a Library of Congress record available from OCLC. In order to expedite cataloging of these items, the Cataloging Coordinator re-examined and streamlined the procedures for copy cataloging. Old procedures had a lot of excessive verification built into them, and a number of steps could be eliminated; for example, we discontinued verifying the size of a book, editing punctuation in the record, and shelf listing. It was determined to be more efficient to correct an occasional duplicate call number when it is detected by Circulation. The old procedures were in place for many years and staff were used to them. Many times Heinrich heard the comment "it only takes a second"; however, those seconds add up into minutes, and minutes into hours. We changed our load tables in order to automate the remaining record editing. The load tables were adjusted to strip out "foreign fields," like non-LC subject headings. As a result, within a month we achieved a 50% increase in productivity by simply revising copy–cataloging procedures. Automating cataloging by implementing PromptCat was still to come!

We looked into eliminating duplication, such as the repeated searching of the same title along the materials movement cycle. Despite of years of changing technology and modernization, there still existed unnecessary, tasks held over from many years ago. At the library, we continued to stripe the edges of periodicals with red ink for easy identification during the bag checks. Exit detectors replaced the bag checks long ago, but the procedures were not adjusted accordingly. Another, more high-tech example was the creation of a local authority record for every heading that did not have a record in National Authority File, even for the headings that did not have cross-references. This rule was a vestige of an old integrated library system (ILS) requirement but, as with the periodical striping, those practices were never questioned by staff and came up to light only during the reorganization. Examples like that prompted a tongue-in-cheek motto from Cataloging Coordinator: *Less work, not more people!*

In addition to the specific changes in the workflow, we needed to adjust the quality standards to correspond to reality. This method is especially important for cataloging. Now that so much of imperfect publishers' and vendors' metadata flows into the catalog, it's not worth editing and massaging to perfection every record that comes from OCLC and bringing it to the standards of olden times. "There is no reason why the data model currently in operation in academic libraries to continually fix, update, and localize bibliographic records should be maintained" notes Eden (2008). In most cases, we will provide better service by having more records that are "good enough," rather than fewer records of perfect quality.

To make changes that would have the biggest impact, we adhered to the principle of "low hanging fruit." First and foremost, we focused on changes that were easy to make but yielded big results. For example, we started by making changes to copy cataloging, which constitutes about 80% of the Cataloging unit's workflow.

Maximizing the use of staff expertise was the cornerstone of the reorganization. As was revealed during the workflow study, experienced and highly skilled staff spent a lot of time on tasks that could be delegated to personnel in more appropriate categories. Therefore, we shifted tasks for which we could use templates, constant and automatically populated data to less skilled staff and began fully utilizing expert staff for challenging tasks.

Providing cross training enabled us to put effort where it was most needed and distribute the workload more efficiently; there is no time wasted when someone else can do the job. This approach helped us promote "one-touch handling," where we aimed to reduce passing of an item through the least number of hands, ideally one.

Oviatt Library TS consists of people with various backgrounds and levels of technological acumen. Not surprisingly, trust in technology emerged as an issue. For example, it has been a long-standing practice to claim periodicals we receive from EBSCO by corresponding via email with an EBSCO representative, as personal contact was considered more reliable that system-generated claiming. Personal contact provided a "paper" trail and confirmation. Our latest ILS performs electronic claiming directly into the EBSCO portal, with no need for correspondence. We invited an EBSCO representative to demonstrate the function and illustrate the claims reporting feature. Despite initial reservations, the new auto claiming feature worked flawlessly, saving TS employee labor and cutting down on turnaround time. As a bonus, we convinced some technological skeptics along the way.

Reorganize

The consolidation of related functions reduced fragmentation and provided tighter control over the affected workflows. For example, cataloging of government documents was split between two people, according to the publication format: print versions were handled by the Government Document Specialist and electronic format items were cataloged by the Serials Cataloger. We eliminated this division by assigning all government documents cataloging to the Government Document Specialist. It cleared the confusion of where to place a request for cataloging and improved management of government documents collection.

Communication is important in creating an efficient workflow. During the workflow study, it became apparent that there was a breakdown in communication between the Acquisitions and Cataloging units. This led to unnecessary steps in the workflow that drained resources, but did not yield results. For example, Acquisitions staff intended to help Cataloging find a title in the catalog by writing a 10-digit bibliographic record number on every purchasing slip that came with a book. But Cataloging never used that number! They were searching the items by title and ISBN and never relied on the record number that Acquisitions painstakingly took time to write down. (Now, after the implemented shelf-ready options, Cataloging searches by just scanning the barcode.)

The division of the department into numerous sub-units, such as Continuations, Firm Orders, Approval Orders, etc., led to the lack of communication, fragmentation and duplication of functions. With lines blurring between the TS functions, we were able to merge small sub-units into the bigger ones which also allowed us to absorb a couple of supervisory positions vacated through attrition.

Trusting the expertise of colleagues emerged as an important issue. Confidence in a colleague's work helps distribute the workflow evenly and eliminates double-checking because there is no expectation that somebody will make a mistake. A flagrant example in CSUN's case: the claiming of periodicals included verification that issues displayed as "late" or "not-yet-received" in the check-in card were indeed not received and instead mistakenly shelved without checking-in. A student assistant with a list of not-received issues made weekly runs to check the shelves and verify that the issues were not actually there. This has been done in order to avoid claiming the received issues by mistake. We adopted the new default thought that information displayed in the check-in record is indeed accurate; i.e. an issue that was not checked-in was, in fact, not received. Stopping the control runs saved the unit an hour of employee time per week, which translates into 52 hours a year saved.

We abandoned perfectionism! TS personnel everywhere are well known for their meticulousness and drive for perfection. What it may develop into (and in CSUN's case it did), is a steadfast determination to avert a mistake by building a complex workflow to prevent that mistake from happening. However, it may be more efficient to correct an occasional mistake when it occurs than to build an entire workflow to prevent it. A 5% chance for an error should not define 95% of work. "Our infatuation with order, perfection, and control does not work in today's information environment" (p. 38).

For the changes to be effective, it was important to ensure continuity of efficiencies throughout the cycle. We worked very hard to expedite cataloging only to discover that the increased volume of books cataloged created a bottleneck in materials processing. This invalidated our efforts to speed the availability of new materials to our users. It also spurred us to implement shelf-ready services from our vendors.

Once we identified the areas for improvement, be it in the workflow or in our mindset, it became clear that we needed a method to continue this type of imperative change that improves our service. The department's workflow "is a dynamic process that require [sic] constant re-examination" (Roitberg, 2000). In order for such a technology-rich department as Technical Services to function at an optimal level, it is crucial that the responsibility for knowing about new processes and technologies and introducing efficiencies is part of someone's job duties. To avoid stagnation and the perpetuation of outdated practices, someone has to attend conferences, subscribe to the online lists, and read the latest articles.

Technology

Technology is the foundation of the workflow in Technical Services. Therefore, leveraging existing technology and knowing and taking advantage of the advances in the field are the key issues for a reorganization. The following are some of the time- and resource-saving changes that we introduced by leveraging available technologies (see Figures 1 and 2):

- Activated OpenURL capabilities in the portals of our two approval vendors, Blackwell and YBP. This enabled us to check for duplication between new selections in the vendor portal and our catalog from one-point entry.

- Added more data (such as list price, fund code, initials, etc.) to the vendor output records to eliminate editing each record in our ILS to add those elements.

- Changed the load tables in Millennium to automatically enrich records with local elements.

- Utilized batch processing to apply constant data, delete or activate holdings in OCLC.

Finally, straightforward things like providing needed equipment made a difference. Some of our staff do not have printers at their workstations, so many labels were hand-written or the labeling process was broken down in two steps between printer-haves and have-nots.

Collaboration with Vendors

Vendors are crucial part of work of TS. First, we buy books and receive invoices from them. Second, they enable many of the changes that can optimize TS functions. Creating partnerships with vendors facilitates the implementation of the latest advances in the electronic information exchange. In the case of CSUN, working closely with Blackwell, YBP, OCLC and EBSCO gave us a tremendously advantaged.

Below are some of the workflow changes that helped propel Oviatt Library Technical Services into the age of optimized processes and improved efficiency:

- Paced spending evenly throughout the year. This spread the workload of TS more evenly throughout the year by setting milestones of spending for bibliographers.

- Began ordering from fewer "firm" vendors. Scouring large numbers of vendors in search of the best discounts may not justify the time spent looking for those discounts.

- Discontinued outdated auditing trail practices.

- Simplified and streamlined procedures.

- Automated copy cataloging by implementing WorldCat Partners program.

- Discontinued unnecessary practices.

- Reassigned staff to leverage expertise in needed areas.

- Reduced claiming by implementing a time limit. If we do not receive an issue after the window for claiming expired, chances are we are not going to get it, so instead we order the issue from a loose-issue vendor. Time is saved and the user receives the issue much sooner.

- Reduced filing by reviewed filing procedures. For example, we were processing and filing government documents shipping lists before discovering that they are available online.

- Simplified physical processing. Many of our practices date back to the times when they were affordable. For example, we added a tip-in sheet to every paperback in order to paste on a date-due slip, even if the half-title page could be used.

- Outsourced some materials processing.

These are other changes that were implemented during the workflow study and reorganization produced some tangible results:

- Manual transactions saved: 28,000

- Bibliographic searches saved: 14,000

- Time savings in Acquisitions: 11 weeks

- Time savings in Cataloging with PromptCat: 11 weeks

- Overall savings: 5 months of FTE time

- Eliminated backlog of newly purchased materials

- Merger of two positions into one (through attrition)

- Reduction in student employee budget in processing: 50%

- Reduction in turnaround time in receipt-to-shelf cycle: 75%

Conclusion

The value of library services is greater than the sum of its individual service areas. This is especially true for Technical Services. TS is not only an integral part of the library's mission to serve but is key to the provision of many of the library's high-demand, electronic resources. "Library technology provides the power to maximize the use of library resources… [enabling] patrons to search every virtual nook and cranny of the library and increase the likelihood of satisfying a user's needs" (Heinrich, 2007, p. 218).

More than most departments in the library, TS feels the pressure of bridging the two realities, print and virtual one, without losing the speed or diminishing customer satisfaction. With shrinking resources and growing costs, how do we maintain the equilibrium?

At CSUN we made a successful attempt to look within for the answer.

References

Diaz, J.R. & Pintozzi, C. (1999). Helping teams work: lessons learned from the University of Arizona library reorganization. *Library Administration & Management. 13*(1), 27-36. Retrieved January 26, 2009, from Library Literature & Information Full Text database.

Deeken, J., Webb, P.L., & Taffurelli, V. (2008). We are all winners: training silents to millenials to work as a team. *The Serials Librarian. 54* (3-4), 211-216. Retrieved January 18, 2009, from Haworth Press database.

Eden, B.L. (2008). Ending the status quo: the future of information organization. *American Libraries. 39*(3), 38. Retrieved January 18, 2009, from Library Lit & Inf Full Text database.

Heinrich, H, (2007). *E-journal invasion: A cataloger's guide to survival.* Oxford: Chandos Publishing.

Roitberg, N. (2000). The influence of the electronic library on library management: A technological university library experience. *Conference Proceedings: IFLA Council and General Conferecen* (66th, Jerusalem, Israel, August 13-18, 2000). The Hague: IFLA. Retrieved September 23, 2008 at http://www.ifla.org/IV/ifla66/papers/050-132e.htm

Skekel, D. (2008). Ethical, unethical, or benign: technical services decisions and access to information. *Journal of Information Ethics. 17* (1), 20-27. doi: 10.3172/JIE.17.1.20

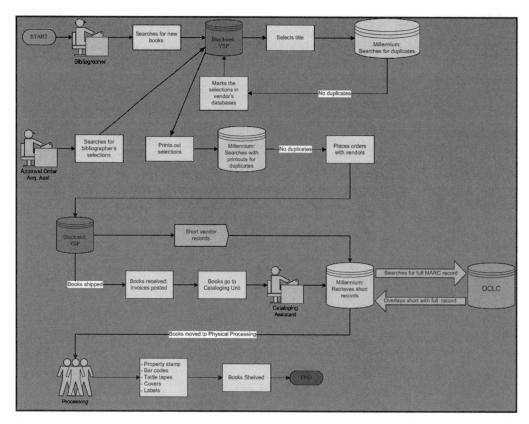

Figure 1: The Approval Ordering Workflow before the implementation of recommendations from the TS reorganization.

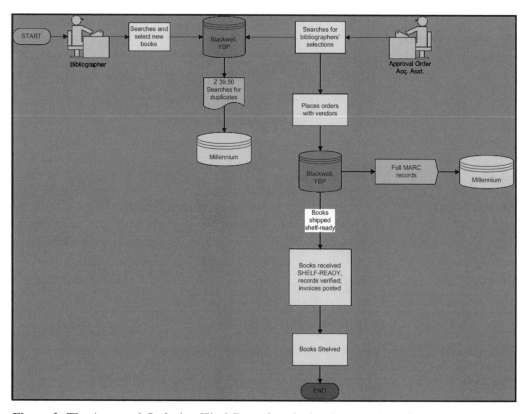

Figure 2: The Approval Ordering Workflow after the implementation of recommendations from the TS reorganization.

PRACTICAL USES OF ACCESS DATABASES IN ACQUISITIONS

Jack Fisher, Acquisitions Librarian, Valdosta State University, Valdosta, Georgia

"Practical Uses of Access Databases in Acquisitions" was presented at the Saturday November 8 morning Innovation Session. Jack Fisher, Acquisitions Librarian at Valdosta State University was the presenter. Since beginning a career in library science in 2002 I have found that Microsoft Access can be intimidating. However, once I learned a little about Access and the ease of constructing tables and data entry forms I found that Access allows the creation of tools to help with, among other acquisitions activities, organizing ordering information, preserving data, and recording financial activity. The session provided some basic, practical ideas in creating Access databases that may serve as a replacement to paper systems, enhance Excel data, and provide a supplement to the ILS.

Initial Database Project

Previously, orders for the acquisitions department were generated by department liaisons on paper cards as seen in Figure 1. In addition, there was a desire to provide an online form to make the data entry easier. The cards were kept in old card catalog drawers and pulled for ordering. I created the database form to mimic the paper card and make data entry easy. I also added fields that not only allowed for sorting by department, but also suggested vendor, priority, requester, and ordering information to name but a few. The data entry form is seen in Figure 2.

Figure 1: Order card

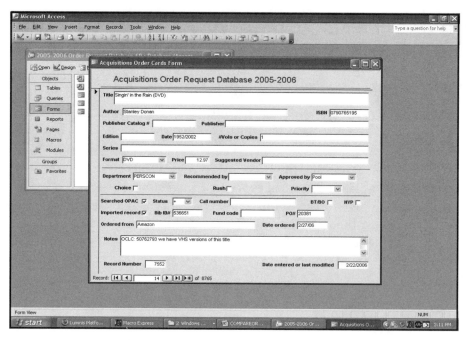

Figure 2: Access database data entry form

Over the years the order database has remained much the same but I have added additional fields to allow for quicker sorting and reports. Some additional fields that have been helpful are "Not Yet Published," and "Choice Card." To make the database accessible online I created an email group that only authorized liaisons have access to through their email password. They can download an empty file to their computer, enter data, and then upload the file back to the group. I then copy the data into a master database I have for each fiscal year. Some liaisons don't have Access installed on their computers so I have an Excel version that copies easily into Access.

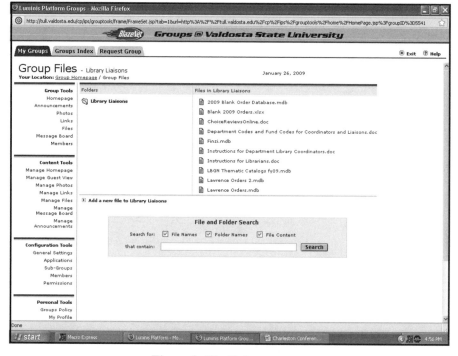

Figure 3: The liaison group

Other Database Projects

Once the order database was running smoothly I worked on another paper form to database project. The original purpose was to generate a monthly bindery list. Previously, a monthly pulling of paper forms from a file of alphabetized journal titles generated the list. A monthly bindery list was then typed and the paper forms were returned to the file. I took the data from the bindery forms and added some other fields from another paper file form called the "Periodical Work Sheet." This data included fields such as ISSN, frequency, and supplement information. Now, as publication frequently changes or print titles are cancelled, I can easily update the monthly binding list.

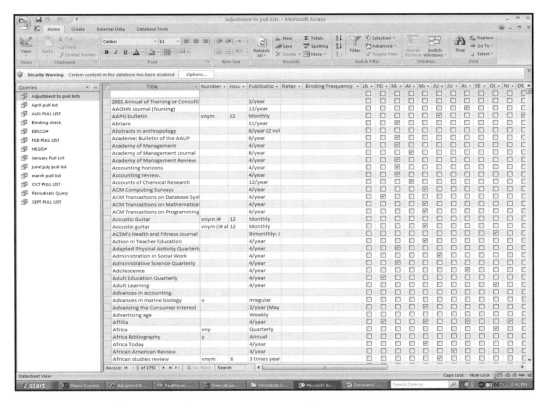

Figure 4: Form for changing or selecting a monthly bindery list

The acquisitions department used to process gifts. That workflow has now changed but the process used to include a lot of manual sorting and typing. Gift books were alphabetized on a book cart and a list was typed in the MS Word. Then the books were selected either for addition to the collection or disposal. Another list was then typed for the donor. By using Access I was able to sort titles alphabetically, by donor, and whether they were accepted or not. Generating a list for a donor letter was a matter of adjusting a query. I was also able to sort by format type for statistical reporting.

Another opportunity to use an Access database was the archives of the Georgia Library Association. Odum Library at Valdosta State holds the archives and I have volunteered to serve as the archivist. There is a description of the archives but no detailed listing of the contents of the many boxes. I created a database that would be easy for students or interns to use yet contain enough information that I would be able to find requested material. The main feature of this database is a memo field that contains the folder or box contents. If the folder or box contents were long we could type this in Microsoft Word and then paste it into the memo field; however one issue we had to deal with was formatting marks that appeared in the text when we copied. These were simple to edit out. To make searching easy we all use a consistent date format of mm/dd/yy.

Since Access worked so well with copying information into a memo field I created a database to use as storage for email content. We use purchasing cards in the acquisitions department and I frequently get emails from online purchases that can serve as receipts or invoices. Each fiscal year I create a database to store these financial transaction messages. These emails are frequently large file sizes and so storing them off the email server allows me to keep within the limits of my inbox. Frequently these emails have provided backup when the invoice is not included in the shipment. I now have an additional Access database of non-financial emails that I keep as an archive. I also keep a database archive of wiki message that I receive via email.

Two of the most useful Access databases I create each year are the EBSCO subscriptions and changes to EBSCO subscriptions. I use the Excel spreadsheet from EBSCO of all the titles we receive to instantly create a database of titles that is easy to sort for department reports, formats, etc. I also use Access to create a database for periodical changes. Reports from both these databases can be converted easily into a Word document and printed or sent easily via email attachment.

One of the most recent databases I constructed is the Visa card and check request database. This serves as our electronic log, replacing individual paper logs, of purchases that the department makes. Figure 5 shows the various fields in the data entry form. One very useful aspect is the boxes that allow you to enter multiple shipments as they are received from a single order. I can also note the use of a special fund and then when the order is complete.

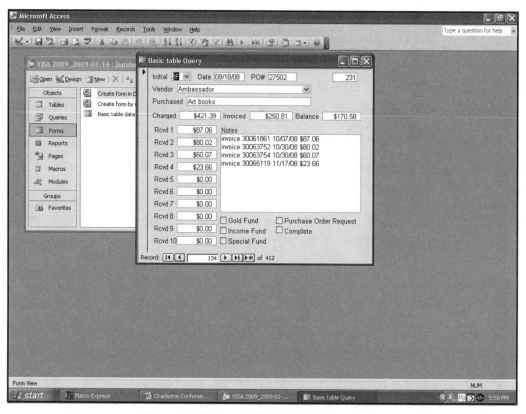

Figure 5: Various fields in data entry form

One special feature of this database is the use of calculating fields on the form. Unlike Excel, which is designed for calculations, this is a little complicated. The calculations appear only on the form or on the datasheet view of the form as seen is Figure 6.

Microsoft Access - [Basic table Query]

Initial	Date	PO#	Vendor	Purchased	Charged	Invoiced	Balance	Rcvd 1	Rcvd 2
SP	08/13/08	27231	Amazon	Ten seeds	$78.08	$78.08	$0.00	$78.08	$0.00
SP	08/13/08	27232	Amazon	A Lark Ascends...	$54.49	$54.49	$0.00	$54.49	$0.00
SP	01/12/08	29366	Amazon	6 books	$161.37	$161.37	$0.00	$69.37	$92.00
JF	10/23/08	28308	Ambassador	Psychology titles	$2,727.80	$2,558.85	$168.95	$79.57	$1,239.21
JF	09/17/08	27501	Ambassador	4 ACED titles	$565.76	$565.76	$0.00	$417.79	$147.97
JF	09/04/08	27293	Ambassador	MGED titles	$343.39	$343.39	$0.00	$25.36	$60.25
JF	09/18/08	27502	Ambassador	Art books	$421.39	$250.81	$170.58	$87.06	$80.02
JF	09/18/08	27508	Ambassador	Chemistry titles	$1,552.90	$1,438.88	$114.02	$193.71	$1,245.17
JF	09/18/08	27509	Ambassador	Chemistry titles	$677.81	$677.81	$0.00	$286.36	$306.27
JF	09/19/08	27546	Ambassador	CLT titles	$592.47	$0.00	$592.47	$0.00	$0.00
JF	11/14/08	28866	Ambassador	AA studies titles	$155.59	$155.59	$0.00	$155.59	$0.00
JF	11/14/08	28861	Ambassador	Psychology titles	$424.50	$388.07	$36.43	$388.07	$0.00
JF	09/29/08	27757	American Mathematical		$361.25	$361.21	$0.04	$361.21	$0.00
JF	07/09/08	27147	American Orff-Schulwerk	Subscription	$45.00	$45.00	$0.00	$45.00	$0.00
JF	09/16/08	27472	American Psychological	books	$681.40	$681.40	$0.00	$681.40	$0.00
JF	09/16/08	27474	American Psychological	DVDs	$4,559.22	$4,559.22	$0.00	$4,559.22	$0.00
JF	09/16/08	27469	American Psychological	DVD	$219.89	$219.89	$0.00	$219.89	$0.00
JF	09/19/08	27521	American Psychological		$0.00	$0.00	$0.00	$0.00	$0.00
JF	11/21/08	29137	American Society of Ass		$76.70	$76.70	$0.00	$76.70	$0.00
JF	09/11/08	27415	American String Teache	order 16792	$337.70	$337.70	$0.00	$337.70	$0.00
JF	11/14/08	28887	Annenberg Media	Exploring the world of music	$295.90	$295.90	$0.00	$295.90	$0.00
JF	08/18/09	27503	Art Video World	4 dvds	$79.85	$79.85	$0.00	$79.85	$0.00
JF	07/29/08	27168	ASCD	3 DVD series	$362.00	$362.00	$0.00	$362.00	$0.00
JF	09/19/08	27549	ASCD	Differentiated literacy	$25.95	$25.95	$0.00	$25.95	$0.00
JF	10/23/08	28310	Ashgate	Driver behaviour and training	$404.46	$404.46	$0.00	$127.46	$277.00
JF	10/21/08	28217	B & T	International whos who in classical	$363.35	$363.35	$0.00	$363.35	$0.00
SP	09/03/08	27292	B & T	10 books	$528.30	$528.30	$0.00	$528.30	$0.00
SP	09/04/08	27296	B & T	10 books	$303.83	$303.83	$0.00	$303.83	$0.00
SP	09/04/08	27295	B & T	9 books	$386.38	$386.38	$0.00	$386.38	$0.00
SP	09/04/08	27294	B & T	10 books	$265.93	$265.93	$0.00	$265.93	$0.00
SP	08/01/08	27192	Baker & Taylor	Bizarre Bugs	$15.17	$15.17	$0.00	$15.17	$0.00
SP	10/01/08	27816	Baker & Taylor		$222.11	$222.11	$0.00	$222.11	$0.00

Record: 134 of 412

Datasheet View

Figure 6: Data sheet view

The use of Access databases has made my job much easier because of the ease with which I can sort and organize data and create statistical reports. Access does have some weak points. I can't currently upgrade to Access 2007 because it is not compatible with the current version of Voyager, our ILS system that relies on Access 2003 to generate reports. Calculations are tricky. Changing or adding to the database fields each fiscal year has created some problems in moving data between databases. I wanted to have multiple users and use Access on our network but our network was not reliable and we have worked around that issue with external storage that the department shares. It is possible to just duplicate paper forms in Access and receive benefits but a little extra planning of the fields you might use and the sorting or reports you want to get as a result of all your data should drive the construction of your database tables. I urge the reader to take an Access workshop or purchase one of the basic software instruction books and make use of this wonderful tool.

Brief Bibliography Used in the Presentation

Atinmo, Morayo Ibironke (2007). Setting up a computerized catalog and distribution database of alternative format materials for blind and visually impaired persons in Nigeria. *Library Trends*, 55(4), 830-846.

> Without the assistance of a national library, this project sought to audit the materials in various formats available to the blind and visually impaired. The research project sought to use the database to create a catalog of collections, analyze the collections by subject for strengths and weaknesses, determine all organizations serving the blind and visually impaired, and profile the use of these resources. A template of appropriate fields was created using Microsoft Access. An ADA compliant website became the front door of the database http://www.alvi-laris.org. Since the creation of this database users have been able to find easier access to the materials they need. Although this article does not delve into the actual creation and workings of the Access database, it was inspiring to read of the use of off the shelf technology to help people in need.

DePalo, Lisa, & Rossignol, Lucien R. (2001). Navigating the waves of change in serials management: employing MS Access database management software. *Serials Librarian*, 40(3-4), 267-270.

> The authors describe a workshop that emphasized the use of Microsoft Access in a library with limited time and financial resources for the purpose of a serials project at College of Staten Island. Data from a paper survey was entered into the database. In her presentation DePalo pointed out the information from Excel and even Word can be imported into Access where data can then be manipulated and then retrieved in various combinations. She notes that data input can be labor intensive depending on the quantity and original format. Careful construction of the data tables is also important. Access allows more specific or narrower querying than Excel for example and the user can easily manipulate the appearance of the reports generated by the query.

Doering, William, & Chilton, Galadriel (2008). A locally created ERM: how and why we did it. *Computers in Libraries*, 28(8), 46-48.

> Doering and Chilton needed a basic, inexpensive, yet effective ERM for the University of Wisconsin La Crosse Murphy Library. The web site http://murphylibrary.uwlax.edu/erm/ allows anyone to use their work. The article describes the process of creating the ERM. They are pleased with the results as the ERM was developed quickly, cheaply, has no vendor fees, and yet it provides reports and functionality that help the Murphy Library track the management of their electronic resources. The "before and after" chart on page 47 of the article is especially informative. They have concluded that although perhaps not as robust or complex as a commercial product their ERM is a vast improvement over past practice and may be especially useful for smaller libraries that choose not to purchase a vendor management system.

Reichardt, Karen (2000). Using Microsoft Access for journal collection management. *Serials Librarian*, 37(4), 69-78.

> The article shows how an extensive serial and database review was conducted at The Citadel. Funds, space, and use via the curriculum were prime reasons for this review. The Daniel Library study used a similar journal review database developed at the University of Florida Health Sciences Center Library as a model. The team points out that Access was already had other uses in the library including but not limited to acquisitions process-

ing and ad hoc reporting. The article goes on to show the creation of the database tables and then outlines the faculty review process. The project allowed for a 50% reduction in the budget for the reviewed titles.

Richardson, Joshua (2005). Can't afford a big database application?: MS Access works well in smaller organizations. *Information Outlook*, 9(1), 35-37.

Richardson's article describes the creation of a catalog of resources using Access rather than more powerful server-based database applications such as MySQL. The advantages of using Access in this application was that it is inexpensive, it was quick to set up (because much of the data was already entered into an Access database), and it was unknown whether a skilled cataloger would be available to manage the catalog in the future. Richardson worked to adapt the existing database and then created tables to support various functions such as serial holdings and patron information. Part of the adapting involved utilizing only core MARC information. ASP, Active Server Page, code was added to create a functioning online catalog with circulation management. Reports available from the system have also allowed collection analysis. Growth in the Anshen + Allen organization has created some doubt as to the scalability of the use of Access in the long term.

Robbins, Laura Pope (2002). Creating an integrated periodicals listing using Microsoft Access and ASP scripts. *OCLC Systems & Services*, 18(2) 24-31.

This article presents steps on creating a web accessible database of journals from both the physical collection and aggregators at Dowling College Library. http://library.dowling.edu/ Search page - http://www.dowling.edu/library/journaldb/jrnl.html

Taglienti, Paolina, & Srivastava, Sandhya D. (2002). Reinventing the wheel: the Microsoft Access alternative. *Against the Grain,* 14(2) 20-26.

Taglienti writes about the library acquisitions department and their work with Access in designing databases to handle ordering, receiving, and invoicing of library materials as well as check-in of periodicals and claiming. Previously paper methods and Excel were used. The database use proved successful particularly in report flexibility however there were networking issues. The article delves into the construction of various pieces of the database and has screen shots for illustration. Work progressed into a second generation version that collapsed multiple forms onto one for ease of data entry and update. In addition, a monograph database was created. The department considered the work with Access time well spent in creating efficiency of department functions.

USING BLOG TECHNOLOGY TO GET THEIR ATTENTION

Audrey Powers, Associate Librarian, Research Services and Collections, University of South Florida, Tampa, Florida

Cheryl McCoy, University Librarian, University of South Florida, Tampa, Florida

Gina Clifford, Web Administrator, University of South Florida, Tampa, Florida

Sue Polanka, Head of Reference and Instruction, University of South Florida, Tampa, Florida

The University of South Florida is a metropolitan university with a large student population and the academic library has an extensive collection of resources. In order to better serve the research needs of the faculty and graduate students, the Research Services and Collections librarians began to use blog technology to inform faculty of subject specific collection development issues. Use of blog technology enabled communication with discipline specific faculty groups. It also captured the attention of the faculty, provided librarians with an outreach tool, reminded faculty about existing library services and served as evidence to faculty that librarians are proactive on their behalf. The blogs are used as newsletters and are distributed electronically on a regular basis. Two of four subject specific blogs that are currently being published are STM News @ USF Libraries and CVPA News @ USF Libraries.

The blog, or newsletter, STM News @ USF Libraries, provides a forum in which to communicate with the science, technology and medical faculty. It was started at the time when participation in a national science survey was impending and became a primary avenue for disseminating information about the survey. Upon complete examination of these disciplines, it became evident that we were in a position to facilitate interdisciplinary communication and enhance research collaboration through this blog.

The development of another blog, CVPA News @ USF Libraries was specifically targeted for faculty and graduate students in the College of Visual and Performing Arts. The disciplines included are Architecture, Art, Art History, Music, Theatre and Dance. The goal for the development of this blog was to raise awareness of new resources, begin a dialogue with faculty about collection development work and communicate collection development initiatives to the faculty.

Each month these blogs are distributed to faculty in the disciplines that are targeted; therefore, subject specific library news is generated and distributed in a timely fashion. Each newsletter includes new acquisitions received during the month, updates and training schedules for databases, and reminders of existing library services. It also provides a forum for collection development projects such as the Information Seeking Behavior of Science Researchers, Center for Research Libraries proposals, and library surveys that require faculty feedback with the goal toward enhancing resources and services.

The benefits of using blog technology to advance library initiatives is that it communicates discipline specific library news, disseminates information efficiently and effectively, and creates an overall awareness of the library. From the collection development perspective, it disseminates collection development information and initiatives which encourage a deeper understanding of how collection development work is done, engages faculty in the collection development process, and conveys the organizational structure of collection development to the faculty.

Needless to say, there are challenges that every editor of a blog recognizes when working with a group of people who are posting information to the blog. Some of these challenges include obtaining consistent participation from other librarian bloggers, keeping up with posting information in a timely manner, distributing the blog regularly, blog design impediments and software issues.

In order to disseminate these blogs, faculty are emailed a link to the current issue of the blog with a corresponding Table of Contents with links to each posting. Use of RSS feeds is encouraged. Each issue is announced on the library web page under "News" and the blogs can be searched and found using Google. Because we are unable to obtain a list of graduate students in each discipline, faculty are requested to forward the email with a link to the current issue to their students.

To date, the USF Library has four subject specific blogs: Visual & Performing Arts, Science & Technology, Education and Business. Usage statistics have proven that these blogs are consistently read by a large number of faculty. You can access these blogs by linking to them as follows:

Visual & Arts	CVPA News @ USF Libraries http://usflibraries.typepad.com/arts
Science & Technology	STM News @ USF Libraries http://usflibraries.typepad.com/stmnews/
Education	The EdLib Report @ USF Libraries http://usflibraries.typepad.com/edlibreport/
Business	The Bull: **Bu**siness **L**ibrary **L**inks http://usflibraries.typepad.com/businessnews/

Why Blogs? – Gina Clifford

Unfortunately, many people think of blogs as online outlets for extended political rants, streams of consciousness or pages full of personal minutiae.

Fortunately, blogs are really just mini-websites and come with powerful content management systems built-in. If you call a blog by another name, say "newsletter," "website," or "portal," it is a legitimate business tool with lots to offer.

Think of your content as the trunk of a large tree with deep roots, which represents your organizational knowledge. Now, think of the direct branches of the tree as avenues for connecting with your constituency. On one branch there are built-in RSS feeds. Another branch holds the comment management tools. Other main branches contain tagging and categorizing capabilities, a built-in Google search and team authoring. These branches ultimately support your online communities, connecting you with your target audience and providing your organization with a neatly organized, searchable and categorized knowledge management system. Custom-built websites containing all of these features cost thousands of dollars, not counting the IT infrastructure necessary to support them.

Which Blog Solution?

First of all, let us assume that your primary goal is not to become a professional blogger who gets paid to blog. Blog solutions for people in the professional blogging realm are outside the scope of this paper. We will focus on blogs that target a specific audience within a university community, are highly specialized, and do not host advertisements. In their purest form, blogs can be simply more personalized and focused "extensions" of academic websites.

Three hosted blog products that fit well for our purposes are Blogger, WordPress and TypePad. Hosted blogs are blogs that host your content so that your blog's default URL has the hosted company's name in it. Each hosted blog product has benefits and drawbacks, and choosing the appropriate hosted blog is sometimes a matter of personal choice and circumstance.

If you have little technical web design skills or resources, Blogger.com provides some basic design templates and widgets that a novice can easily add. Blogger's "What You See is What You Get" (WYSIWYG) editor also allows novices to change font colors, font faces, etc. WordPress.com is much more restrictive. Although WordPress.com does provide basic design templates, by default, it doesn't allow users to add many widgets, change font, background or font colors. For a small fee, WordPress.com does allow users to change the cascading style sheet, allowing for a more customized design, but there is no WYSIWYG editor to assist the novice. However, WordPress does have a fairly nice statistics package built into it, so page view and referrer statistics are just a click away. Blogger doesn't come with such a simple statistics solution, but users can configure the Blogger blog to use a Google Analytics account. For those with web design skills, the TypePad Pro account is by far the best choice. Although not free, TypePad Pro offers almost unlimited possibilities for blog designs, including customized navigation, integrated Google custom searches, complete control of cascading style sheets, and many technical "hacks." TypePad offers basic, built-in statistics, but technical users can set up tracking with Google Analytics. TypePad lets users create unlimited blogs through the same account, but allows only one administrator account. As a result, maintenance issues (design changes, adding new categories, and creating Typelists) can only be completed using the single administrator account. If you need complete control of blog design/branding and have good web design skills, TypePad is tough to beat.

Essential Design Elements

Blogger, WordPress.com and TypePad all provide methods for adding the following important blog features: RSS Feed link, Google search box and an "About" page. However, Blogger doesn't seem to allow split or excerpted posts and it doesn't provide a method for "featuring" a post. WordPress and TypePad both have these useful features.

The RSS feed link is very important because it allows your viewers to "subscribe" to your updates without visiting your blog directly. When you add an important new post, your viewers see your headline in their RSS reader, click on the headline link and are viewing your blog without even remembering your blog URL. The search box is another important element on your blog. Both the RSS link and the search box should be placed near the top of your blog. Keep in mind that if you have chosen to keep your blog private, Google won't index it and the search feature won't return any results from your blog.

Content Presentation

Whether writing copy for a website or a blog, there are several key strategies for making your information easier to read. Usability tests demonstrate that web viewers determine within 5 seconds whether or not to continue reading your website or blog. Bob Johnson of Bob Johnson Consulting recommends some simple ways to make your content more readable. First, write short titles, short sentences and short paragraphs. Use bullet points to outline major ideas and use meaningful images to break up text. Finally, avoid using vague words to describe important ideas. These practices also set the stage for optimizing your content for search engines, which will be discussed in the next section.

Text is most readable when black text is contrasted against white or a very light background color. Keep users from squinting to read your text by using 10-12pt. serif fonts.

Basic Search Engine Optimization

Many times, people start their quest for information with a Google search. Even your blog readers may prefer to start with a Google search rather than typing your blog URL into the location bar. For this reason, it is important to take a few steps to improve your rankings in a Google search result set.

Within your short titles, always use descriptive rather than vague words. If you are posting about a specific book title, use the actual book title in the blog post title instead of something generic like "New Book."

Next, be sure to use the same key words within the body of the post. Reusing your key words lets search engines know that these are the important words to index within your post.

Within blog posts, link to information located on your main website and provide links from your main website back to your blog. Frequently link to past, related posts from your current posts, too.

Post to your blog regularly. If you post less than once per month, your readers (and search engines) may lose interest in your blog.

Once you have established your blog and have a regular update schedule, ask others to link to your blog.

Read related blogs and post thoughtful comments. Usually, you can post a link back to your blog within a comment to provide readers with broader information or a different perspective on a subject.

Create a descriptive title for your blog and pages and add a blog description using descriptive key words.

Using Blog Technology to Get Their Attention – Sue Polanka

No Shelf Required was developed to disseminate information about the growing eBook market to librarians and publishers. Specifically it was developed to:

Create an awareness of ebooks, platforms, new technologies, business models, aggregators, etc.

Share ideas and opinions about ebooks and ebook technology

Provide a resource for those implementing ebook collections

No Shelf Required, therefore, is a moderated discussion of the issues surrounding eBooks for librarians and publishers. Sue Polanka serves as the moderator, with several librarians and industry professionals as an advisory board.

Prior to launch, the following items were completed to develop the blog:

• Organized existing eBook content in the form of online articles (got persistent links) and pre-loaded this in an "articles" section.

• Developed poll questions using a widget enabling voting and vote tallies. A poll archive was put in place to keep track of previous polls.

• Solicited board members from various reference publishers/aggregators. Board members were asked to publicize the blog to their clients and add content/comments to the blog.

• Pre-loaded several posts with significant content related to eBooks.

At launch, the blog was marketed via listservs, posts on other blogs, in direct email messages from Board members to clients, and at the ALA conference in the form of business cards and posters at each Board member booth. Additionally, Booklist online, and print, were able to refer/link to the blog since the moderator is on the Reference Books Bulletin Advisory Board.

Benefits of the blog include:

• The Advisory Board was initially able to spread the word and add some content

- RBB/Booklist – my connection with them provided many links to and from Booklist Online, generating lots of traffic

- My University offered to host the blog and offer design and development support to me. They helped me switch the blog from its first home on Blogspot to its new home on WordPress.

- Networking with colleagues about ebooks

Challenges include:

- Stimulating discussion on the blog. Most are info stalkers, not contributors. This led to the discussion to moderate or not moderate. The spammers are evil in blog comments, but does moderation prohibit many from commenting? I stayed with moderation in the end.

- Getting feedback and input from the advisory board. I had hoped they would be more active, but alas, I'm the biggest contributor.

- I Wish I would have done categories instead of a tag cloud. The cloud is out of control!

Technology Used:

- Started on Blogspot, moved to Word Press with various plug-ins because my university wanted to host the page.

- To analyze statistics, we use Google analytics and Feedburner stats on subscribers. From May 1 to October 27, 2008, the blog had 4,858 visits from 3,830 unique visitors.

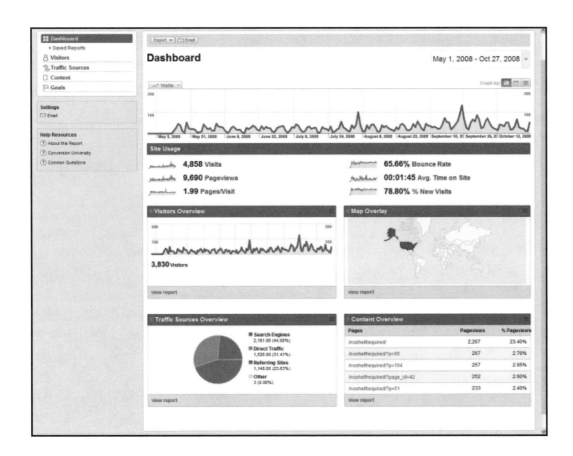

The Charleston Conference is a venue for all types of presentations. This section includes an interesting look at creating better processes to improve services, and what to do with usage statistics.

Miscellaneous

LEARNING TOGETHER: VENDORS AND LIBRARIES CREATING BETTER PROCESSES TO IMPROVE SERVICES

Mildred L. Jackson, Associate Dean for Collections, The University of Alabama

Robin Champieux, Director of Sales and Customer Experience, Blackwell

Beth Holley, Head of Acquisitions, The University of Alabama

Janet Lee-Smeltzer, Head of Cataloging & Metadata Services, The University of Alabama

Introduction

In June 2007, The University of Alabama Libraries began exploring possibilities for new workflows in the Acquisitions and Cataloging departments. Through discussions with a new Associate Dean for Collections, the possibilities for change quickly became apparent. Both acquisitions and cataloging were still using paper intensive processes and had not taken advantage of many of the improvements offered by either Blackwell or OCLC's technology, or the Library's Voyager system. They wanted to, however.

Many opportunities to eliminate repetitive searching in OCLC, paper forms, and printing records that could be better managed electronically quickly became obvious. Some improvements in workflow had been implemented in Acquisitions due to the use of Blackwell's Collection Manager. Collection Manager was used to identify titles for ordering and EDI ordering and invoicing was in place. Many selectors were using electronic slips and notifications, rather than paper slips. The creation of orders remained a primarily manual process, however. Although Collection Manager's electronic Request function was implemented in 2006, orders were still being created with one title per purchase order. The Cataloging Department reorganized a few years ago due to some staffing changes. FastCat and DLC/DLC cataloging moved to Acquisitions at that time. The Cataloging Department previously imported OCLC PromptCat records in batch but ceased using the records when OCLC Connexion was implemented. It was time to examine all processes and determine the future of the departments and their workflow.

Over the summer, the Associate Dean began discussing possibilities for change with John Laraway, our Blackwell Regional Representative. Through those discussions, UA began working with Robin Champieux, then Library Partnership Manager, to conduct an in-depth analysis of workflow across both departments. This partnership became a key element and advantage in the process. Blackwell staff did not treat discussions of workflow as solely connected to ordering from Blackwell though the examples of changes were tied to Collection Manager. Examining the processes related to ordering titles from Blackwell allowed us to begin discussing workflows with other vendors and exploring the technological changes they had been putting in place. We began testing more than just Blackwell services, spreading our testing to vendors such as EBSCO, Harrassowitz and Coutts. The analysis and discussions allowed us to broadly examine services, workflows and reorganization.

The University of Alabama developed several goals for changing processes and procedures:

- Increased efficiencies

- Quicker ordering processes

- Cost savings

- Providing opportunities for staff

- Moving the library forward

Even when change is desired, it can be difficult. Analyzing processes and procedures, as well as implementing changes, has taken almost 18 months. We continue to work to implement changes and to adjust workflows. This article describes how we analyzed and adjusted workflow, how we reorganized staff, and how we carried out the goals listed above and our plans for the coming year.

Blackwell

Blackwell's workflow consulting services are rooted in the understanding that vendors are stakeholders in a library's practices and processes. Our services and consultation can contribute to an institution meeting its goals and successfully implementing change. Conversely, bad service can make achieving success difficult. For instance, when vendors support seemingly inefficient workflows and do not consult with our customers to understand goals and possibly suggest alternatives, we can contribute to higher and unnecessary costs for both the customer and the vendor. This is an unacceptable scenario, especially in our current economic climate.

How do we engage to avoid this outcome? At Blackwell, for both small implementations and large workflow transitions we consult with a library to define and understand its goals and current processes. With this understanding, as well as our valuable knowledge of best practices and system interfaces, we can make service and workflow recommendations that reflect a customers needs, capabilities, and goals. In this capacity, it is important that a vendor does not tie evaluations and recommendations to its services and capabilities. We must focus on customer needs and goals as independent of our company's capabilities.

In September and October 2007, librarians, staff and students in the University of Alabama Libraries' Acquisitions and Cataloging departments created descriptions of their workflow and tasks for Blackwell's analysis. Throughout this process, the Blackwell consultant and Alabama's Associate Dean for Collections communicated often, clarifying the purpose of existing practices and exploring alternatives that are more efficient. In November 2007, Blackwell presented a recommended monographic acquisitions workflow to the AD, Acquisitions, and Cataloging staff. Blackwell's recommendations included the implementation of batched-based EDI ordering via Voyager, OCLC WorldCat Cataloging Partners service to replace title-by-title copy cataloging, and an electronic rather than paper-based system for tracking orders. In March 2008, Blackwell asked UA to be a beta user of a new partnership service with OCLC, WorldCat Cataloging Partners (WCP) at Time-of-Order, because we believed the new capabilities would better meet UA's desire to have full cataloging records available at the time of order and the inclusion of an OCLC control number.

This meeting was followed by frequent consultation between the Blackwell consultant, Blackwell staff, the Associate Dean of Collections, and UA Cataloging and Acquisitions Staff to clarify and refine processes, especially those related to interfaces with Voyager and the implementation of WCP at Time of Order. In May 2008, the Blackwell team returned for two days of continued discussions and training. Key players in the Acquisitions and Cataloging and Metadata Services staff, the Blackwell team, and the AD of Collections mapped the new workflows and addressed outstanding questions. This session was profitable and resulted in the implementation moving forward.

Changing the Acquisitions Workflow

The workflow analysis and discussion of new ways to use Blackwell's technology provided options for Acquisitions. As a result of examining the workflow and beginning the implementation of WorldCat Cataloging Partners Time of Order and Time of Invoice functions, procedures began to change dramatically in the Spring of 2008. We also began testing and implementing additional changes in conjunction with the changes we were implementing with Blackwell.

We began with a small test group of records. Using the Education library as a source of orders, we started testing the Export function in Collection Manager in order to have a control group. Paper order request forms were eliminated because the selector was tagging orders in Collection Manager. The most significant change implemented was the automatic creation of multi-lined purchase orders based on the information exported from Blackwell.

Previously, a single PO was created by searching OCLC and importing the correct record into the Cataloging module title by title. A PO was then created by attaching the BIB record to the PO and filling in vendor, fund code, location, and price.

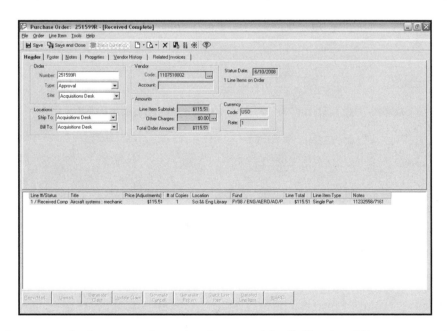

Under the new ordering procedures implemented in Collection Manager, a multi-lined PO is automatically created with all pertinent information needed, thus saving time and effort, as we are no longer creating one PO per title, nor searching, and importing records from OCLC. The new procedures are helping us realize cost savings in staff and in OCLC charges.

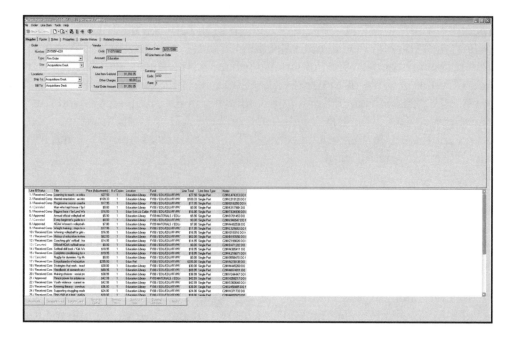

To implement the new procedures, codes for shelf-ready profiles were mapped for firm orders for Gorgas and the four branch libraries. Profiles were created for both shelf-ready and non–shelf-ready materials. This allowed selectors to order all available titles found in Collection Manager regardless of their suitability for shelf-ready processing, such as reference and rush materials. We also examined and made adjustments to profiles and funds.

Selectors play a major role in making these new procedures work correctly. They must set their request template preferences to reflect the correct order data. In the next version of Collection Manager, each selector will have the capability to create multiple templates, one for each fund code for which they are responsible, further eliminating the chance for error.

Steps in the new procedure are:

Selector requests or tags titles in Collection Manager.

Acquisitions retrieve titles by JUAU+ code.

Acquisitions exports file to Blackwell who sends information to OCLC.

OCLC sends Time of Order Records.

Acquisitions/Cataloging review records.

Acquisitions loads multi-lined PO into Voyager.

Acquisitions delete any problem orders from pending PO.

Acquisitions EDIs file to Blackwell for fulfillment.

OCLC sends Time of Invoice Records

Testing a small group of orders allowed us to discover where the problems were prior to implementing the new ordering procedures for all funds. We were able to work with individuals to determine incorrect coding and clarify instructions for those who do not work in Acquisitions and Cataloging on a daily basis.

We have identified some materials that should not come shelf-ready. These materials will vary from library to library, depending on local processing practices. The following materials were identified as problematic for shelf-ready processing:

- Curriculum materials

- School Library materials

- Books with media and/or instructional materials

- Special Collection materials

- Musical scores

- Materials to be book plated and/or purchased with endowment funds

- Bibliographies

- Reference

- Added volumes

    Multi-volume sets

    Serials

    Monographic series treated as serials

- Added copies

- Rush materials

Since identifying this list in our initial tests, we have worked with Blackwell to identify ways in which they can be processed through Collection Manager. There will always be books which need to be re-labeled or receive special handling due to their nature or content. The bulk of our materials can go through these new processes, however.

We had initially decided to add only one more profile when Acquisitions came back up in the new fiscal year. However, in the Fall we decided to move forward and implement all profiles. This has proven efficient and has helped us identify other issues that needed to be addressed in workflow or in understanding the new procedures.

Cataloging and Metadata Implementation

Additional components in the planning and implementation of the new workflow were establishing WorldCat Cataloging Partner (WCP) Time-of-Invoice profiles, and the review of processing specifications with Blackwell to receive shelf-ready books. In the WCP profiles, we specified our desire to receive records of all encoding levels and cataloging sources. When UA was using PromptCat, we received only DLC/DLC records. The books come in shelf-ready: property-stamped, tattle-taped and labeled. The call number labels on books going to the three branch libraries (Education, Business, and Science and Engineering) include location text.

At the end of March 2008, Blackwell approached us about beta testing a new service they developed with OCLC. The new service, WCP at Time-of-Order, delivers WorldCat records, if available, at the point of ordering. If WorldCat records are not available, Partnering Data Records (PDR) are delivered.

We decided to beta test the new service. Having WorldCat records in the library catalog as "order" records would provide users with much better access to on-order titles. We completed A Time-of-Order profile to receive "order" records from OCLC. The diagram below illustrates the WCP Time-of-Order workflow between the library, Blackwell, and OCLC.

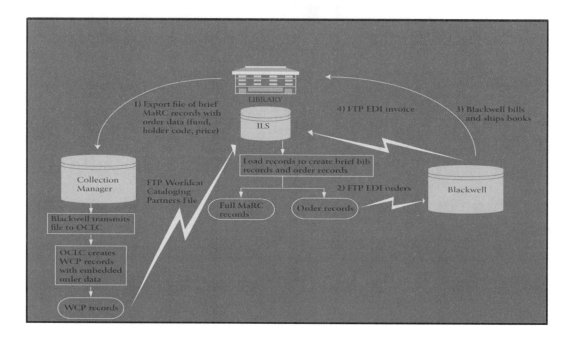

The ILS & Electronic Resources Management Unit participated in the planning process from the beginning. They needed to know the system work required to implement the new workflow. Voyager, the library ILS, had to be set up to batch load the Time-of-Order records delivered by OCLC and to generate orders from the acquisitions data imbedded in the bibliographic records during the "order" bibliographic records loading process. The "cataloging" records, WCP Time-of-Invoice records, later overlay the "order" records, WCP Time-of-Order records, based on the overlay number inserted in the 024 field of both the "order" and the "cataloging" records. The overlay numbers are generated automatically when titles are exported from the Collection Manager.

As stated, we tested the process with Education orders. The first batch of test orders was exported from Collection Manager in May 2008. We tested approximately 150 orders before orders for the main library and the other two branch libraries were activated for both WCP Time-of-Order and Time-of-Invoice.

The automated and batch ordering process using Blackwell Collection Manager and OCLC WCP made the ordering much more efficient. The new workflow afforded the Technical Services the opportunity to re-examine the staffing in both the Acquisitions and the Cataloging & Metadata Services and resulted in a major reorganization of the Technical Services. Three Acquisitions staff members were reassigned to the Cataloging & Metadata Services.

Reorganization

One result of the workflow analysis was a change in the organization of departments in what is traditionally called Technical Services. As we began implementing new workflows, we realized that there were different ways to group staff and that staff needed to be assigned to work at appropriate levels for their classification and training. Overlapping efforts and unnecessary steps became evident. The resulting reorganization is below. The first chart is from the summer of 2007 when Cataloging and Metadata were still separate departments. In addition, some copy cataloging was being completed in Acquisitions. By the summer of 2008, we merged Cataloging and Metadata into one department and all copy cataloging was moved to Cataloging & Metadata Services

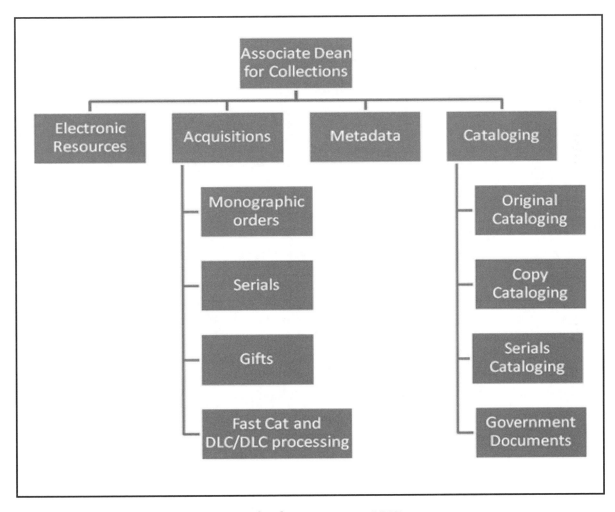

Organization — Summer 2007

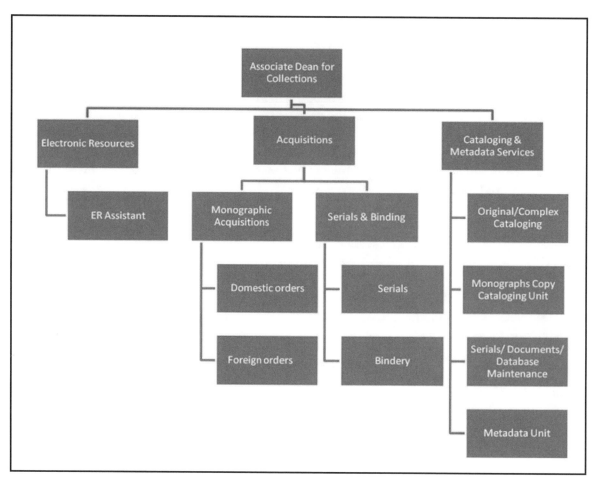

Organization Fall 2008

The new organizational structure offers several advantages. Workflow within and between departments are more efficient. In addition, units and staff are grouped in a logical way. The new organization takes advantage of streamlined processes and procedures. It also places staff in areas where they have the greatest potential for advancement. As procedures and policies are refined, work will continue to be redistributed and redefined. Other processes for approval plans and e-books which we have not yet implemented will be completed.

Training has been provided for all staff; this has been another advantage. While staff had been cross-trained as individuals and in small groups, large group training had not taken place. Further training opportunities are being discussed and planned.

Keys to Success

We are continuing to plan the next steps for implementing change. We have examined shelf ready processing and have already made a few changes to our profiles so that costs can be shifted. As we implement WCP processing for our Approval Plans, we will review and update our shelf ready processing requirements. These changes will create further efficiencies and will help us realize further cost savings.

There must be staff and faculty involvement to engender support when changes such as the ones we have described take place. This can be a difficult step, but it is necessary for success. Open lines of communication on all levels create an environment of trust and flexibility. There are varying levels of tolerance for change in organizations and we must be aware of this and allow time to adjust to new processes, ideas and ways of thinking. Training, as mentioned, is also a key element. It is important not to overlook faculty and staff who have been involved in library work for years, as it is important to provide them training and a forum for asking questions.

Changes such as the ones implemented at The University of Alabama provide tangible results that are realized not only in the departments affected, but throughout the Library and should be shared with Administration. Such changes provide impressive results and are to be celebrated by those who have worked through the processes and by those who benefit from the changes by receiving materials in a quicker and more efficient manner, ultimately providing better service to patrons.

APPLICATIONS OF USAGE STATISTICS

Hana Levay, Information Resources Librarian, University of Washington Libraries, Seattle, Washington

Historically, usage statistics have been cumbersome, from collection to their analysis once they have been gathered. Several recent developments, including the release of COUNTER and SUSHI standards, the service offered by ScholarlyStats, and features of electronic resource management systems (ERMS), have made the collecting and analysis of usage statistics much more manageable. I will summarize these recent developments and then show how the University of Washington Libraries is using them to help make collection assessment decisions.

Usage statistics for electronic resources have undergone many changes in the past several years. It used to be that every provider counted use differently, which made it very difficult to compare between resources. Even worse, providers might change how they count as time went on, making it difficult to even track trends in one resource. COUNTER (Counting Online Usage of NeTworked Electronic Resources; see http://www.projectcounter.org/) was developed as a collaboration of librarians and resource providers as a standard way to count use. For example, for electronic journals, usage is now measured by how many article downloads a title receives. There are defined uses for electronic journals, databases, and e-books. The COUNTER standard also defines how these reports should look, so now different reports from different vendors will all look the same and will be reporting the same kinds of counts. This means they can be compared against each other, and, perhaps most importantly, automated processes can be developed to manipulate the data.

COUNTER reports were hailed as a great step in easing the Herculean task of managing usage data, but it quickly became obvious that, although all of the data now looked and acted the same, there was still the matter of collecting all of the reports. For a library with several hundred resources such as ours, that takes time. At one point, we estimated it took 30-40 hours for one usage collection cycle. Two developments have helped with this problem.

A company called ScholarlyStats (http://www.scholarlystats.com) entered the scene in 2006. For a fee based on the number of resources covered, they collect usage statistics for you and provide not only a large file of all the compiled statistics, but also several reports based on these statistics, such as a list of journals with the lowest usage. This service has saved the University of Washington an estimated 8-10 hours of work per usage collection cycle. Since we collect statistics once a month, this is significant savings.

The other major development in this area was the development of the SUSHI (Standardized Usage Statistics Harvesting Initiative; see: http://www.niso.org/workrooms/sushi) standard. This standard allows software (usually an ERMS, but sometimes a library-developed system) to send a request to a SUSHI-compliant vendor, which automatically responds with a COUNTER-formatted usage report. This data would then be stored as desired.

The University of Washington Libraries uses Innovative's Millennium ERM. Their recent release in 2007 supports the SUSHI standard. That means, once the initial set up is complete, our ERM system retrieves and stores usage reports once a month with no further effort on our part. A person interested in the usage for a resource would simply navigate to that resource in ERM and open the usage report from that screen. Also, since the usage is stored in the same system as our ordering information, ERM can easily calculate cost-per-use based on our payment data and the usage data.

All taken together, these developments have greatly improved the usage collection and management process. However, there are still some problems. First, since SUSHI is a new development, there are not yet many SUSHI-compliant vendors. This will improve with time, especially since the recent release of COUNTER 3.0 which now requires the vendor to be SUSHI-compatible to be considered COUNTER-compliant. For now, we are fortunate that ScholarlyStats has a SUSHI server, so any data they collect for us can be retrieved using the SUSHI protocol even though the original resource providers are not yet SUSHI compatible.

Secondly, not all of our resources are covered by ScholarlyStats. We do not subscribe to all possible resources covered by ScholarlyStats, but even if we did, there are still many resources, especially the smaller ones, that are not covered by ScholarlyStats. So, although the process I will demonstrate works for a large number of our electronic journals, there are even more that are not covered, especially the smaller resources. The resources that are covered in the process demonstrated here are:

- American Chemical Society
- Annual Reviews
- BioOne
- Blackwell Synergy
- Cambridge Journals Online
- EBSCOhost
- Elsevier Science Direct
- Gale
- HighWire Press
- HW Wilson
- Informaworld
- IngentaConnect
- Institute of Electrical and Electronics Engineers (IEEE)

- Institute of Physics Publishing
- JSTOR
- Meta Press
- Nature Publishing Group
- Ovid (Wolters Kluwer)
- Oxford Journals Online
- Project MUSE
- ProQuest
- Sage
- Springer
- Thomson Gale
- Wiley InterScience

I will now demonstrate how the University of Washington Libraries configured Innovative's Millennium ERM to automatically collect usage data using the SUSHI protocol. First, you must edit the ERM AutoStat Configuration menu, found in Admin>Parameters> ERM>ERM AutoStat Configuration. Figure 1 shows the menu for the configuration screens.

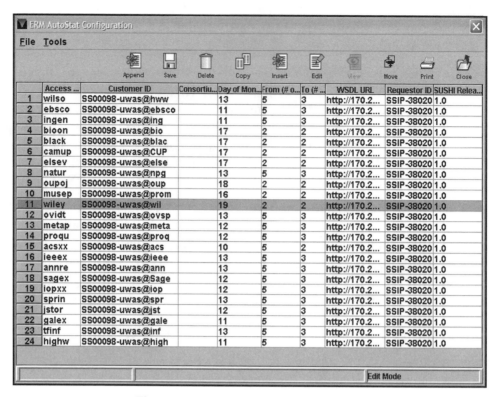

Figure 1 - ERM AutoStat Configuration

Clicking the "append" or "insert" button or double clicking on an existing row opens the configuration screen for a resource (see Figure 2). For each resource, you will need to fill out the following fields: Access Provider, Customer ID, Day of Month, From (# of months back), To (# of months back), WSDL URL, Requestor ID, and SUSHI Release.

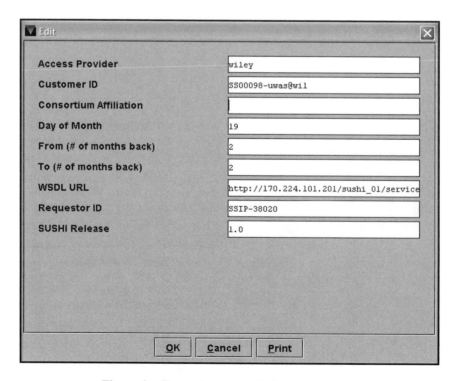

Figure 2 - Example of AutoStat configuration

The "Access Provider" field should be the code for access provider in the related ERM resource record. "Customer ID" will be your ScholarlyStats code followed by @ and the short code used by ScholarlyStats for that resource. "Day of month" is which day you would like ERM to send the request. Since ScholarlyStats data is made available mid-month, use a date after the data will be available. "From (# of months back)" is how many months back you want to go for usage data. Since ScholarlyStats data is generally provided with a six week lag, you would use 2 months here. Use the same number in the field "To (# of months back)", 2 in this case, if you only want to collect one month of usage. You would use something like 14 and 2 in these two fields if you wanted to collect an entire year of data at once. Keep in mind, however, that Millennium ERM can only collect data within the same calendar year at one time. The WSDL URL is the URL ERM will use to contact ScholarlyStats. That URL is http://170.224.101.201/sushi_01/services/SushiServicePort?wsdl. The Requestor ID is the same for all Innovative Millennium users: SSIP-38020. For SUSHI Release, use 1.0 for now, but I expect Millennium to be SUSHI 1.6 compatible soon.

Once this is set up for each resource, and the date given in "Day of Month" has passed, check your resource. Navigate to the Usage Statistics tab in the ERM record for that resource, and if statistics are available, the available dates of usage statistics will be automatically filled in. Clicking the "export" button will launch a Microsoft Excel spreadsheet containing the statistics.

Figure 3 shows an example of a usage statistics spreadsheet generated via ERM using data gathered with the SUSHI process. Note that in addition to the usage data, there is also cost and cost per use information. This is because Millennium ERM is connected to our order records where the payment information is stored. The titles are connected using the coverage database and the Resource ID field. The Resource ID in the resource record must match the name in the coverage database for the titles to match appropriately. Finally, the costs are associated only when the "Payment From" and "Payment To" columns are filled in on the payments tab in the related order record. These are new columns in ERM 2007, and tell ERM what calendar year to apply payments to. For example, a payment in October 2006 might actually apply to a 2007 subscription. Therefore, to get cost per use, ERM takes the payment, sees the 2007 date, and divides by 2007 usage. If the "Payment From" and "Payment To" columns are empty, cost per use will show as 0.

Cost per use calculations are made as follows. For a package that is paid for with one lump sum, ERM uses this algorithm (see figure 3 for values):

Average cost per title (2007)	= Total cost for 2007 subscription / number of titles in package
	= $26108/360 =$72.53
CPU per title (2007)	= Average cost per title / Use for title
CPU: Africa Today	= $72.52/270
	= $0.27

For titles that are paid for on a line by line basis, ERM uses this calculation (see figure 4; use Genesis as the example):

2007 payment / 2007 Use	= 2007 CPU
$1950.71 / 649	= $3.00

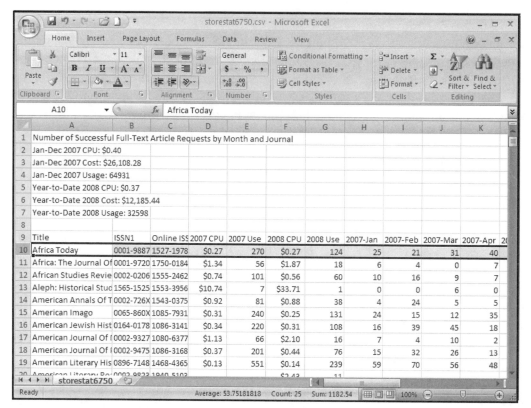

Figure 3 - Project Muse usage statistics export

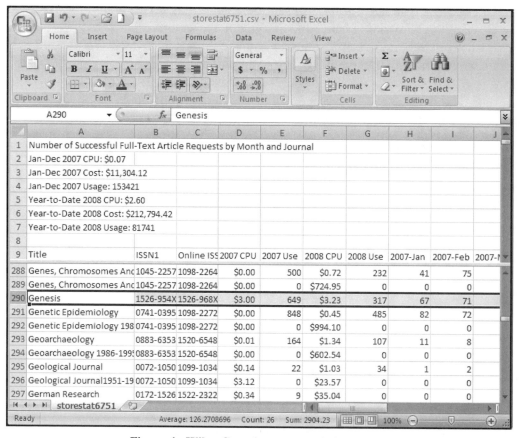

Figure 4 - Wiley Genesis usage statistics export

For years that aren't complete, such as 2008 in these figures when the screenshots were taken, ERM still performs the calculations but then prorates the cost to reflect the partial year.

Integrating data retrieved via SUSHI with cost data in ERM is an excellent start to solving the usage collection and analysis problem. However, there are still some issues. First, not all of our resources are covered with this method. We can adjust our ScholarlyStats subscription to fine tune this, or hope that other resources become SUSHI compatible. For now, we are limited to those resources covered in ScholarlyStats. Also, we still have some complaints about the reporting features in ERM. The reports are not customizable at this time. We would like to see other data elements in the reports, for example, fund code. Also, usage data and cost per use data are not accessible from other areas of Millennium. For example, we cannot pull this information using the Create Lists feature. To solve this problem, we had to step back from Millennium and design a tool that could compile all of the data of interest.

Using Create Lists to export data from Millennium, I was able to create a spreadsheet containing information about our subscription titles. Then, I used Access to associate those titles with usage data by matching on ISSN. I could also pull in Portico titles and bibliometrics such as ISI Impact Factor and Eigenfactor, also matching on ISSN. Finally, I also pulled in information from the resource and license records (matching between order and resource records with SLK link) to provide information on cancellation restrictions and perpetual access notes. See figure 5 for the complete relationship diagram I used in this database.

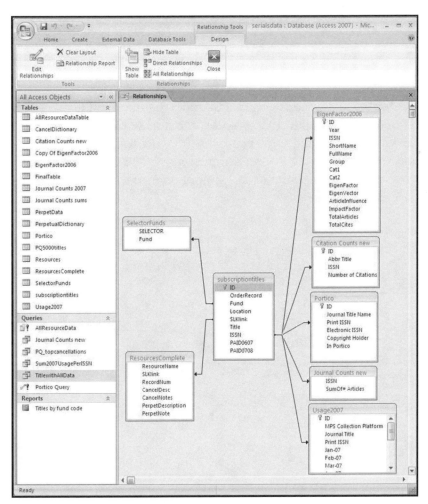

Figure 5 - Database relationships

Once the relationships were established, I could run a query pulling all of the fields of interest and export that in spreadsheet form. One of the uses of this data at the University of Washington is to generate a report showing all of the titles paid for with a certain fund. See figure 6 to see a portion of the report for the social sciences fund.

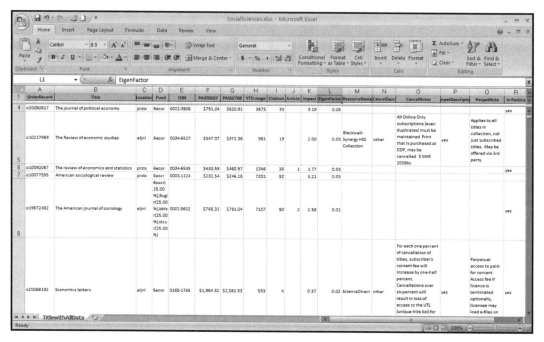

Figure 6 - Sample spreadsheet

The other use for this database is to generate reports at the fund level. I used the report feature in Access to develop a report that would contain most of the essential information that could fit onto the width of one landscape page, thus making a report that can easily be printed and brought to meetings. See figure 7 for a sample report. The user ideally would use the printable report for initial considerations, and simply refer to the large Excel spreadsheet for further details on specific titles.

Record#	Subscription	Location	PAID0607	PAID0708	2007 e-Use	UW Articles	UW Citation	ISI Impact	EigenFactor	Cancel	In Portico
o10112911	International journal of government auditing	baper									
o17904328	International journal of industrial organization	eljnl	$1,182.63	$1,241.76	87		1	0.562000	0.0087510	other	yes
o12603673	International journal of information and management sciences	baper									
o10219778	International journal of market research :|the journal of the Market Research Society /	baper	$570.14	$638.10							
o17885814	International journal of project management	eljnl	$1,019.18	$1,070.14	240					other	yes
o10112960	International journal of research in marketing	eljnl	$610.55	$641.07	121	1	7	1.280000	0.0018777	other	yes
o15017540	Investext plus	elind	$8,844.62								
o10254663	Investor's business daily	bastx	$316.21	$343.53							
o10104239	Ivey business journal	bastx			3						
o16612565	Japan company handbook.	bastx	$279.50								
o16612590	Japan company handbook.	bastx	$279.50	$604.26							
o12603399	Japan research quarterly	baper									
o10120415	JMR, Journal of marketing research	baper	$296.27	$363.68	1018		62	2.389000	0.0125010		yes
o10176160	Journal of accountancy	baper	$75.07	$75.14	78						
o17904365	Journal of accounting & economics	eljnl	$1,022.06	$1,073.17	752	1	43	3.360000	0.0150790	other	yes
o10113125	Journal of accounting and public policy	eljnl	$591.32	$620.88	45					other	yes
o10113162	Journal of accounting education	eljnl	$476.90	$500.74	19					other	yes

Figure 7 - Sample Report

These reports have proven to be valued tools for fund managers to use in cancellation projects.

Recent developments in the field of usage statistics have eased the task of collecting and analyzing usage statistics. Widely adopted standards such as COUNTER and SUSHI have helped data to be more uniform and useful. As more data meets these criteria, we can more easily automate the process and use tools to help with the analysis. Knowing which titles are heavily used helps librarians know which titles to keep; conversely, less used journals should either be canceled, or better marketed to increase use to get the full value.

HOW NOT TO READ A MILLION BOOKS

Tanya Clement, PhD Candidate, English Literature and Digital Studies, University of Maryland, College Park, Maryland

Sara Steger, PhD Candidate, Department of English, University of Georgia, Athens, Georgia

John Unsworth, Dean, School of Information and Library Science, University of Illinois, Urbana, Illinois

Kirsten Uszkalo, Assistant Professor, Department of English, Simon Fraser University, Burnaby, British Columbia, Canada

First of all, where does the trope of "a million books" come from? It originates, as far as I know, with the Universal Library and its Million Books Project, which began in 2001. The Universal Library is directed by Raj Reddy, professor and former Dean of Computer Science at Carnegie Mellon University; the million books project (funded by NSF and others) was a kind of very large pilot, aimed at digitizing a million books ("less than 1% of all books in all languages ever published"[1]), beginning with partners in India and later expanding to China and Egypt. The "million book" goal was accomplished in 2007, by which time it had been eclipsed by some large commercial projects, including most notably Google Print (now known as Google Book Search) that had begun in secret in 2002 and was unveiled at the Frankfurt Book Fair in October 2004, and had Harvard's library as one of its initial partners. Google Books aims to scan as many as 30 million books, a number equal to all the titles in WorldCat—and for all we know, they are already about halfway there.[2] Libraries and others have been digitizing books for years, but these massive digitization projects really changed the landscape and raised the question "What do you do with a million books?"—a question first asked, I think, by Greg Crane, in D-Lib Magazine, in March of 2006.[3] My answer to that question is that whatever you do, you don't read them, because you can't.

As Franco Moretti points out, in *Graphs, Maps, Trees*, we focus on a "minimal fraction of the literary field":

> . . . a canon of two hundred novels, for instance, sounds very large for nineteenth-century Britain (and is much larger than the current one), but is still less than one per cent of the novels that were actually published: twenty thousand, thirty, more, no one really knows—and close reading won't help here, a novel a day every day of the year would take a century or so... And it's not even a matter of time, but of method: a field this large cannot be understood by stitching together separate bits of knowledge about individual cases, because it isn't a sum of individual cases: it's a collective system, that should be grasped as such, as a whole."[4]

I think that what Moretti calls "the quantitative approach to literature" acquires a special importance when millions of books are equally at your fingertips, all eagerly responding to your Google Book Search: you can no longer as easily ignore the books you don't know, nor can you grasp the collective systems they make up without some new strategy—a strategy for not reading.

Martin Mueller is my collaborator and co-PI on the MONK project, and professor of classics and English at Northwestern University. Martin is fond of citing this poem about not reading, called "The Spectacles":

Korf reads avidly and fast.
Therefore he detests the vast
bombast of the repetitious,
twelvefold needless, injudicious.

Most affairs are settled straight
just in seven words or eight;
in as many tapeworm phrases
one can prattle on like blazes.

Hence he lets his mind invent
a corrective instrument:
Spectacles whose focal strength
shortens texts of any length.

Thus, a poem such as this,
so beglassed one would just — miss.
Thirty-three of them will spark
nothing but a question mark.[5]

Korf is the kind of reader for which some text-mining tools are intended: I'm sure he would approve of text-summarization technology, for example—the sort of thing that tells you what a newspaper article is about, so you don't have to go through the tiresome and inkstained exercise of actually reading it.

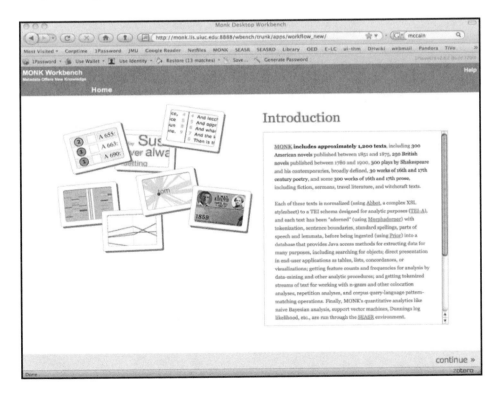

What we're trying to do, by contrast, in the Mellon-funded MONK project, is to use text-mining techniques as a provocation for reading, but also to cast the net for that provocation much more broadly than one could do without computers. In other words, although we expect that our users may end up reading, even reading closely, we begin by not reading. Sometimes we don't read single unreadable texts, sometimes we don't read the collected works of an author, sometimes we don't read all of the books in the MONK datastore—but we never don't not read.

225. Dering, Edward
    1. A fruitfull sermon, vpon the 3.4.5.6.7.&8. verses ...
    2. A sermo[n] preached before the Quenes Maiestie. By...
    3. A sermon preached at the Tower of London, by M. De...
226. Dickens, Charles
    1. A Christmas Carol. In Prose. Being a Ghost Story o...
    2. A Tale of Two Cities. By Charles Dickens. With Ill...
    3. Barnaby Rudge [in, Master Humphrey's Clock. By Cha...
    4. Bleak House. By Charles Dickens. With Illustration...
    5. Dombey and Son. By Charles Dickens. With Illustrat...
    6. Great Expectations: By Charles Dickens: In Three V...
    7. Hard Times. For These Times. By Charles Dickens
    8. Little Dorrit. By Charles Dickens. With Illustrati...
    9. Oliver Twist; or, The Parish Boy's Progress. By "B...
   10. Our Mutual Friend. By Charles Dickens. With Illust...
   11. The Life and Adventures of Martin Chuzzlewit. By C...
   12. The Life and Adventures of Nicholas Nickleby. By C...
   13. The Mystery of Edwin Drood. By Charles Dickens. Wi...
   14. The Old Curiosity Shop [in, Master Humphrey's Cloc...
   15. The Personal History of David Copperfield. By Char...
   16. The Posthumous Papers of the Pickwick Club. By Cha...
227. Disraeli, Benjamin, Earl of Beaconsfield
    1. Coningsby; or The New Generation. By B. Disraeli ....
    2. Lothair. By the Right Honourable B. Disraeli. In T...
    3. Sybil; or, The Two Nations. By B. Disraeli
    4. Tancred: or, The New Crusade. By B. Disraeli
    5. Vivian Grey
228. Dod, John
    1. Foure godlie and fruitful sermons two preached at ...
229. Donne, John

That MONK datastore currently includes a small fraction of the literary field that Moretti describes, but still, it includes enough to be interesting. It has the complete text of approximately 1,200 works, including 300 American novels published between 1851 and 1875, 250 British novels published between 1780 and 1900, 300 plays by Shakespeare and his contemporaries, 30 works of 16th and 17th century poetry, and 300 works of 16th and 17th prose, including fiction, sermons, travel literature, and witchcraft texts. 250 of these works, by 104 authors, come from Chadwyck-Healey's Nineteenth-Century Fiction collection; 658 works by 366 authors come from the Text Creation Partnership at the University of Michigan, with an emphasis on Early English Books Online; 244 works by 172 authors come from The Wright American Fiction collection at Indiana University. Taken together, these 1152 works contain about 81.5 million words, and they represent a reasonable sample of printed literature in English from the 16th, 17th, 18th, and 19th centuries. There's also a single 20th-century text that we've been working with—Gertrude Stein's The Making of Americans—about which more in a moment. And we've just learned that we'll be able to include a substantial subset of the Early American Fiction collection from the University of Virginia: that set of texts, along with the Wright American Fiction collection, make up a very solid representation of American fiction before 1875, and one that we will be able to make publicly available for text-mining, in just a few months, when the MONK project ends.

```xml
- <p xml:id="para112">
  - <seg part="N" rend="186,1706,1855,1846" xml:id="seg112">
      <lb/>
      <c> </c>
      <w eos="0" lem="""" pos="""" reg="""" spe="""" tok="""" xml:id="adventuresoftoms00twai2_TEI_MERGED-000340" ord="17" part="N">"</w>
      <w eos="0" lem="what|be" pos="q-crq|vbz" reg="What's" spe="What's" tok="What's" xml:id="adventuresoftoms00twai2_TEI_MERGED-000350" ord="18" part="N">What's</w>
      <c> </c>
      <w eos="0" lem="go" pos="vvn" reg="gone" spe="gone" tok="gone" xml:id="adventuresoftoms00twai2_TEI_MERGED-000360" ord="19" part="N">gone</w>
      <c> </c>
      <w eos="0" lem="with" pos="pp" reg="with" spe="with" tok="with" xml:id="adventuresoftoms00twai2_TEI_MERGED-000370" ord="20" part="N">with</w>
      <c> </c>
      <w eos="0" lem="that" pos="d" reg="that" spe="that" tok="that" xml:id="adventuresoftoms00twai2_TEI_MERGED-000380" ord="21" part="N">that</w>
      <c> </c>
      <w eos="0" lem="boy" pos="n1" reg="boy" spe="boy" tok="boy" xml:id="adventuresoftoms00twai2_TEI_MERGED-000390" ord="22" part="N">boy</w>
      <w eos="0" lem="," pos="," reg="," spe="," tok="," xml:id="adventuresoftoms00twai2_TEI_MERGED-000400" ord="23" part="N">,</w>
      <c> </c>
      <w eos="0" lem="i" pos="pns11" reg="I" spe="I" tok="I" xml:id="adventuresoftoms00twai2_TEI_MERGED-000410" ord="24" part="N">I</w>
      <c> </c>
      <w eos="0" lem="wonder" pos="vvb" reg="wonder" spe="wonder" tok="wonder" xml:id="adventuresoftoms00twai2_TEI_MERGED-000420" ord="25" part="N">wonder</w>
      <w eos="1" lem="?" pos="?" reg="?" spe="?" tok="?" xml:id="adventuresoftoms00twai2_TEI_MERGED-000430" ord="26" part="N">?</w>
      <c> </c>
      <w eos="0" lem="you" pos="pn22" reg="You" spe="You" tok="You" xml:id="adventuresoftoms00twai2_TEI_MERGED-000440" ord="27" part="N">You</w>
      <lb/>
      <c> </c>
```

In the process of assembling these texts into the MONK datastore, each of them is transformed (using routines written by Brian Pytlik Zillig at the University of Nebraska) from their native markup to markup that follows an XML schema designed (again, at Nebraska) for analytic purposes. Each text is then analyzed by software (written by Phil Burns at Northwestern University) that identifies word boundaries, sentence boundaries, standard spellings, parts of speech and lemmata. This software, called MorphAdorner, differs from other NLP toolkits by having special features for dealing with orthographic and morphological variance of dialectal or Early Modern English texts. Finally, the texts are ingested into a database (also designed at Northwestern, by John Norstad) that provides Java access methods for extracting data for many purposes, including searching for objects; direct presentation in end-user applications as tables, lists, concordances, or visualizations; getting feature counts and frequencies for analysis by data-mining and other analytic procedures; and getting tokenized streams of text for doing analysis of collocation and repetition, and other pattern-matching operations.

MONK's analytic routines include supervised learning methods for text-classification, like Naive Bayesian analysis and support vector machines (the sorts of things that the spam filter in your email client uses, with a little training from you, to decide whether to put something in your junk mailbox), as well as tools for unsupervised text-classification (for fully automated clustering of texts), and tools for evaluating probability (for example, measuring word frequencies in a single work vs. in other works of the same period). These analytics are run using something called the Software Environment for the Advancement of Scholarly Research (SEASR), developed by Michael Welge's Automated Learning Group at the National Center for Supercomputing Applications, with help from Amit Kumar, at the University of Illinois.

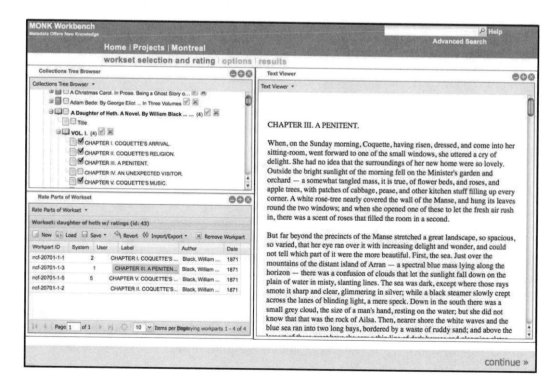

MONK's user interface combines these texts and tools to enable literary research through the discovery, exploration, and visualization of patterns—which may be patterns in a single work, in a subset of the MONK collection, or across everything we have. The interface for this is being developed by colleagues at the University of Alberta (Matt Bouchard and others, under the supervision of Stan Ruecker), McMaster University (Andrew MacDonald and others, under the supervision of Stefan Sinclair), the University of Maryland (Anthony Don and others, under the supervision of Catherine Plaisant), and the University of Illinois (Amit Kumar and Duane Searsmith). It is designed as a kind of workbench, where users can assemble collections, choose tools, create worksets, save results of analysis, and submit those results to various kinds of visualization, or export them for use in other systems; I should point out that some of the things I will show you are experiments done along the way that have not been fully incorporated in the workbench. In general, though, the MONK user interface is a browser-based client: it talks to the datastore and to SEASR over the Web, and these transactions are mediated by middleware developed at Illinois—an intermediate layer of software that turns input from the client into queries for datastore, ships results from the datastore off to SEASR's analytics engine, and takes results from SEASR and sends them back to the client, managing queuing and communication all the while.

Without a doubt, though, the most important component of the MONK project is the scholarly user. These patient and persistent people provide real-world requirements for the tools that we are trying to build, and they are involved in every step of the process, from the initial design onward. I'll present here several use cases—two being pursued by graduate students in English (Sarah Steger at the University of Georgia and Tanya Clement at the University of Maryland, both in English), one by a junior faculty member at Simon Fraser University (also in English), and two by a senior faculty member, Martin Mueller, in English and Classics at Northwestern University. These experiments will be presented in order of increasing breadth but decreasing depth, from an examination of the structure of a single work (Gertrude Stein's *The Making of Americans*), to tracing the emergence of archetypes (the gentleman devil; the haggard witch) across dozens of texts, to understanding the characteristics of a literary movement (sentimentalism) by examining hundreds of exemplars, to identifying the sources of a multi-volume, multi-author encyclopedia.

The Making of Americans

My first example, then, is Tanya Clement's work on Gertrude Stein's *The Making of Americans*. This work is part of her dissertation in the English Department at the University of Maryland, and it will also appear in the next issue of *Literary and Linguistic Computing*, published by Oxford University Press. *The Making of Americans*, Tanya writes,

> was criticized by [those] like Malcolm Cowley who said Stein's "experiments in grammar" made this novel "one of the hardest books to read from beginning to end that has ever been published."[6] More recent scholars have attempted to aid its interpretation by charting the correspondence between structures of repetition and the novel's discussion of identity and representation. Yet, the use of repetition in Making is far more complicated than manual practices or traditional word-analysis programs (such as those that make concordances or measure word-frequency occurrence) could indicate. The highly repetitive nature of the text, comprising almost 900 pages and 3174 paragraphs with only approximately 5,000 unique words,[7] makes keeping tracks of lists of repetitive elements unmanageable and ultimately incomprehensible.

```
3:|it of anyone whether they are enjoying a thing , whether they know that they are hurting someone , whether they have b|
3:|it of anyone whether they are enjoying a thing , whether they know that they are hurting someone , whether they have b|
3:|anyone whether they are enjoying a thing , whether they know that they are hurting someone , whether they have been pl|
3:|, in some when they are not so young , in some when they are getting older , in some when they are old ones|clearer wh|
3:|, in some when they are not so young , in some when they are getting older , in some when they are old ones|clearer wh|
3:|, in some when they are not so young , in some when they are getting older , in some when they are old ones|clearer wh|
3:|, in some when they are not so young , in some when they are getting older , in some when they are old ones|clearer wh|
3:|, in some when they are not so young , in some when they are getting older , in some when they are old ones|clearer wh|
3:|, in some when they are not so young , in some when they are getting older , in some when they are old ones|clearer wh|
3:|, in some when they are not so young , in some when they are getting older , in some when they are old ones|clearer wh|
3:|, in some when they are not so young , in some when they are getting older , in some when they are old ones|clearer wh|
3:|, in some when they are not so young , in some when they are getting older , in some when they are old ones|clearer wh|
3:|, in some when they are not so young , in some when they are getting older , in some when they are old ones|clearer wh|
3:|clearer when they are very young , in some when they are young , in some when they are not so young , in some|they are|
3:|clearer when they are very young , in some when they are young , in some when they are not so young , in some|is clear|
3:|clearer when they are very young , in some when they are young , in some when they are not so young , in some|is clear|
3:|clearer when they are very young , in some when they are young , in some when they are not so young , in some|is clear|
3:|are young , in some when they are not so young , in some when they are old ones . Always in each one it|clearer when t|
3:|are young , in some when they are not so young , in some when they are old ones . Always in each one it|clearer when t|
3:|are young , in some when they are not so young , in some when they are old ones . Always in each one it|clearer when t|
3:|clearer when they are very young , in some when they are young , in some when they are not so young , in some|they are|
3:|clearer when they are very young , in some when they are young , in some when they are not so young , in some|they are|
3:|clearer when they are very young , in some when they are young , in some when they are not so young , in some|they are|
3:|one to me . Sometime the bottom nature in each one , the other nature or natures in each one , the mixing or not|one c|
3:|one to me . Sometime the bottom nature in each one , the other nature or natures in each one , the mixing or not|one c|
3:|one to me . Sometime the bottom nature in each one , the other nature or natures in each one , the mixing or not|one c|
3:|one to me . Sometime the bottom nature in each one , the other nature or natures in each one , the mixing or not|one c|
3:|one comes to be a whole one to me . Sometime the bottom nature in each one , the other nature or natures in each|a who|
3:|be a whole one to me . Sometime the bottom nature in each one , the other nature or natures in each one , the|a whole |
3:|be a whole one to me . Sometime the bottom nature in each one , the other nature or natures in each one , the|a whole |
3:|be a whole one to me . Sometime the bottom nature in each one , the other nature or natures in each one , the|a whole |
3:|a whole one to me . Sometime the bottom nature in each one , the other nature or natures in each one , the mixing|
3:|it takes many years of hearing the repeating in one before the whole being is clear to the understanding of one who ha|
3:|it takes many years of hearing the repeating in one before the whole being is clear to the understanding of one who ha|
3:|it takes many years of hearing the repeating in one before the whole being is clear to the understanding of one who ha|
3:|it takes many years of hearing the repeating in one before the whole being is clear to the understanding of one who ha|
3:|it takes many years of hearing the repeating in one before the whole being is clear to the understanding of one who ha|
3:|it takes many years of hearing the repeating in one before the whole being is clear to the understanding of one who ha|
3:|it takes many years of hearing the repeating in one before the whole being is clear to the understanding of one who ha|
```

Thinking that she might get a bird's-eye view of repetition in the novel by using text-mining tools, Tanya applied "a frequent pattern analysis algorithm"[8] that looked at every sequence of three words in the book, and any patterns across those trigrams, but "executing the algorithm on making generated thousands of patterns since each slight variation in a repetition generated a new pattern."[9] Working with the MONK partners at the University of Maryland's Human Computer Interaction Lab, Tanya's use-case helped to drive the development of a new tool called FeatureLens. FeatureLens, in Tanya's words, highlights

> trends such as co-occurring patterns that tend to increase or decrease in frequency "suddenly" across a distribution of data points (area "A" in Figure 7).[10] It allows the user to choose particular patterns for comparison (area "B"), charts those patterns across the text's nine chapters at the chapter level and at the paragraph[11] level (area "C"), and facilitates finding these patterns in context (area "D"). Ultimately, while text mining allowed me to use statistical methods to chart repetition across thousands of paragraphs, FeatureLens facilitated my ability to read the results by allowing me to sort those results in different ways and view them within the context of the text. As a result, by visualizing clustered patterns across the text's 900 pages of repetitions, I discovered two sections that share, verbatim, 495 words and form a bridge over the center of the text. This discovery provides a new key for reading the text as a circular text with two corresponding halves, which substantiates and extends the critical perspective that Making is neither inchoate nor chaotic, but a highly systematic and controlled text. This perspective will change how scholars read and teach *The Making of Americans*.

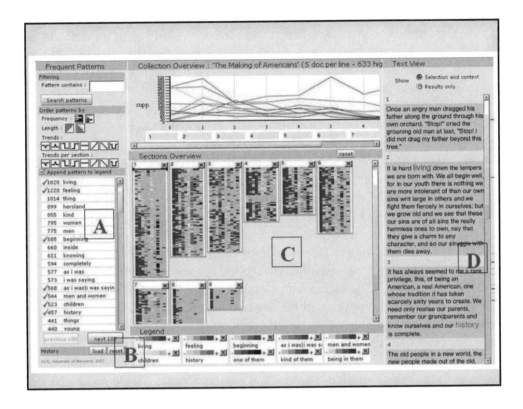

Working with the Devil

Kirsten Uszkalo, junior faculty in English at Simon Fraser University, and she is, as she says, "working with the Devil right now—trying to figure out when the gentleman devil showed up in English witchcraft tracts" and also investigating the literary emergence of his diabolical creature, the witch. Kirsten says,

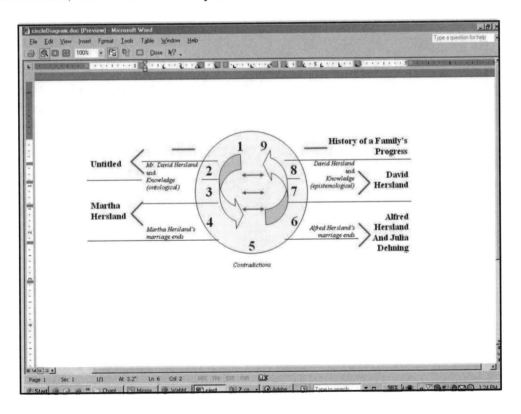

I began the first trial run of the witchcraft sample set, starting with a small sample set — those of the anonymous witchcraft tracts which we had morphadorned. This was actually a pretty useful way to begin to look at what witchcraft meant in early modern England, because the tracts themselves tell the story of the social, literary, and legal representation of witchcraft in not only small text chunks, but provide a useful span across the chronology of witchcraft texts. I set down to write a kind of classification system, based on the schema I had developed in "hard coding" the paper versions of the texts, with flags and highlighters. One of the most fascinating results of this pass through was a result I had not intended to find, but that which spoke volumes about Richard Head's construction of Mother Shipton's diabolical upbringing. MONK returned a sample I had not realized was there and may have been a kind of source text, or framework on which Head drew an expanded version of Shipton's life. Although I was looking for sex as a signifier of diabolism, I found that a number of the texts I was getting returned spoke to the idea of the prodigious birth as a sign of the Devil's presence. This makes all sorts of sense; witchcraft, monster babies, comets, and two-headed chickens all belong to the same kind of "enquirer" genre in early modern England. So although Head's version of Shipton's life has not been digitized, the computer returned a result that shares eerie similarities because it is part of the same genre . . . MONK showed what it should have showed; it returned findings like those I told it to find. However, beyond showing what couldn't be seen with the naked eye, the computer suggested connections I hadn't thought of. It ranked texts based on similarities I hadn't "ranked" as there. In searching the computer results, I was able to see sub-groupings of texts in the displayed results. In that way, did not just tell me what was similar, but presented texts which illustrated similarities I hadn't thought of. I've had to rethink essential ideas like the ways witches are linked, the way sex functions, and the role of the monstrous in early modern witchcraft.

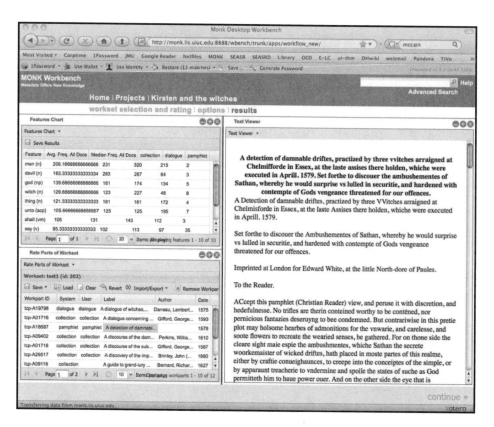

Sentimentalism

Sara Steger, a graduate student in English at the University of Georgia, has (like Tanya Clement) been using MONK as a research tool for her dissertation, which is on sentimentalism in British Literature. Sara describes the questions she's examining with MONK as follows:

> Can you train the computer to recognize sentimentality and return "more like these?" I have results from running naïve bayes routines on a training set of 409 mid-Victorian novels that I classified sentimental and unsentimental. The testbed was 3,921 novels and the system returned 1,348 chapters as sentimental. I'm going through these results and am talking with [experienced data miners] about ways to assess the success of this experiment. It seems that the system is really good at recognizing sentimentality in Dickens.

Sara used Dunning's log likelihood to compare various aspects of sentimental novels with the rest of her testbed of texts. Martin Mueller was the person who first called our attention in MONK to the simplicity and power of Dunning's log likelihood as a technique for understanding the differences that make a difference. Martin learned about it from Paul Rayson (Lancaster University), who has used it in his wmatrix program. Martin notes that

> Dunning's log likelihood ratio is a statistic that does more or less the same thing as a Chi-square, but it is supposed to be more suitable for textual data. It supports a "figure and ground" operation where you choose one set of texts or words, called the Analysis Corpus, compare it with another set of texts or words, the Reference Corpus, and find words that are, in comparison with the Reference corpus, disproportionately common or rare in the Analysis Corpus. The resultant log likelihood ratio maps to a probability table that you interpret in the same way as a chi-square statistic. For the analysis of lexical differences, Dunning's log likelihood ratio is a powerful tool whose results can be easily interpreted by users who do not understand the details of the underlying math. And the elegant word-cloud program Wordle, from IBM's ManyEyes project, turns out to be an excellent for visualizing Dunning results.

Just to show a couple of Martin's initial examples here, he produced a visualization of the "words Jane Austen Avoids" by comparison to other novelists of her era . . . and he produced these visualizations of the vocabulary characteristic of male authors, and of female authors, in the same period.

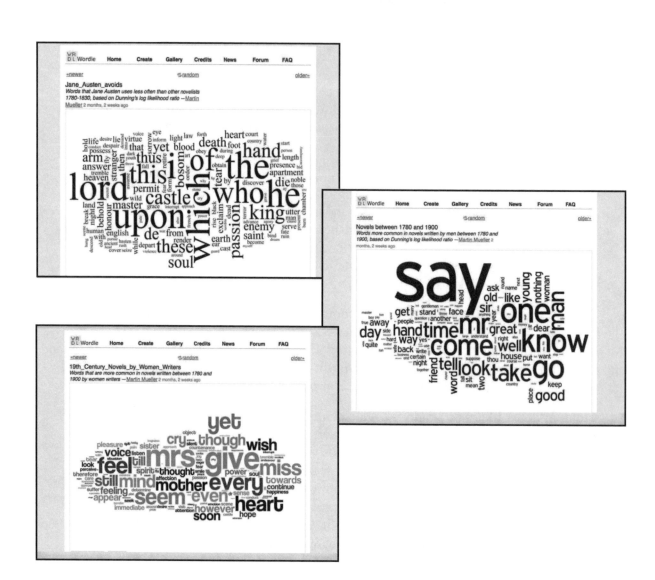

In using these same tools and techniques to explore sentimentalism in British fiction, Sara Steger was particularly interested in that most sentimental of situations, the deathbed scene. Sara says,

> I've run both a comparison of my training set of sentimental vs. unsentimental and a comparison using the machine-classified texts. Not surprisingly, "mother," "child," "heart," and "love" stand out as markers of the sentimental in both lists. . . . The words that are over-represented in deathbed scenes set the scene, hinting at descriptions of the bed, the room, the pillow, the chamber, and even the hospital. Words corresponding to illness also are prominent, including "fever," "sick," "nurse," "doctor," and "sick-room." Moreover, that word cloud is a reminder of how death is a domestic affair. Not only is there an emphasis on that most domestic of spaces, the bedroom, but the vocabulary emphasizes intimate relationships—"mamma," "papa," "darling," and "child." This latter word also crosses over into demonstrating a concern with innocence and diminutiveness, especially when read with to the related "baby," and "little." Moreover, the visualization reflects the thematic importance of last words and touches—the "lips" that "speak," "whisper," or "kiss," the "last" "farewell," the final "breath." . . . While a close reader may be able to get a sense of which words

are used more often in sentimental scenes, the algorithm enabled me to discover information that a scholar would never be able to obtain without these technologies: that which is absent. What the word cloud does not include is almost as informative as what it does. Given the prominence of mourning in Victorian culture, there is almost no trace of the formal trappings of mourning in this snapshot of deathbed scenes. While the words "coffin," "archdeacon," and "grave" appear, the visualization shows that the topos is much more concerned with describing the death than with detailing the mourning. A description of the moment is sufficient to convey the "good death" of the character; the burial and the mourning – the public moments in the church and graveyard – are largely absent.

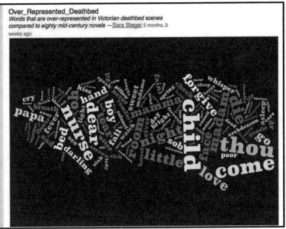

This makes the list and visualization of the words that are under-represented in deathbed scenes even more striking. One of the most under-represented words is "holy," and it is followed by "church," "saint," "faith," "believe" and "truth." It seems the Victorian deathbed scene is more concerned with relationships, marked by words such as "forgiveness," "mercy," "forgive," and "comfort" than with personal convictions and declarations of faith. . . . Words that have to do with business and class ("money," "power," "business," "lord," and "gentleman") don't belong at the deathbed. . . . Tellingly, words of uncertainty also appear prominent in the visualization of under-used words in deathbed scenes, including "suppose," "perhaps," and "doubt." The deathbed scene, by nature a scene of resolution, leaves no room for incertitude. Altogether, the words that are not used, the "negatives," serve as a sort of shadow to the "positives," giving dimension to the themes and patterns that stood out in the first visualization.

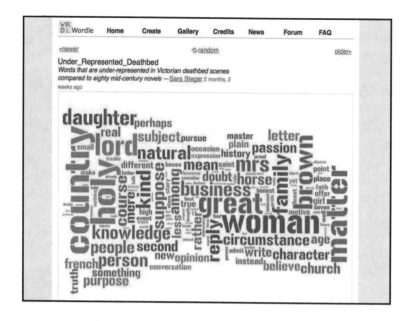

Literary DNA

Martin Mueller, has provided some of the most imaginative use-cases for MONK, and I recommend to your attention his writings on the MONK wiki—they are a pleasure and an education to read. Martin is one of those people who is open to ideas from all quarters, and one of his sources of inspiration is his daughter Rachel, a biologist who works on sequencing DNA. They often talk about the fact that there are many resemblances between tracing DNA sequences and verbal borrowings across genomes or literary corpora. He became very interested in the use of sequence alignment techniques by Mark Olsen and his team at Philologic. They have been tracking the sources of Diderot's *Encyclopedie.*[12] This work is very much along the lines of Tanya Clements' analysis of repetition in *The Making of Americans*. In the Philologic application of sequence analysis, Martin writes,

> the fragments are fragments of text considered as overlapping n-grams [an n-gram is just a series of n words]. These overlapping "shingles" of text are then examined for patterns of repetition. A variant and simpler version of this technology was used by Brian Vickers in a recent TLS essay, where he argued for Kyd's authorship of several Elizabethan plays, including the old Lear Play, on the basis of phrasal echoes or shingles (discovered by submitting *King Lear* and three of the plays of Thomas Kyd to some open source plagiarism detection software).[13] We will work with the Philologic folks to track shingle patterns across the entire corpus of Early Modern drama.

Meaning and Mining

I began with a skeptical verse, and I want to end with a skeptical essay, called "Meaning and Mining: The Impact of Implicit Assumptions in Data Mining for the Humanities," by D. Sculley and Bradley M. Pasanek. This essay is forthcoming in the same issue of *Literary and Linguistic Computing* that will include Tanya Clement's essay on Stein, and the essay begins with this headnote, from Hans Georg Gadamer's *Truth and Method*:

A person who is trying to understand a text is always projecting. He projects a meaning for the text as a whole as some initial meaning emerges in the text. Again, the initial meaning only emerges because he is reading the text with particular expectations in regard to a certain meaning. Working out this fore-projection, which is constantly revised in terms of what emerges as he penetrates into the meaning, is understanding what is there.

Pasanek and Sculley argue that text-mining is of doubtful value for literary studies, because readers—especially professional readers—can make meaning out of almost anything: "just because results are statistically valid and humanly interpretable does not guarantee that they are meaningful." Specifically, they point out that there are some key practices and assumptions in data-mining and machine learning that literary users of these tools may not fully appreciate or understand, and that without an understanding of fundamental principles, it is easy to misinterpret or overstate the significance of statistical results:

> The temptation in applying machine learning methods to humanities data is to interpret a computed result as some form of proof or determinate answer. In this case, the validity of the evidence lies inherent in the technology. This can be problematic when the methods are treated as a black box, a critic ex machina.

Table 1: Confusion matrix with balanced class sizes, cross validation by metaphor, no word stemming, stop word removal, or feature selection.

	PREDICTED WHIG	PREDICTED TORY	PREDICTED RADICAL	RECALL
ACTUAL WHIG	434	134	68	0.69
ACTUAL TORY	149	456	56	0.66
ACTUAL RADICAL	76	83	486	0.72
PRECISION	0.62	0.70	0.69	INF. GAIN: 0.69

Table 2: Confusion matrix with balanced class sizes, cross validation by author, no word stemming, stop word removal, or feature selection.

	PREDICTED WHIG	PREDICTED TORY	PREDICTED RADICAL	RECALL
ACTUAL WHIG	249	211	198	0.38
ACTUAL TORY	275	199	167	0.31
ACTUAL RADICAL	256	139	250	0.39
PRECISION	0.32	0.36	0.41	INF. GAIN: 0.04

After reviewing some of those fundamental principles, they lay out a case study in which they applied text-mining techniques to a database of metaphors culled from 18th-century British political writing, in order to demonstrate or disprove George Lakoff's hypothesis "that political debates are contests between root conceptual metaphors (Lakoff, 2002). Party affiliation is rooted in metaphorically structured mental models (in 'pictures' not 'propositions')." They apply Support Vector Machines (one of the tools we use in MONK) to sort the metaphors into clusters, and then ask whether the resulting clusters support Lakoff's hypothesis. I won't go into the details of this part of the argument here, though if you look at the figure in the bottom right-hand cell in each of these two tables, and consider that a random distribution in this case would be about .33, you can get a sense of how much and then how little Lakoff's hypothesis seems to be supported by the data, as Pasanek and Sculley except "prove" and "disprove" it several times over, using different representations of the data, different forms of cross-validation, and different clustering techniques. "One of the ironies here," say the authors,

> is that machine learning methods, which seemed so promising as a way of performing what Moretti calls distant reading or what Martin Mueller calls, perhaps even more provocatively, not-reading, is that they require us to trade in a close reading of the original text for something that looks like a close reading of experimental results – a reading that must navigate ambiguity and contradiction. Where we had hoped to explain or understand those larger structures within which an individual text has meaning in the first place, we find ourselves acting once again as interpreters. The confusion matrix, authored in part by the classifier, is a new text, albeit a strange sort of text, one that sends us back to those texts it purports to be about.

I would agree with that, and I think we see that in the use-cases that I've presented here—Tanya Clement reads the patterns of repetition in order to discover the structure of a notoriously unreadable novel; Kirsten Uszkalo reads the clustering of descriptive language in 17th-century texts to identify the emergence of ideas about the supernatural; Sara Steger reads the predictions of sentimentalism as a way of thinking about the components of a genre; and Martin Mueller reads "shingles" of word sequences produced by plagiarism detection techniques as a way of suggesting the authorship of entries in an encyclopedia.

Pasanek and Sculley make some sensible recommendations for best practices in text mining for the humanities, including:

Make assumptions explicit

Use multiple representations and methodologies

Report all trials (including failures)

Make data available and methods reproducible

Engage in peer review of methodology

I might be inclined to add one more, which is to avoid approaching the application of this technology as a matter of proving the truth of a hypothesis. For literary purposes, as I suggested at the outset of this paper and elsewhere, I think it makes more sense to think of text-mining tools as offering provocations, surfacing evidence, suggesting patterns and structures, or adumbrating trends. Whereas text mining is usually about prediction, accuracy, and ground truth, in literary study, I think it is more about surprise, suggestion, and negative capability—and on that point, Sculley and Pasanek concur:

> The virtue of automated analysis is not ready delivery of objective truth, but instead the more profound virtue of bringing us up short, of disturbing us in our preconceptions and our basic assumptions so that we can exist, if only for a moment, in uncertainties, mysteries, and doubts. Should we learn to forestall interpretation, we may come to revise our prejudices, theories, and fore-projections in terms of what emerges.

The tendency to leap to conclusions is understandable, not least because it is impossible to operate without preconceptions or to make sense of things without paying selective attention across a field of information. But the value of these tools, especially with a large full-text collection, is that they can bring to your attention works that otherwise might be overlooked, they can expose patterns that are so fine-grained that they would otherwise escape notice, and they can allow you to not-read a million books on your way to reading a period, or reading a genre, or even reading a book.

Notes

1. http://www.ulib.org/ULIBAboutUs.htm#goalsBkMark
2. Jeffrey Toobin, "Google's Moon Shot: The Quest for The Universal Library." *New Yorker*, Feb. 5, 2007. http://www.newyorker.com/reporting/2007/02/05/070205fa_fact_toobin
3. http://www.dlib.org/dlib/march06/crane/03crane.html
4. Franco Moretti. *Graphs, Maps, Trees: Abstract Models for a Literary History*. 3-4.
5. Christian Morgenstern, "Die Brille" from *Galgenlieder*, 1905. Trans. Max Knight, 1964.
6. Cowley, Malcolm (2000). "Gertrude Stein, Writer or Word Scientist." *The Critical Response to Gertrude Stein*. Westport, CT: Greenwood Press, 147-150, 148.
7. Please see http://www.wam.umd.edu/~tclement/samplesMoa.html for a comparison chart showing that texts such as *Moby Dick* or *Ulysses* which have approximately half the number of words as *The Making of Americans* also have, respectively, three times and five times as many unique words. [Clement's note.]
8. J. Pei, J. Han, and R. Mao, " 'CLOSET: An Efficient Algorithm for Mining Frequent Closed Itemsets (PDF)," Proc. 2000 ACM-SIGMOD Int. Workshop on Data Mining and Knowledge Discovery (DMKD'00), Dallas, TX, May 2000. [Clement's note.]
9. Examples of frequent co-occurring patterns from the text may be found at ftp://ftp.ncsa.uiuc.edu/alg/tanya/withstem (any file on this list opens in a browser to reveal thousands of patterns). [Clement's note.]
10. All figures are located on my samples page at http://wam.umd.edu/~tclement/Nebraska2008Samples.html. [Clement's note.]
11. Each line in Area C represents five paragraphs in order that the user may see the whole text at once. [Clement's note.]
12. The Encyclopédie ou Dictionnaire raisonné des sciences, des arts et des métiers, par une Société de Gens de lettres was published under the direction of Diderot and d'Alembert, with 17 volumes of text and 11 volumes of plates between 1751 and 1772. Containing 72,000 articles written by more than 140 contributors, the Encyclopédie was a massive reference work for the arts and sciences, as well as a machine de guerre which served to propagate the ideas of the French Enlightment. The impact of the Encyclopédie was enormous. Through its attempt to classify learning and to open all domains of human activity to its readers, the Encyclopédie gave expression to many of the most important intellectual and social developments of its time. — ARTFL web site, http://www.lib.uchicago.edu/efts/ARTFL/projects/encyc/
13. Brian Vickers, "Thomas Kyd, Secret Sharer." *TLS*, April 18, 2008. 13-15.

112012